Microsoft®
Access® 2013

ILLUSTRATED

Brief | **Introductory** | Complete

Microsoft® Access® 2013

ILLUSTRATED

Brief | **Introductory** | Complete

Lisa Friedrichsen

CENGAGE
Learning®

Australia • Brazil • Japan • Korea • Mexico • Singapore • Spain • United Kingdom • United States

CENGAGE
Learning

Microsoft® Access® 2013—Illustrated Introductory
Lisa Friedrichsen

Executive Editor: Marjorie Hunt

Associate Acquisitions Editor: Amanda Lyons

Senior Product Manager: Christina Kling-Garrett

Product Manager: Kim Klasner

Editorial Assistant: Brandelynn Perry

Brand Manager: Elinor Gregory

Developmental Editor: Lisa Ruffolo

Full-Service Project Management: GEX Publishing
Services

Copyeditor: Karen Annett

Proofreader: Vicki Zimmer

Indexer: Alexandra Nickerson

QA Manuscript Reviewers: John Freitas, Susan
Pedicini, Susan Whalen, Jeff Schwartz

Cover Designer: GEX Publishing Services

Cover Artist: GEX Publishing Services

Composition: GEX Publishing Services

For product information and technology assistance, contact us at
Cengage Learning Customer & Sales Support, 1-800-354-9706

For permission to use material from this text or product, submit all
requests online at **www.cengage.com/permissions**
Further permissions questions can be emailed to
permissionrequest@cengage.com

Library of Congress Control Number: 2013936199
ISBN-13: 978-1-285-09328-4
ISBN-10: 1-285-09328-3

Cengage Learning
200 First Stamford Place, 4th Floor
Stamford, CT 06902
USA

Cengage Learning is a leading provider of customized learning solutions
with office locations around the globe, including Singapore, the United
Kingdom, Australia, Mexico, Brazil, and Japan. Locate your local office at:
www.cengage.com/global

Cengage Learning products are represented in Canada by
Nelson Education, Ltd.

For your course and learning solutions, visit **www.cengage.com**

Purchase any of our products at your local college store or at our
preferred online store **www.cengagebrain.com**

Printed in the United States of America
1 2 3 4 5 6 7 18 17 16 15 14 13

Brief Contents

Contents

Office 2013

Access 2013

Preface

Welcome to *Microsoft Access 2013—Illustrated Introductory*. This book has a unique design: each skill is presented on two facing pages, with steps on the left and screens on the right. The layout makes it easy to learn a skill without having to read a lot of text and flip pages to see an illustration.

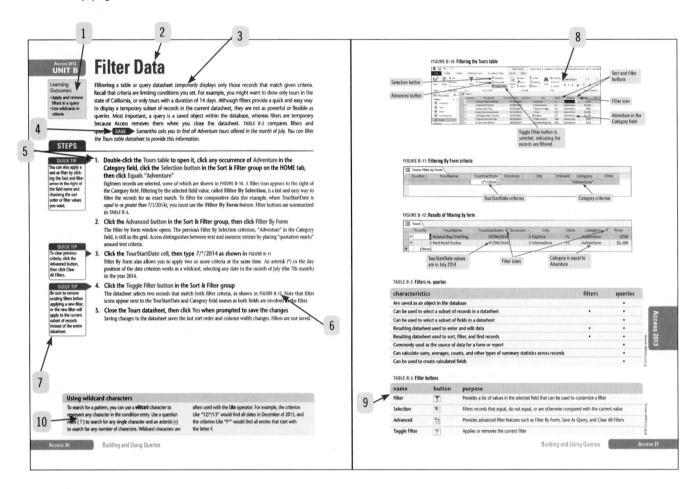

1 New! Learning Outcomes box lists measurable learning goals for which a student is accountable in that lesson.

2 Each two-page lesson focuses on a single skill.

3 Introduction briefly explains why the lesson skill is important.

4 A case scenario motivates the steps and puts learning in context.

5 Step-by-step instructions and brief explanations guide students through each hands-on lesson activity.

6 New! Figure references are now in red bold to help students refer back and forth between the steps and screenshots.

7 Tips and troubleshooting advice, right where you need it—next to the step itself.

8 New! Larger screenshots with green callouts now placed on top keep students on track as they complete steps.

9 Tables provide summaries of helpful information such as button references or keyboard shortcuts.

10 Clues to Use yellow boxes provide useful information related to the lesson skill.

This book is an ideal learning tool for a wide range of learners—the "rookies" will find the clean design easy to follow and focused with only essential information presented, and the "hotshots" will appreciate being able to move quickly through the lessons to find the information they need without reading a lot of text. The design also makes this a great reference after the course is over! See the illustration on the left to learn more about the pedagogical and design elements of a typical lesson.

What's New in this Edition

- **Coverage** — This book helps students learn to use Microsoft Access 2013, including step-by-step instructions on creating tables, queries, forms, and reports. Working in the Cloud appendix helps students learn to use SkyDrive to save, share, and manage files in the cloud and to use Office Web Apps.
- **New! Learning Outcomes** — Each lesson displays a green Learning Outcomes box that lists skills-based or knowledge-based learning goals for which students are accountable. Each Learning Outcome maps to a variety of learning activities and assessments. (See the *New! Learning Outcomes* section on page xiii for more information.)
- **New! Updated Design** — This edition features many new design improvements to engage students — including larger lesson screenshots with green callouts placed on top, and a refreshed Unit Opener page.
- **New! Independent Challenge 4: Explore** — This new case-based assessment activity allows students to explore new skills and use creativity to solve a problem or create a project.

Assignments

This book includes a wide variety of high quality assignments you can use for practice and assessment. Assignments include:

- **Concepts Review** — Multiple choice, matching, and screen identification questions.
- **Skills Review** — Step-by-step, hands-on review of every skill covered in the unit.
- **Independent Challenges 1-3** — Case projects requiring critical thinking and application of the unit skills. The Independent Challenges increase in difficulty. The first one in each unit provides the most hand-holding; the subsequent ones provide less guidance and require more critical thinking and independent problem solving.
- **Independent Challenge 4: Explore** — Case projects that let students explore new skills that are related to the core skills covered in the unit and are often more open ended, allowing students to use creativity to complete the assignment.
- **Visual Workshop** — Critical thinking exercises that require students to create a project by looking at a completed solution; they must apply the skills they've learned in the unit and use critical thinking skills to create the project from scratch.

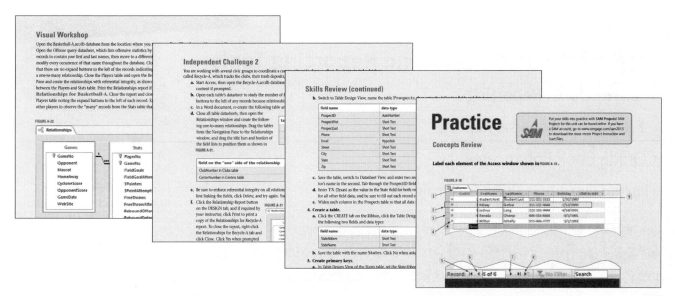

WHAT'S NEW FOR SAM 2013?

Get your students workplace ready with *SAM*

The market-leading assessment and training solution for Microsoft Office

SAM 2013

Exciting New Features and Content

- ➤ Computer Concepts Trainings and Assessments *(shown on monitor)*
- ➤ Student Assignment Calendar
- ➤ All New SAM Projects
- ➤ Mac Hints
- ➤ More MindTap Readers

More Efficient Course Setup and Management Tools

- ➤ Individual Assignment Tool
- ➤ Video Playback of Student Clickpaths
- ➤ Express Assignment Creation Tool

Improved Grade Book and Reporting Tools

- ➤ Institutional Reporting
- ➤ Frequency Analysis Report
- ➤ Grade Book Enhancements
- ➤ Partial Credit Grading for Projects

SAM's active, hands-on environment helps students master Microsoft Office skills and computer concepts that are essential to academic and career success.

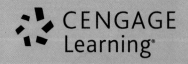

CENGAGE Learning®

New! Learning Outcomes

Every 2-page lesson in this book now contains a green **Learning Outcomes box** that states the learning goals for that lesson.

- **What is a learning outcome?** A learning outcome states what a student is expected to know or be able to do after completing a lesson. Each learning outcome is skills-based or knowledge-based and is *measurable*. Learning outcomes map to learning activities and assessments.

- **How do students benefit from learning outcomes?** Learning outcomes tell students exactly what skills and knowledge they are *accountable* for learning in that lesson. This helps students study more efficiently and effectively and makes them more active learners.

- **How do instructors benefit from learning outcomes?** Learning outcomes provide clear, measurable, skills-based learning goals that map to various high-quality learning activities and assessments. A **Learning Outcomes Map**, available for each unit in this book, maps every learning outcome to the learning activities and assessments shown below.

Learning Outcomes Map to These Learning Activities:

1. **Book lessons:** Step-by-step tutorial on one skill presented in a two-page learning format
2. **SAM Training:** Short animations and hands-on practice activities in simulated environment

Learning Outcomes Map to These Assessments:

1. **End-of-Unit Exercises: Concepts Review** (screen identification, matching, multiple choice); **Skills Review** (hands-on review of each lesson); **Independent Challenges** (hands-on, case-based review of specific skills); **Visual Workshop** (activity that requires student to build a project by looking at a picture of the final solution).
2. **Exam View Test Banks:** Objective-based questions you can use for online or paper testing.
3. **SAM Assessment:** Performance-based assessment in a simulated environment.
4. **SAM Projects:** Auto-graded projects for Word, Excel, Access, and PowerPoint that students create live in the application.
5. **Extra Independent Challenges:** Extra case-based exercises available in the Instructor Resources that cover various skills.

Learning Outcomes Map

A **Learning Outcomes Map**, contained in the Instructor Resources, provides a listing of learning activities and assessments for each learning outcome in the book.

Learning Outcomes Map
Microsoft Access 2013 Illustrated
Unit A--Getting Started with Microsoft Office 2013

KEY:
IC=Independent Challenge   EIC=Extra Independent Challenge
VW=Visual Workshop

	Concepts Review	Skills Review	IC1	IC2	IC3	IC4	VW	EIC 1	EIC 2	Test Bank	SAM Assessment	SAM Projects	SAM Training
Understand the Office 2013 Suite													
Identify Office suite components	✔		✔							✔			
Describe the features of each program			✔							✔			
Start an Office App													
Start an Office App			✔							✔	✔	✔	✔
Explain the purpose of a template										✔			
Start a new blank document			✔							✔			
Identify Office 2013 Screen Elements													
Identify basic components of the user interface	✔									✔			
Display and use Backstage view			✔							✔			
Adjust the Zoom level	✔		✔							✔	✔	✔	✔
Create and Save a File													
Create a file			✔							✔	✔	✔	✔
Save a file	✔		✔							✔	✔	✔	✔
Explain SkyDrive			✔										

Instructor Resources

This book comes with a wide array of high-quality technology-based teaching tools to help you teach and to help students learn. The following teaching tools are available for download at our Instructor Companion Site. Simply search for this text at *login.cengage.com*. An instructor login is required.

- **New! Learning Outcomes Map** — A detailed grid for each unit (in Excel format) shows the learning activities and assessments that map to each learning outcome in that unit.

- **Instructor's Manual** — Available as an electronic file, the Instructor's Manual includes lecture notes with teaching tips for each unit.

- **Sample Syllabus** — Prepare and customize your course easily using this sample course outline.

- **PowerPoint Presentations** — Each unit has a corresponding PowerPoint presentation covering the skills and topics in that unit that you can use in lectures, distribute to your students, or customize to suit your course.

- **Figure Files** — The figures in the text are provided on the Instructor Resources site to help you illustrate key topics or concepts. You can use these to create your own slide shows or learning tools.

- **Solution Files** — Solution Files are files that contain the finished project that students create or modify in the lessons or end-of-unit material.

- **Solutions Document** — This document outlines the solutions for the end-of-unit Concepts Review, Skills Review, Independent Challenges and Visual Workshops. An Annotated Solution File and Grading Rubric accompany each file and can be used together for efficient grading.

- **ExamView Test Banks** — ExamView is a powerful testing software package that allows you to create and administer printed, computer (LAN-based), and Internet exams. Our ExamView test banks include questions that correspond to the skills and concepts covered in this text, enabling students to generate detailed study guides that include page references for further review. The computer-based and Internet testing components allow students to take exams at their computers, and also save you time by grading each exam automatically.

Key Facts About Using This Book

Data Files are needed: To complete many of the lessons and end-of-unit assignments, students need to start from partially completed Data Files, which help students learn more efficiently. By starting out with a Data File, students can focus on performing specific tasks without having to create a file from scratch. All Data Files are available as part of the Instructor Resources. Students can also download Data Files themselves for free at cengagebrain.com. (For detailed instructions, go to www.cengage.com/ct/studentdownload.)

System requirements: This book was developed using Microsoft Office 2013 Professional running on Windows 8. Note that Windows 8 is not a requirement for the units on Microsoft Office; Office 2013 runs virtually the same on Windows 7 and Windows 8. Please see Important Notes for Windows 7 Users on the next page for more information.

Screen resolution: This book was written and tested on computers with monitors set at a resolution of 1366 x 768. If your screen shows more or less information than the figures in this book, your monitor is probably set at a higher or lower resolution. If you don't see something on your screen, you might have to scroll down or up to see the object identified in the figure.

Tell Us What You Think!

We want to hear from you! Please email your questions, comments, and suggestions to the Illustrated Series team at: **illustratedseries@cengage.com**

Important Notes for Windows 7 Users

The screenshots in this book show Microsoft Office 2013 running on Windows 8. However, if you are using Microsoft Windows 7, you can still use this book because Office 2013 runs virtually the same on both platforms. There are only two differences that you will encounter if you are using Windows 7. Read this section to understand the differences.

Dialog boxes

If you are a Windows 7 user, dialog boxes shown in this book will look slightly different than what you see on your screen. Dialog boxes for Windows 7 have a light blue title bar, instead of a medium blue title bar. However, beyond this superficial difference in appearance, the options in the dialog boxes across platforms are the same. For instance, the screenshots below show the Font dialog box running on Windows 7 and the Font dialog box running on Windows 8.

FIGURE 1: Font dialog box in Windows 7

FIGURE 2: Font dialog box in Windows 8

Alternate Steps for Starting an App in Windows 7

Nearly all of the steps in this book work exactly the same for Windows 7 users. However, starting an app (or program/ application) requires different steps for Windows 7. The steps below show the Windows 7 steps for starting an app. (Note: Windows 7 alternate steps also appear in red Trouble boxes next to any step in the book that requires starting an app.)

Starting an app (or program/application) using Windows 7

1. Click the **Start button** on the taskbar to open the Start menu.
2. Click **All Programs**, then click the **Microsoft Office 2013 folder**. See Figure 3.
3. Click the app you want to use (such as **Access 2013**).

FIGURE 3: Starting an app using Windows 7

Acknowledgements

Author Acknowledgements

The Access portion is dedicated to my students, and all who are using this book to teach and learn about Access. Thank you. Also, thank you to all of the professionals who helped me create this book.

–Lisa Friedrichsen

Advisory Board Acknowledgements

We thank our Illustrated Advisory Board who gave us their opinions and guided our decisions as we developed all of the new editions for Microsoft Office 2013.

They are as follows:

Merlin Amirtharaj, Stanly Community College

Londo Andrews, J. Sargeant Reynolds Community College

Rachelle Hall, Glendale Community College

Terri Helfand, Chaffey Community College

Sheryl Lenhart, Terra Community College

Dr. Jose Nieves, Lord Fairfax Community College

Coming Soon: MindTap

MindTap is a fully online, highly personalized learning experience built upon Cengage Learning content. MindTap combines student learning tools - readings, multimedia, activities, and assessments - into a singular Learning Path that guides students through their course. Instructors personalize the experience by customizing authoritative Cengage Learning content and learning tools, including the ability to add SAM trainings, assessments, and projects into the Learning Path via a SAM app that integrates into the MindTap framework seamlessly with Learning Management Systems. Available in 2014.

Getting Started with Microsoft Office 2013

CASE This unit introduces you to the most frequently used programs in Office, as well as common features they all share.

Unit Objectives

After completing this unit, you will be able to:

- Understand the Office 2013 suite
- Start an Office app
- Identify Office 2013 screen elements
- Create and save a file

- Open a file and save it with a new name
- View and print your work
- Get Help, close a file, and exit an app

File You Will Need

OFFICE A-1.xlsx

Learning
Outcomes
• Identify Office
suite components
• Describe the
features of each
program

Understand the Office 2013 Suite

Microsoft Office 2013 is a group of programs--which are also called applications or apps--designed to help you create documents, collaborate with coworkers, and track and analyze information. You use different Office programs to accomplish specific tasks, such as writing a letter or producing a presentation, yet all the programs have a similar look and feel. Microsoft Office 2013 apps feature a common, context-sensitive user interface, so you can get up to speed faster and use advanced features with greater ease. The Office apps are bundled together in a group called a **suite**. The Office suite is available in several configurations, but all include Word, Excel, and PowerPoint. Other configurations include Access, Outlook, Publisher, and other programs. **CASE** ▶ *As part of your job, you need to understand how each Office app is best used to complete specific tasks.*

DETAILS

The Office apps covered in this book include:

• **Microsoft Word 2013**

When you need to create any kind of text-based document, such as a memo, newsletter, or multipage report, Word is the program to use. You can easily make your documents look great by inserting eye-catching graphics and using formatting tools such as themes, which are available in most Office programs. **Themes** are predesigned combinations of color and formatting attributes you can apply to a document. The Word document shown in **FIGURE A-1** was formatted with the Organic theme.

• **Microsoft Excel 2013**

Excel is the perfect solution when you need to work with numeric values and make calculations. It puts the power of formulas, functions, charts, and other analytical tools into the hands of every user, so you can analyze sales projections, calculate loan payments, and present your findings in a professional manner. The Excel worksheet shown in **FIGURE A-1** tracks personal expenses. Because Excel automatically recalculates results whenever a value changes, the information is always up to date. A chart illustrates how the monthly expenses are broken down.

• **Microsoft PowerPoint 2013**

Using PowerPoint, it's easy to create powerful presentations complete with graphics, transitions, and even a soundtrack. Using professionally designed themes and clip art, you can quickly and easily create dynamic slide shows such as the one shown in **FIGURE A-1**.

• **Microsoft Access 2013**

QUICK TIP
In Word, Excel, and
PowerPoint, the
interface can be
modified to auto-
matically open a
blank document,
workbook, or pre-
sentation. To do this,
click the FILE tab,
click Options, click
Show the Start
screen when this
application starts
(to deselect it), then
click OK. The next
time the program
opens, it will open a
blank document.

Access is a relational database program that helps you keep track of large amounts of quantitative data, such as product inventories or employee records. The form shown in **FIGURE A-1** was created for a grocery store inventory database. Employees use the form to enter data about each item. Using Access enables employees to quickly find specific information such as price and quantity.

Microsoft Office has benefits beyond the power of each program, including:

• **Common user interface: Improving business processes**

Because the Office suite programs have a similar **interface**, or look and feel, your experience using one program's tools makes it easy to learn those in the other programs. In addition, Office documents are **compatible** with one another, meaning that you can easily incorporate, or **integrate**, an Excel chart into a PowerPoint slide, or an Access table into a Word document.

• **Collaboration: Simplifying how people work together**

Office recognizes the way people do business today, and supports the emphasis on communication and knowledge sharing within companies and across the globe. All Office programs include the capability to incorporate feedback—called **online collaboration**—across the Internet or a company network.

Newsletter created in Word

Checkbook register created in Excel

Tourism presentation created in PowerPoint

Store inventory form created in Access

What is Office 365?

Until the release of Microsoft Office 2013, most consumers purchased Microsoft Office in a traditional way: by buying a retail package from a store or downloading it from Microsoft.com. You can still purchase Microsoft Office 2013 in this traditional way--but you can also now purchase it as a subscription service called Microsoft Office 365 (for businesses) and

Microsoft Office 365 Home Premium (for consumers). Office 365 requires businesses to pay a subscription fee for each user. Office 365 Home Premium Edition allows households to install Office on up to 5 devices. These subscription versions of Office provide extra services and are optimized for working in the cloud.

Start an Office App

To get started using Microsoft Office, you need to start, or **launch**, the Office app you want to use. If you are running Microsoft Office on Windows 8, an easy way to start the app you want is to go to the Start screen, type the app name you want to search for, then click the app name In the Results list. If you are running Windows 7, you start an app using the Start menu. (If you are running Windows 7, follow the Windows 7 steps at the bottom of this page.) **CASE** ▶ *You decide to familiarize yourself with Office by starting Microsoft Word.*

STEPS

1. **Go to the** Windows 8 Start screen

   Your screen displays a variety of colorful tiles for all the apps on your computer. You could locate the app you want to open by scrolling to the right until you see it, or you can type the app name to search for it.

2. **Type** word

   Your screen now displays "Word 2013" under "Results for 'word'", along with any other app that has "word" as part of its name (such as WordPad). See **FIGURE A-2**.

3. **Click** Word 2013

   Word 2013 launches, and the Word **start screen** appears, as shown in **FIGURE A-3**. The start screen is a landing page that appears when you first start an Office app. The left side of this screen displays recent files you have opened. (If you have never opened any files, then there will be no files listed under Recent.) The right side displays images depicting different templates you can use to create different types of documents. A **template** is a file containing professionally designed content that you can easily replace with your own. You can also start from scratch using the Blank Document option.

Starting an app using Windows 7

1. Click the Start button 🟦 on the taskbar
2. Click All Programs on the Start menu, click the Microsoft Office 2013 folder as shown in FIGURE A-4, then click Word 2013

Word 2013 launches, and the Word start screen appears, as shown previously in FIGURE A-3. The start screen is a landing page that appears when you first start an Office app. The left side of this screen displays recent files you have opened. (If you have never opened any files, then there will be no files listed under Recent.) The right side displays images depicting different templates you can use to create different types of documents. A **template** is a file containing professionally designed content that you can easily replace with your own. Using a template to create a document can save time and ensure that your document looks great. You can also start from scratch using the Blank Document option.

Using shortcut keys to move between Office programs

You can switch between open apps using a keyboard shortcut. The [Alt][Tab] keyboard combination lets you either switch quickly to the next open program or file or choose one from a gallery. To switch immediately to the next open program or file, press [Alt][Tab]. To choose from all open programs and files, press and hold [Alt], then press and release [Tab] without releasing [Alt]. A gallery opens on screen, displaying the filename and a thumbnail image of each open program and file, as well as of the desktop. Each time you press [Tab] while holding [Alt], the selection cycles to the next open file or location. Release [Alt] when the program, file, or location you want to activate is selected.

FIGURE A-2: Searching for Word app from the Start screen in Windows 8

Word 2013 app appears as a search result when you type "word"

FIGURE A-3: Word start screen

Word 2013 Preview

Recent

Task List.docx
Your Name's SkyDrive » Documents » shared d...

Task List.docx
Documents » Word Unit C

To do list.docx
Documents » Word Unit C

Memo.docx
Your Name's SkyDrive » Documents

sale flyer.docx
Your Name's SkyDrive

Open Other Documents

Recently opened documents appear here

Your name will appear here if you signed in using a Microsoft account

Take a tour

Templates let you create a certain type of document fast using professionally designed content you can modify

FIGURE A-4: Starting an app using Windows 7

Using the Office Clipboard

You can use the Office Clipboard to cut and copy items from one Office program and paste them into others. The Office Clipboard can store a maximum of 24 items. To access it, open the Office Clipboard task pane by clicking the dialog box launcher ⬚ in the Clipboard group on the HOME tab. Each time you copy a selection, it is saved in the Office Clipboard. Each entry in the Office Clipboard includes an icon that tells you the program it was created in. To paste an entry, click in the document where you want it to appear, then click the item in the Office Clipboard. To delete an item from the Office Clipboard, right-click the item, then click Delete.

Identify Office 2013 Screen Elements

One of the benefits of using Office is that the programs have much in common, making them easy to learn and making it simple to move from one to another. Individual Office programs have always shared many features, but the innovations in the Office 2013 user interface mean even greater similarity among them all. That means you can also use your knowledge of one program to get up to speed in another. A **user interface** is a collective term for all the ways you interact with a software program. The user interface in Office 2013 provides intuitive ways to choose commands, work with files, and navigate in the program window. **CASE** ▶ *Familiarize yourself with some of the common interface elements in Office by examining the PowerPoint program window.*

STEPS

1. **Go to the Windows 8** Start screen, **type** pow, **click** PowerPoint 2013, **then click** Blank Presentation

   PowerPoint becomes the active program displaying a blank slide. Refer to **FIGURE A-5** to identify common elements of the Office user interface. The **document window** occupies most of the screen. At the top of every Office program window is a **title bar** that displays the document name and program name. Below the title bar is the **Ribbon**, which displays commands you're likely to need for the current task. Commands are organized onto **tabs**. The tab names appear at the top of the Ribbon, and the active tab appears in front.

2. **Click the** FILE **tab**

   The FILE tab opens, displaying **Backstage view**. It is called Backstage view becausee the commands available here are for working with the files "behind the scenes." The navigation bar on the left side of Backstage view contains commands to perform actions common to most Office programs.

3. **Click the** Back button ← **to close Backstage view and return to the document window, then click the** DESIGN tab **on the Ribbon**

   To display a different tab, click its name. Each tab contains related commands arranged into **groups** to make features easy to find. On the DESIGN tab, the Themes group displays available design themes in a **gallery**, or visual collection of choices you can browse. Many groups contain a **dialog box launcher**, which you can click to open a dialog box or pane from which to choose related commands.

4. **Move the mouse pointer** ⍢ **over the** Ion theme **in the Themes group as shown in** FIGURE A-6, **but** *do not click* **the mouse button**

   The Ion theme is temporarily applied to the slide in the document window. However, because you did not click the theme, you did not permanently change the slide. With the **Live Preview** feature, you can point to a choice, see the results, then decide if you want to make the change. Live Preview is available throughout Office.

5. **Move** ⍢ **away from the Ribbon and towards the slide**

   If you had clicked the Ion theme, it would be applied to this slide. Instead, the slide remains unchanged.

6. **Point to the** Zoom slider |— ——|— + 100%| **on the status bar, then drag to the right until the Zoom level reads** 166%

   The slide display is enlarged. Zoom tools are located on the status bar. You can drag the slider or click the Zoom In or Zoom Out buttons to zoom in or out on an area of interest. **Zooming in** (a higher percentage), makes a document appear bigger on screen but less of it fits on the screen at once; **zooming out** (a lower percentage) lets you see more of the document at a reduced size.

7. **Click the** Zoom Out button ▬ **on the status bar to the left of the Zoom slider until the Zoom level reads** 120%

FIGURE A-5: PowerPoint program window

Quick Access toolbar

Ribbon

Dialog box launcher

Title bar

Tabs

Document window

Click to add title

Click to add subtitle

FIGURE A-6: Viewing a theme with Live Preview

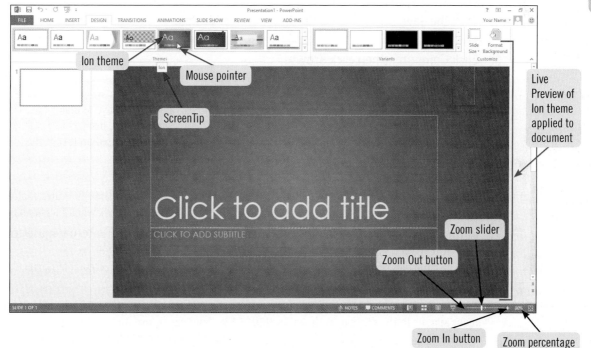

Ion theme

Mouse pointer

ScreenTip

Live Preview of Ion theme applied to document

Click to add title

CLICK TO ADD SUBTITLE

Zoom slider

Zoom Out button

Zoom In button

Zoom percentage

Using Backstage view

Backstage view in each Microsoft Office program offers "one stop shopping" for many commonly performed tasks, such as opening and saving a file, printing and previewing a document, defining document properties, sharing information, and exiting a program. Backstage view opens when you click the FILE tab in any Office program, and while features such as the Ribbon, Mini toolbar, and Live Preview all help you work *in* your documents, the FILE tab and Backstage view help you work *with* your documents. You can return to your active document by pressing the Back button.

Create and Save a File

Learning Outcomes
• Create a file
• Save a file
• Explain SkyDrive

When working in an Office program, one of the first things you need to do is to create and save a file. A **file** is a stored collection of data. Saving a file enables you to work on a project now, then put it away and work on it again later. In some Office programs, including Word, Excel, and PowerPoint, you can open a new file when you start the program, then all you have to do is enter some data and save it. In Access, you must create a file before you enter any data. You should give your files meaningful names and save them in an appropriate location, such as a folder on your hard drive or SkyDrive so they're easy to find. **SkyDrive** is the Microsoft cloud storage system that lets you easily save, share, and access your files from anywhere you have Internet access. See "Saving Files to SkyDrive" for more information on this topic. **CASE** ▶ *Use Word to familiarize yourself with creating and saving a document. First you'll type some notes about a possible location for a corporate meeting, then you'll save the information for later use.*

STEPS

1. **Click the Word program button** 🗄 **on the taskbar, click Blank document, then click the Zoom In button** ➕ **until the level is 120%, if necessary**

2. **Type Locations for Corporate Meeting, then press [Enter] twice**
   The text appears in the document window, and the **insertion point** blinks on a new blank line. The insertion point indicates where the next typed text will appear.

QUICK TIP
A filename can be up to 255 characters, including a file extension, and can include upper- or lowercase characters and spaces, but not ?, ", /, \, <, >, *, |, or :.

3. **Type Las Vegas, NV, press [Enter], type San Diego, CA, press [Enter], type Seattle, WA, press [Enter] twice, then type your name**

4. **Click the Save button** 🖫 **on the Quick Access toolbar**
   Backstage view opens showing various options for saving the file, as shown in **FIGURE A-7**.

5. **Click Computer, then click Browse**
   Because this is the first time you are saving this document, the Save As command is displayed. Once you choose a location where you will save the file, the Save As dialog box displays, as shown in **FIGURE A-8**. Once a file is saved, clicking 🖫 saves any changes to the file *without* opening the Save As dialog box. The Address bar in the Save As dialog box displays the default location for saving the file, but you can change it to any location. The File name field contains a suggested name for the document based on text in the file, but you can enter a different name.

QUICK TIP
Saving a file to the Desktop creates a desktop icon that you can double-click to both launch a program and open a document.

6. **Type OF A-Potential Corporate Meeting Locations**
   The text you type replaces the highlighted text. (The "OF A-" in the filename indicates that the file is created in Office Unit A. You will see similar designations throughout this book when files are named.)

7. **In the Save As dialog box, use the Address bar or Navigation Pane to navigate to the location where you store your Data Files**
   You can store files on your computer, a network drive, your SkyDrive, or any acceptable storage device.

QUICK TIP
To create a new blank file when a file is open, click the FILE tab, click New on the navigation bar, then click the option for the style document you want.

8. **Click Save**
   The Save As dialog box closes, the new file is saved to the location you specified, and the name of the document appears in the title bar, as shown in **FIGURE A-9**. (You may or may not see the file extension ".docx" after the filename.) See **TABLE A-1** for a description of the different types of files you create in Office, and the file extensions associated with each.

TABLE A-1: Common filenames and default file extensions

file created in	is called a	and has the default extension
Word	document	.docx
Excel	workbook	.xlsx
PowerPoint	presentation	.pptx
Access	database	.accdb

FIGURE A-7: Save As screen in Backstage view

Saves to your SkyDrive account

Click to change location for file

Click to save to your computer or alternate storage device

FIGURE A-8: Save As dialog box

Address bar

Navigation pane; your links and folders may differ

File name field; your computer may not display file extensions

Save as type list

FIGURE A-9: Saved and named Word document

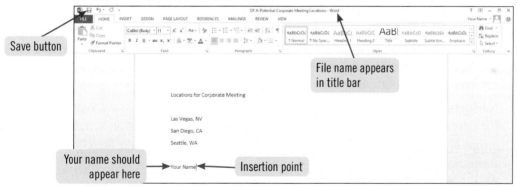

Save button

File name appears in title bar

Your name should appear here

Insertion point

Locations for Corporate Meeting

Las Vegas, NV

San Diego, CA

Seattle, WA

Saving files to SkyDrive

All Office programs include the capability to incorporate feedback—called **online collaboration**—across the Internet or a company network. Using **cloud computing** (work done in a virtual environment), you can take advantage of commonly shared features such as a consistent interface. Using SkyDrive, a free file storage service from Microsoft, you and your colleagues can create and store documents in the cloud and make the documents available anywhere there is Internet access to whomever you choose. To use SkyDrive, you need a free Microsoft Account, which you obtain at the signup.live.com website. You can find more information about SkyDrive in the "Working in the Cloud" appendix. When you are logged into your Microsoft account and you save a file in any of the Office apps, the first option in the Save As screen is your SkyDrive. Double-click your SkyDrive option and the Save As dialog box opens displaying a location in the address bar unique to your SkyDrive account. Type a name in the File name text box, then click Save and your file is saved to your SkyDrive. To sync your files with SkyDrive, you'll need to download and install the SkyDrive for Windows app. Then, when you open Explorer, you'll notice a new folder called SkyDrive has been added to the Users folder. In this folder is a sub-folder called Documents, in which an updated copy of your Office app files resides. This means if your Internet connection fails, you can work on your files offline. The SkyDrive folder also displays Explorer in the list of Favorites folders.

Open a File and Save It with a New Name

Learning Outcomes
• Open an existing file
• Save a file with a new name

In many cases as you work in Office, you start with a blank document, but often you need to use an existing file. It might be a file you or a coworker created earlier as a work in progress, or it could be a complete document that you want to use as the basis for another. For example, you might want to create a budget for this year using the budget you created last year; instead of typing in all the categories and information from scratch, you could open last year's budget, save it with a new name, and just make changes to update it for the current year. By opening the existing file and saving it with the Save As command, you create a duplicate that you can modify to suit your needs, while the original file remains intact. **CASE** ▶ *Use Excel to open an existing workbook file, and save it with a new name so the original remains unchanged.*

STEPS

TROUBLE
If you are running WIndows 7, click the Start button on the taskbar, type excel, then click Excel 2013.

1. **Go to the Windows 8 Start screen, type exc, click Excel 2013, click Open Other Workbooks, click Computer on the navigation bar, then click Browse**

   The Open dialog box opens, where you can navigate to any drive or folder accessible to your computer to locate a file. You can click Recent Workbooks on the navigation bar to display a list of recent workbooks; click a file in the list to open it.

2. **In the Open dialog box, navigate to the location where you store your Data Files**

   The files available in the current folder are listed, as shown in **FIGURE A-10**. This folder displays one file.

TROUBLE
Click Enable Editing on the Protected View bar near the top of your document window if prompted.

3. **Click OFFICE A-1.xlsx, then click Open**

   The dialog box closes, and the file opens in Excel. An Excel file is an electronic spreadsheet, so the new file displays a grid of rows and columns you can use to enter and organize data.

4. **Click the FILE tab, click Save As on the navigation bar, then click Browse**

   The Save As dialog box opens, and the current filename is highlighted in the File name text box. Using the Save As command enables you to create a copy of the current, existing file with a new name. This action preserves the original file and creates a new file that you can modify.

5. **Navigate to the location where you store your Data Files if necessary, type OF A-Budget for Corporate Meeting in the File name text box, as shown in FIGURE A-11, then click Save**

   A copy of the existing workbook is created with the new name. The original file, Office A-1.xlsx, closes automatically.

6. **Click cell A19, type your name, then press [Enter], as shown in FIGURE A-12**

   In Excel, you enter data in cells, which are formed by the intersection of a row and a column. Cell A19 is at the intersection of column A and row 19. When you press [Enter], the cell pointer moves to cell A20.

7. **Click the Save button 🖫 on the Quick Access toolbar**

   Your name appears in the workbook, and your changes to the file are saved.

Exploring File Open options

You might have noticed that the Open button in the Open dialog box includes a list arrow to the right of the button. In a dialog box, if a button includes a list arrow you can click the button to invoke the command, or you can click the list arrow to see a list of related commands that you can apply to a selected file in the file list. The Open list arrow includes several related commands, including Open Read-Only and Open as Copy.

Clicking Open Read-Only opens a file that you can only save with a new name; you cannot make changes to the original file. Clicking Open as Copy creates and opens a copy of the selected file and inserts the word "Copy" in the file's title. Like the Save As command, these commands provide additional ways to use copies of existing files while ensuring that original files do not get changed by mistake.

FIGURE A-10: Open dialog box

FIGURE A-11: Save As dialog box

FIGURE A-12: Your name added to the workbook

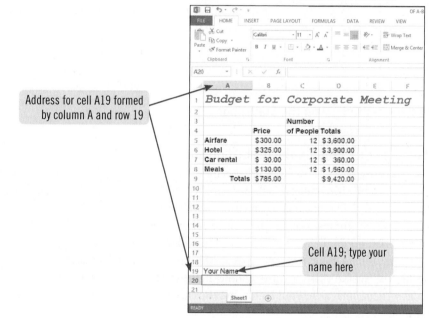

Address for cell A19 formed by column A and row 19

Cell A19; type your name here

Working in Compatibility Mode

Not everyone upgrades to the newest version of Office. As a general rule, new software versions are **backward compatible**, meaning that documents saved by an older version can be read by newer software. To open documents created in older Office versions, Office 2013 includes a feature called Compatibility Mode. When you use Office 2013 to open a file created in an earlier version of Office, "Compatibility Mode" appears in the title bar, letting you know the file was created in an earlier but usable version of the program. If you are working with someone who may not be using the newest version of the software, you can avoid possible incompatibility problems by saving your file in another, earlier format. To do this in an Office program, click the FILE tab, click Save As on the navigation bar, click the location where you want to save the file, then click Browse. In the Save As dialog box, click the Save as type list arrow in the Save As dialog box, then click an option on the list. For example, if you're working in Excel, click Excel 97-2003 Workbook format in the Save as type list to save an Excel file so it can be opened in Excel 97 or Excel 2003.

View and Print Your Work

Each Microsoft Office program lets you switch among various **views** of the document window to show more or fewer details or a different combination of elements that make it easier to complete certain tasks, such as formatting or reading text. Changing your view of a document does not affect the file in any way, it affects only the way it looks on screen. If your computer is connected to a printer or a print server, you can easily print any Office document using the Print button on the Print tab in Backstage view. Printing can be as simple as **previewing** the document to see exactly what a document will look like when it is printed and then clicking the Print button. Or, you can customize the print job by printing only selected pages. The Backstage view can also be used to share your document with others, or to export it in a different format. **CASE** *Experiment with changing your view of a Word document, and then preview and print your work.*

STEPS

1. Click the Word program button 📰 on the taskbar

Word becomes the active program, and the document fills the screen.

2. Click the VIEW tab on the Ribbon

In most Office programs, the VIEW tab on the Ribbon includes groups and commands for changing your view of the current document. You can also change views using the View buttons on the status bar.

3. Click the Read Mode button in the Views group on the VIEW tab

The view changes to Read Mode view, as shown in **FIGURE A-13**. This view shows the document in an easy-to-read, distraction-free reading mode. Notice that the Ribbon is no longer visible on screen.

4. Click the Print Layout button 📄 on the Status bar

You return to Print Layout view, the default view in Word.

5. Click the FILE tab, then click Print on the navigation bar

The Print tab opens in Backstage view. The preview pane on the right side of the window displays a preview of how your document will look when printed. Compare your screen to **FIGURE A-14**. Options in the Settings section enable you to change margins, orientation, and paper size before printing. To change a setting, click it, and then click a new setting. For instance, to change from Letter paper size to Legal, click Letter in the Settings section, then click Legal on the menu that opens. The document preview updates as you change the settings. You also can use the Settings section to change which pages to print. If your computer is connected to multiple printers, you can click the current printer in the Printer section, then click the one you want to use. The Print section contains the Print button and also enables you to select the number of copies of the document to print.

6. If your school allows printing, click the Print button in the Print section (otherwise, click the Back button ⊙)

If you chose to print, a copy of the document prints, and Backstage view closes.

Customizing the Quick Access toolbar

You can customize the Quick Access toolbar to display your favorite commands. To do so, click the Customize Quick Access Toolbar button ⚐ in the title bar, then click the command you want to add. If you don't see the command in the list, click More Commands to open the Quick Access Toolbar tab of the current program's Options dialog box. In the Options dialog box, use the Choose commands from list to choose a category, click the desired command in the list on the left, click Add to add it to the Quick Access toolbar, then click OK. To remove a button from the toolbar, click the name in the list on the right in the Options dialog box, then click Remove. To add a command to the Quick Access toolbar as you work, simply right-click the button on the Ribbon, then click Add to Quick Access Toolbar on the shortcut menu. To move the Quick Access toolbar below the Ribbon, click the Customize Quick Access Toolbar button, and then click Show Below the Ribbon.

FIGURE A-13: Web Layout view

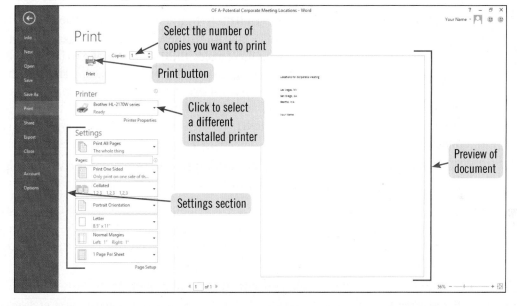

Print Layout button

View buttons on status bar

FIGURE A-14: Print settings on the FILE tab

Print

Select the number of copies you want to print

Print button

Printer

Click to select a different installed printer

Settings

Settings section

Preview of document

Creating a screen capture

A **screen capture** is a digital image of your screen, as if you took a picture of it with a camera. For instance, you might want to take a screen capture if an error message occurs and you want a Technical Support person to see exactly what's on the screen. You can create a screen capture using features found in Windows 8 or Office 2013. Both Windows 7 and Windows 8 come with the Snipping Tool, a separate program designed to capture whole screens or portions of screens. To open the Snipping Tool, click the Start screen thumbnail, type "sni", then click the Snipping Tool when it appears in the left panel. After opening the Snipping Tool, click New, then drag the pointer on the screen to select the area of the screen you want to capture. When you release the mouse button, the screen capture opens in the Snipping Tool window, and you can save, copy, or send it in an email. In Word, Excel, and PowerPoint 2013, you can capture screens or portions of screens and insert them in the current document using the Screenshot button in the Illustrations group on the INSERT tab. And finally, you can create a screen capture by pressing [PrtScn]. (Keyboards differ, but you may find the [PrtScn] button in or near your keyboard's function keys.) Pressing this key places a digital image of your screen in the Windows temporary storage area known as the **Clipboard**. Open the document where you want the screen capture to appear, click the HOME tab on the Ribbon (if necessary), then click the Paste button in the Clipboard group on the HOME tab. The screen capture is pasted into the document.

Learning
Outcomes
• Display a
  ScreenTip
• Use Help
• Close a file
• Exit an app

Get Help, Close a File, and Exit an App

You can get comprehensive help at any time by pressing [F1] in an Office app or clicking the Help button on the right end of the title bar. You can also get help in the form of a ScreenTip by pointing to almost any icon in the program window. When you're finished working in an Office document, you have a few choices regarding ending your work session. You close a file by clicking the FILE tab, then clicking Close; you exit a program by clicking the Close button on the title bar. Closing a file leaves a program running, while exiting a program closes all the open files in that program as well as the program itself. In all cases, Office reminds you if you try to close a file or exit a program and your document contains unsaved changes. **CASE** ▶ *Explore the Help system in Microsoft Office, and then close your documents and exit any open programs.*

STEPS

1. **Point to the Zoom button in the Zoom group on the VIEW tab of the Ribbon**
   A ScreenTip appears that describes how the Zoom button works and explains where to find other zoom controls.

2. **Click the Microsoft Word Help (F1) button ? in the upper-right corner of the title bar**
   The Word Help window opens, as shown in **FIGURE A-15**, displaying the home page for help in Word. Each entry is a hyperlink you can click to open a list of topics. The Help window also includes a toolbar of useful Help commands such as printing and increasing the font size for easier readability, and a Search field. If you are not connected to Office.com, a gold band is displayed telling you that you are not connected. Office.com supplements the help content available on your computer with a wide variety of up-to-date topics, templates, and training. If you are not connected to the Internet, the Help window displays only the help content available on your computer.

3. **Click the Learn Word basics link in the Getting started section of the Word Help window**
   The Word Help window changes, and a list of basic tasks appears below the topic.

4. **If necessary, scroll down until the Choose a template topic fills the Word Help window**
   The topic is displayed in the pane of the Help window, as shown in **FIGURE A-16**. The content in the window explains that you can create a document using a template (a pre-formatted document) or just create a blank document.

5. **Click in the Search online help text box, type Delete, then press [Enter]**
   The Word Help window now displays a list of links to topics about different types of deletions that are possible within Word.

6. **Click the Keep Help on Top button ⚲ in the upper-right corner (below the Close button)**
   The Pin Help button rotates so the pin point is pointed towards the bottom of the screen: this allows you to read the Help window while you work on your document.

7. **Click the Word document window, then notice the Help window remains visible**

8. **Click a blank area of the Help window, click ⚲ to Unpin Help, click the Close button ✕ in the Help window, then click the Close button ✕ in the upper-right corner of the screen**
   Word closes, and the Excel program window is active.

9. **Click the Close button ✕ to exit Excel, click the Close button ✕ to exit the remaining Excel workbook, click the PowerPoint program button 🖼 on the taskbar if necessary, then click the Close button ✕ to exit PowerPoint**
   Excel and PowerPoint both close.

FIGURE A-15: Word Help window

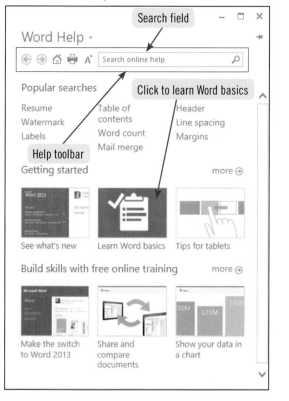

FIGURE A-16: Create a document Help topic

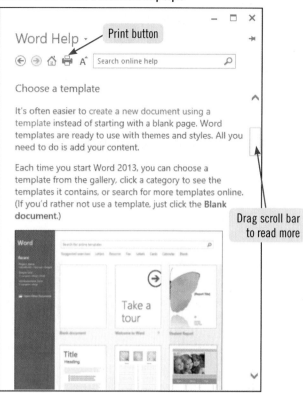

Enabling touch mode

If you are using a touch screen with any of the Office 2013 apps, you can enable the touch mode to give the user interface a more spacious look. Enable touch mode by clicking the Quick Access toolbar list arrow, then clicking Touch/Mouse Mode to select it. Then you'll see the Touch Mode button 👆 in the Quick Access toolbar. Click 👆, and you'll see the interface spread out.

Recovering a document

Each Office program has a built-in recovery feature that allows you to open and save files that were open at the time of an interruption such as a power failure. When you restart the program(s) after an interruption, the Document Recovery task pane opens on the left side of your screen displaying both original and recovered versions of the files that were open. If you're not sure which file to open (original or recovered), it's usually better to open the recovered file because it will contain the latest information. You can, however, open and review all versions of the file that were recovered and save the best one. Each file listed in the Document Recovery task pane displays a list arrow with options that allow you to open the file, save it as is, delete it, or show repairs made to it during recovery.

Practice

Concepts Review

Label the elements of the program window shown in FIGURE A-17.

FIGURE A-17

Match each project with the program for which it is best suited.

8. Microsoft Access   a. Corporate convention budget with expense projections

9. Microsoft Excel   b. Presentation for city council meeting

10. Microsoft Word   c. Business cover letter for a job application

11. Microsoft PowerPoint   d. Department store inventory

Independent Challenge 1

You just accepted an administrative position with a local independently owned produce vendor that has recently invested in computers and is now considering purchasing Microsoft Office for the company. You are asked to propose ways Office might help the business. You produce your document in Word.

a. Start Word, create a new Blank document, then save the document as **OF A-Microsoft Office Document** in the location where you store your Data Files.

b. Change the zoom factor to 120%, type **Microsoft Word**, press [Enter] twice, type **Microsoft Excel**, press [Enter] twice, type **Microsoft PowerPoint**, press [Enter] twice, type **Microsoft Access**, press [Enter] twice, then type your name.

c. Click the line beneath each program name, type at least two tasks you can perform using that program (each separated by a comma), then press [Enter].

d. Save the document, then submit your work to your instructor as directed.

e. Exit Word.

Getting Started with Access 2013

CASE ▶ Samantha Hooper is the tour developer for United States group travel at Quest Specialty Travel (QST), a tour company that specializes in customized group travel packages. Samantha uses Microsoft Access 2013 to store, maintain, and analyze customer and tour information.

Unit Objectives

After completing this unit, you will be able to:

- Understand relational databases
- Explore a database
- Create a database
- Create a table

- Create primary keys
- Relate two tables
- Enter data
- Edit data

Files You Will Need

QuestTravel-A.accdb
RealEstate-A.accdb
Recycle-A.accdb
BusinessContacts-A.accdb
Basketball-A.accdb

Learning
Outcomes
• Describe relational
database concepts
• Explain when to
use a database

Understand Relational Databases

Microsoft Access 2013 is relational database software that runs on the Windows operating system. You use **relational database software** to manage data that is organized into lists, such as information about customers, products, vendors, employees, projects, or sales. Many small companies track customer, inventory, and sales information in a spreadsheet program such as Microsoft Excel. Although Excel offers some list management features and is more commonly used than Access, Access provides many more tools and advantages for managing data. The advantages are mainly due to the "relational" nature of the lists that Access manages. **TABLE A-1** compares the two programs. **CASE** *You and Samantha Hooper review the advantages of database software over spreadsheets for managing lists of information.*

DETAILS

The advantages of using Access for database management include:

• **Duplicate data is minimized**

  FIGURES A-1 and **A-2** compare how you might store sales data in a single Excel spreadsheet list versus three related Access tables. With Access, you do not have to reenter information such as a customer's name and address or tour name every time a sale is made, because lists can be linked, or "related," in relational database software.

• **Information is more accurate, reliable, and consistent because duplicate data is minimized**

  The relational nature of data stored in an Access database allows you to minimize duplicate data entry, which creates more accurate, reliable, and consistent information. For example, customer data in a Customers table is entered only once, not every time a customer makes a purchase.

• **Data entry is faster and easier using Access forms**

  Data entry forms (screen layouts) make data entry faster, easier, and more accurate than entering data in a spreadsheet.

• **Information can be viewed and sorted in many ways using Access queries, forms, and reports**

  In Access, you can save queries (questions about the data), data entry forms, and reports, allowing you to use them over and over without performing extra work to re-create a particular view of the data.

• **Information is more secure using Access passwords and security features**

  Access databases can be encrypted and password protected.

• **Several users can share and edit information at the same time**

  Unlike spreadsheets or word-processing documents, more than one person can enter, update, and analyze data in an Access database at the same time.

FIGURE A-1: Using a spreadsheet to organize sales data

Customer information is duplicated when the same customer purchases multiple tours

Tour information is duplicated when the same tour is purchased by multiple customers

	A	B	C	D	E	F	G	H	I
1	CustNo	FName	LName	SalesNo	SaleDate	TourName	TourStartDate	City	Price
2	1	Gracita	Mayberry	35	7/1/2014	Red Reef Scuba	7/6/2014	Islamadora	1,500.00
3	2	Jacob	Alman	34	7/1/2014	Red Reef Scuba	7/6/2014	Islamadora	1,500.00
4	3	Julia	Bouchart	33	7/1/2014	Red Reef Scuba	7/6/2014	Islamadora	1,500.00
5	3	Julia	Bouchart	7	5/1/2014	Piper-Heitman Wedding	5/30/2014	Captiva	825.00
6	4	Jane	Taylor	13	5/11/2014	Red Reef Scuba	7/6/2014	Islamadora	1,500.00
7	4	Jane	Taylor	20	6/1/2014	American Heritage Tour	8/24/2014	Philadelphia	1,200.00
8	5	Samantha	Braven	30	7/1/2014	Red Reef Scuba	7/6/2014	Islamadora	1,500.00
9	5	Samantha	Braven	52	7/11/2014	Bright Lights Expo	12/1/2014	Branson	200.00
10	6	Kristen	Collins	3	4/30/2014	Ames Ski Club	1/2/2015	Breckenridge	850.00
11	6	Kristen	Collins	21	6/1/2014	Yosemite National Park Great Cleanup	7/20/2014	Sacramento	1,100.00
12	6	Kristen	Collins	29	7/1/2014	American Heritage Tour	8/24/2014	Philadelphia	1,200.00
13	6	Kristen	Collins	40	7/7/2014	Bright Lights Expo	12/1/2014	Branson	200.00
14	7	Tom	Camel	41	7/7/2014	Bright Lights Expo	12/1/2014	Branson	200.00
15	7	Tom	Camel	36	7/1/2014	American Heritage Tour	8/24/2014	Philadelphia	1,200.00
16	7	Tom	Camel	8	5/1/2014	Ames Ski Club	1/2/2015	Breckenridge	850.00
17	7	Tom	Camel	19	6/1/2014	Yosemite National Park Great Cleanup	7/20/2014	Sacramento	1,100.00
18	8	Dick	Tracy	43	7/8/2014	Bright Lights Expo	12/1/2014	Branson	200.00
19	9	Daniel	Cabriella	45	7/9/2014	American Heritage Tour	8/24/2014	Philadelphia	1,200.00
20	9	Daniel	Cabriella	46	7/9/2014	Bright Lights Expo	12/1/2014	Branson	200.00
21	10	Brad	Eahlie	66	7/14/2014	Boy Scout Jamboree	1/13/2015	Vail	1,900.00
22	11	Nancy	Diverman	32	7/1/2014	Red Reef Scuba	7/6/2014	Islamadora	1,500.00

FIGURE A-2: Using a relational database to organize sales data

Customers table

Cust No	First	Last	Street	City	State	Zip	Phone
1	Gracita	Mayberry	52411 Oakmont Rd	Kansas City	MO	64144	(555) 444-1234
2	Jacob	Alman	2505 McGee St	Des Moines	IA	50288	(555) 111-6931
3	Julia	Bouchart	5200 Main St	Kansas City	MO	64105	(555) 111-3081

Sales table

Cust No	TourNo	Date	SalesNo
1	2	7/1/14	35
2	2	7/1/14	34
3	2	7/1/14	33

Tours table

TourNo	TourName	TourStartDate	Duration	City	Cost
1	Stanley Bay Shelling	07/06/2014	3	Captiva	$750.00
2	Red Reef Scuba	07/06/2014	3	Islamadora	$1,500.00
3	Ames Ski Club	01/02/2015	7	Breckenridge	$850.00

TABLE A-1: Comparing Excel with Access

feature	Excel	Access
Layout	Provides a natural tabular layout for easy data entry	Provides a natural tabular layout as well as the ability to create customized data entry screens called forms
Storage	Restricted to a file's limitations	Virtually unlimited when coupled with the ability to use Microsoft SQL Server to store data
Linked tables	Manages single lists of information—no relational database capabilities	Relates lists of information to reduce data redundancy and create a relational database
Reporting	Limited	Provides the ability to create an unlimited number of reports
Security	Limited to file security options such as marking the file "read-only" or protecting a range of cells	When used with SQL Server, provides extensive security down to the user and data level
Multiuser capabilities	Not allowed	Allows multiple users to simultaneously enter and update data
Data entry	Provides limited data entry screens	Provides the ability to create an unlimited number of data entry forms

Explore a Database

You can start Access in many ways. If you double-click an existing Access *database* icon or shortcut, that specific database will open directly within Access. This is the fastest way to open an *existing* Access database. If you start Access on its own, however, you see a window that requires you to make a choice between opening a database and creating a new database. **CASE** *Samantha Hooper has developed a database called QuestTravel-A, which contains tour information. She asks you to start Access 2013 and review this database.*

STEPS

1. **Start Access**

   Access starts, as shown in **FIGURE A-3**. This window allows you to open an existing database, create a new database from a template, or create a new blank database.

2. **Click the Open Other Files link, navigate to the location where you store your Data Files, click the QuestTravel-A.accdb database, click Open, then click the Maximize button ▢ if the Access window is not already maximized**

   The QuestTravel-A.accdb database contains five tables of data named Customers, Sales, States, TourCategories, and Tours. It also contains six queries, six forms, and four reports. Each of these items (table, query, form, and report) is a different type of **object** in an Access database and is displayed in the **Navigation Pane**. The purpose of each object is defined in **TABLE A-2**. To learn about an Access database, you explore its objects.

3. **In the Navigation Pane, double-click the Tours table to open it, then double-click the Customers table to open it**

   The Tours and Customers tables open to display the data they store. A **table** is the fundamental building block of a relational database because it stores all of the data. You can enter or edit data in a table.

4. **In the Navigation Pane, double-click the TourSales query to open it, double-click any occurrence of Heritage (as in American Heritage Tour), type Legacy, then click any other row**

   A **query** selects a subset of data from one or more tables. In this case, the TourSales query selects data from the Tours, Sales, and Customers tables. Editing data in one object changes that information in every other object of the database, demonstrating the power and productivity of a relational database.

5. **Double-click the CustomerRoster form to open it, double-click Tour in "American Legacy Tour," type Rally, then click any name in the middle part of the window**

   An Access **form** is a data entry screen. Users prefer forms for data entry (rather than editing and entering data in tables and queries) because information can be presented in an easy-to-use layout.

6. **Double-click the TourSales report to open it**

   An Access **report** is a professional printout. A report is for printing purposes only, not data entry. As shown in **FIGURE A-4**, the edits made to the American Legacy Rally tour name have carried through to the report.

7. **Click the Close button ✕ in the upper-right corner of the window**

   Clicking the Close button in the upper-right corner of the window closes Access as well as the database on which you are working. Changes to data, such as the edits you made to the American Legacy Rally tour, are automatically saved as you work. Access will prompt you to save *design* changes to objects before it closes.

FIGURE A-3: Opening Microsoft Access 2013 window

Use Custom web app to create a Web-enabled database

Click a database name to open a recently used database; your list will differ

Click to browse for an Access database

Use Blank desktop database to create a new, local Access database

Use Templates to create a new Access database based on a template

FIGURE A-4: Objects in the QuestTravel-A database

Shutter Bar Open/Close button

Tours table tab

Navigation Pane

Path to database; yours will differ

TourSales report tab

CustomerRoster form tab

TourSales query tab

Customers table tab

American Legacy Rally

TABLE A-2: Access objects and their purpose

object	icon	purpose
Table		Contains all of the raw data within the database in a spreadsheet-like view; tables are linked with a common field to create a relational database, which minimizes redundant data
Query		Allows you to select a subset of fields or records from one or more tables; queries are created when you have a question about the data
Form		Provides an easy-to-use data entry screen
Report		Provides a professional printout of data that can contain enhancements such as headers, footers, graphics, and calculations on groups of records

Access 2013

Create a Database

Learning Outcomes
• Create a database
• Create a table
• Define key database terms

You can create a database using an Access **template**, a sample database provided within the Microsoft Access program, or you can start with a blank database to create a database from scratch. Your decision depends on whether Access has a template that closely resembles the type of data you plan to manage. If it does, building your own database from a template might be faster than creating the database from scratch. Regardless of which method you use, you can always modify the database later, tailoring it to meet your specific needs. **CASE** *Samantha Hooper reasons that the best way for you to learn Access is to start a new database from scratch, so she asks you to create a new database that will track customer communication.*

STEPS

1. **Start Access**

2. **Click the Blank desktop database icon, click the Browse button 🖿, navigate to the location where you store your Data Files, type Quest in the File name box, click OK, then click the Create button**

   A new, blank database file with a single table named Table1 is created, as shown in **FIGURE A-5**. Although you might be tempted to start entering data into the table, a better way to build a table is to first define the columns, or **fields**, of data that the table will store. **Table Design View** provides the most options for defining fields.

3. **Click the View button 🔏 on the FIELDS tab to switch to Design View, type Customers in the Save As dialog box as the new table name, then click OK**

   The table name changes from Table1 to Customers, and you are positioned in Table Design View, a window you use to name and define the fields of a table. Access created a field named ID with an AutoNumber data type. The **data type** is a significant characteristic of a field because it determines what type of data the field can store such as text, dates, or numbers. See **TABLE A-3** for more information about data types.

4. **Type CustID to rename ID to CustID, press [▾] to move to the first blank Field Name cell, type FirstName, press [▾], type LastName, press [▾], type Phone, press [▾], type Birthday, then press [▾]**

   Be sure to separate the first and last names into two fields so that you can easily sort, find, and filter on either part of the name later. The Birthday field will only contain dates, so you should change its data type from Short Text (the default data type) to Date/Time.

5. **Click Short Text in the Birthday row, click the list arrow, then click Date/Time**

   With these five fields properly defined for the new Customers table, as shown in **FIGURE A-6**, you're ready to enter data. You switch back to Datasheet View to enter or edit data. **Datasheet View** is a spreadsheet-like view of the data in a table. A **datasheet** is a grid that displays fields as columns and records as rows. The new **field names** you just defined are listed at the top of each column.

6. **Click the View button 🖻 to switch to Datasheet View, click Yes when prompted to save the table, press [Tab] to move to the FirstName field, type *your* first name, press [Tab] to move to the LastName field, type *your* last name, press [Tab] to move to the Phone field, type 111-222-3333, press [Tab], type 1/32/1980, then press [Tab]**

   Because 1/32/1980 is not a valid date, Access does not allow you to make that entry and displays an error message, as shown in **FIGURE A-7**. This shows that selecting the best data type for each field in Table Design View before entering data in Datasheet View helps prevent data entry errors.

TROUBLE
Tab through the CustID field rather than typing a value. The CustID value automatically increments to the next number.

7. **Press [Esc], edit the Birthday entry for the first record to 1/31/1980, press [Tab], enter two more sample records using realistic data, right-click the Customers table tab, then click Close to close the Customers table**

FIGURE A-5: Creating a database with a new table

FIGURE A-6: Defining field names and data types for the Customers table in Table Design View

FIGURE A-7: Entering your first record in the Customers table

TABLE A-3: Data types

data type	description of data
Short Text	Text or numbers not used in calculations such as a name, zip code, or phone number
Long Text	Lengthy text greater than 255 characters, such as comments or notes
Number	Numeric data that can be used in calculations, such as quantities
Date/Time	Dates and times
Currency	Monetary values
AutoNumber	Sequential integers controlled by Access
Yes/No	Only two values: Yes or No
OLE Object	OLE (Object Linking and Embedding) objects such as an Excel spreadsheet or Word document
Hyperlink	Web and e-mail addresses
Attachment	External files such as .jpg images, spreadsheets, and documents
Calculated	Result of a calculation based on other fields in the table
Lookup Wizard	The Lookup Wizard helps you set Lookup properties, which display a drop-down list of values for the field; after using the Lookup Wizard, the final data type for the field is either Short Text or Number depending on the values in the drop-down list

Create a Table

After creating your database and first table, you need to create new, related tables to build a relational database. Creating a table consists of these essential tasks: defining the fields in the table, selecting an appropriate data type for each field, naming the table, and determining how the table will participate in the relational database. **CASE** *Samantha Hooper asks you to create another table to store customer comments. The new table will eventually be connected to the Customers table so each customer record in the Customers table may be related to many records in the Comments table.*

STEPS

1. **Click the CREATE tab on the Ribbon, then click the Table Design button in the Tables group**

   Design View is a view in which you create and manipulate the structure of an object.

2. **Enter the field names and data types, as shown in FIGURE A-8**

   The Comments table will contain four fields. CommentID is set with an AutoNumber data type so each record is automatically numbered by Access. The Comment field has a Long Text data type so a long comment can be recorded. CommentDate is a Date/Time field to identify the date of the comment. CustID has a Number data type and will be used to link the Comments table to the Customers table later.

3. **Click the View button 🔲 to switch to Datasheet View, click Yes when prompted to save the table, type Comments as the table name, click OK, then click No when prompted to create a primary key**

   A **primary key field** contains unique data for each record. You'll identify a primary key field for the Comments table later. For now, you'll enter the first record in the Comments table in Datasheet View. A **record** is a row of data in a table. Refer to **TABLE A-4** for a summary of important database terminology.

4. **Press [Tab] to move to the Comment field, type Interested in future tours to New Zealand, press [Tab], type 1/7/15 in the CommentDate field, press [Tab], then type 1 in the CustID field**

   You entered 1 in the CustID field to connect this comment with the customer in the Customers table that has a CustID value of 1. Knowing which CustID value to enter for each comment is difficult. After you relate the tables properly (a task you have not yet performed), Access can make it easier to link each comment to the correct customer.

5. **Point to the divider line between the Comment and CommentDate field names, and then drag the ↔ pointer to the right to widen the Comment field to read the entire comment, as shown in FIGURE A-9**

6. **Right-click the Comments table tab, click Close, then click Yes if prompted to save the table**

Creating a table in Datasheet View

You can also create a new table in Datasheet View using the commands on the FIELDS tab of the Ribbon. But if you use Design View to design your table before starting the data entry process, you will probably avoid some common data entry errors. Design View helps you focus on the appropriate data type for each field.

Selecting the best data type for each field before entering any data into that field helps prevent incorrect data and unintended typos. For example, if a field is given a Number, Currency, or Date/Time data type, you will not be able to enter text into that field by mistake.

FIGURE A-8: Creating the Comments table

Enter these field names →

Field Name	Data Type
CommentID	AutoNumber
Comment	Long Text
CommentDate	Date/Time
CustID	Number

← Enter these data types

FIGURE A-9: Entering the first record in the Comments table

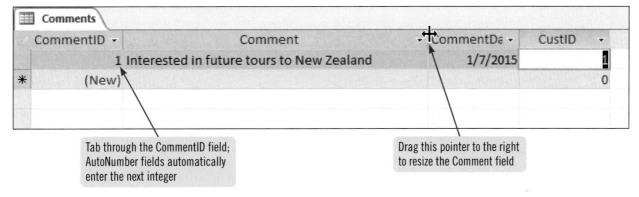

CommentID ▾	Comment	▾ CommentDa ▾	CustID ▾
1	Interested in future tours to New Zealand	1/7/2015	1
* (New)			0

Tab through the CommentID field; AutoNumber fields automatically enter the next integer

Drag this pointer to the right to resize the Comment field

TABLE A-4: Important database terminology

term	description
Field	A specific piece or category of data such as a first name, last name, city, state, or phone number
Record	A group of related fields that describes a person, place, thing, or transaction such as a customer, location, product, or sale
Key field	A field that contains unique information for each record, such as a customer number for a customer
Table	A collection of records for a single subject such as Customers, Products, or Sales
Relational database	Multiple tables that are linked together to address a business process such as managing tours, sales, and customers at Quest Specialty Travel
Objects	The parts of an Access database that help you view, edit, manage, and analyze the data: **tables**, **queries**, **forms**, **reports**, **macros**, and **modules**

© 2014 Cengage Learning

Create Primary Keys

Learning
Outcomes
• Set the primary
  key field
• Define one-to-
  many relationships

The **primary key field** of a table serves two important purposes. First, it contains data that uniquely identifies each record. No two records can have the exact same entry in the field designated as the primary key field. Second, the primary key field helps relate one table to another in a **one-to-many relationship**, where one record from one table may be related to many records in the second table. For example, one record in the Customers table may be related to many records in the Comments table. (One customer may have many comments.) The primary key field is always on the "one" side of a one-to-many relationship between two tables. **CASE** *Samantha Hooper asks you to check that a primary key field has been appropriately identified for each table in the new Quest database.*

STEPS

1. **Right-click the Comments table in the Navigation Pane, then click Design View**

   Table Design View for the Comments table opens. The field with the AutoNumber data type is generally the best candidate for the primary key field in a table because it automatically contains a unique number for each record.

   TROUBLE
   Make sure the DESIGN tab is selected on the Ribbon.

2. **Click the CommentID field if it is not already selected, then click the Primary Key button in the Tools group on the DESIGN tab**

   The CommentID field is now set as the primary key field for the Comments table, as shown in **FIGURE A-10**.

   QUICK TIP
   You can also click the Save button 💾 on the Quick Access toolbar to save a table.

3. **Right-click the Comments table tab, click Close, then click Yes to save the table**

   Any time you must save design changes to an Access object such as a table, Access displays a dialog box to remind you to save the object.

4. **Right-click the Customers table in the Navigation Pane, then click Design View**

   Access has already set CustID as the primary key field for the Customers table, as shown in **FIGURE A-11**.

5. **Right-click the Customers table tab, then click Close**

   You were not prompted to save the Customers table because you did not make any design changes. Now that you're sure that each table in the Quest database has an appropriate primary key field, you're ready to link the tables. The primary key field plays a critical role in this relationship.

FIGURE A-10: Creating a primary key field for the Comments table

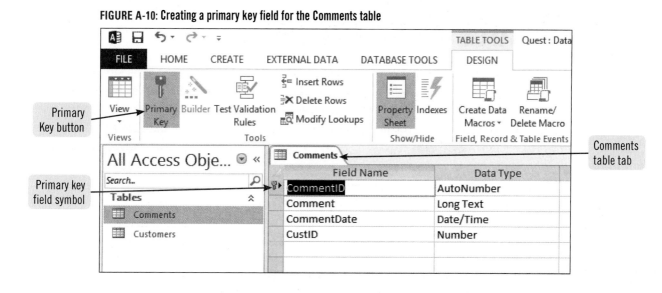

FIGURE A-11: Confirming the primary key field for the Customers table

Learning about field properties

Properties are the characteristics that define the field. Two properties are required for every field: Field Name and Data Type. Many other properties, such as Field Size, Format, Caption, and Default Value, are defined in the Field Properties pane in the lower half of a table's Design View. As you add more property entries, you are generally restricting the amount or type of data that can be entered in the field, which increases data entry accuracy. For example, you might change the Field Size property for a State field to 2 to eliminate an incorrect entry such as FLL. Field properties change depending on the data type of the selected field. For example, date fields do not have a Field Size property because Access controls the size of fields with a Date/Time data type.

Relate Two Tables

Learning Outcomes
• Define common field and foreign key field
• Create one-to-many relationships
• Set referential integrity

After you create tables and set primary key fields, you must connect the tables in one-to-many relationships to enjoy the benefits of a relational database. A one-to-many relationship between two tables means that one record from the first table is related to many records in the second table. You use a common field to make this connection. The common field is always the primary key field in the table on the "one" side of the relationship. **CASE** *Samantha Hooper explains that she has new comments to enter into the Quest database. To identify which customer is related to each comment, you define a one-to-many relationship between the Customers and Comments tables.*

STEPS

1. **Click the DATABASE TOOLS tab on the Ribbon, then click the Relationships button**

> **TROUBLE**
> If the Show Table dialog box doesn't appear, click the Show Table button on the DESIGN tab.

2. **In the Show Table dialog box, double-click Customers, double-click Comments, then click Close**

   Each table is represented by a small **field list** window that displays the table's field names. A key symbol identifies the primary key field in each table. To relate the two tables in a one-to-many relationship, you connect them using a common field, which is always the primary key field on the "one" side of the relationship.

> **QUICK TIP**
> Drag a table's title bar to move the field list.

3. **Drag CustID in the Customers field list to the CustID field in the Comments field list**

   The Edit Relationships dialog box opens, as shown in **FIGURE A-12**. **Referential integrity**, a set of Access rules that governs data entry, helps ensure data accuracy.

> **TROUBLE**
> If you need to delete an incorrect relationship, right-click a relationship line, then click Delete.

4. **Click the Enforce Referential Integrity check box in the Edit Relationships dialog box, then click Create**

   The **one-to-many line** shows the link between the CustID field of the Customers table (the "one" side) and the CustID field of the Comments table (the "many" side, indicated by the **infinity symbol**), as shown in **FIGURE A-13**. The linking field on the "many" side is called the **foreign key field**. Now that these tables are related, it is much easier to enter comments for the correct customer.

> **QUICK TIP**
> To print the Relationships window, click the Relationship Report button on the DESIGN tab, then click Print.

5. **Right-click the Relationships tab, click Close, click Yes to save changes, then double-click the Customers table in the Navigation Pane to open it in Datasheet View**

   When you relate two tables in a one-to-many relationship, expand buttons ⊞ appear to the left of each record in the table on the "one" side of the relationship. In this case, the Customers table is on the "one" side of the relationship.

6. **Click the expand button ⊞ to the left of the first record**

   A **subdatasheet** shows the related comment records for each customer. In other words, the subdatasheet shows the records on the "many" side of a one-to-many relationship. The expand button ⊞ also changed to the collapse button ⊟ for the first customer. Widening the Comment field allows you to see the entire entry in the Comments subdatasheet. Now the task of entering comments for the correct customer is much more straightforward.

> **TROUBLE**
> Be careful to enter complete comments for the correct customer, as shown in **FIGURE A-14**.

7. **Enter two more comments, as shown in FIGURE A-14**

   Interestingly, the CustID field in the Comments table (the foreign key field) is not displayed in the subdatasheet. Behind the scenes, Access is entering the correct CustID value in the Comments table, which is the glue that ties each comment to the correct customer.

8. **Close the Customers table, then click Yes if prompted to save changes**

FIGURE A-12: Edit Relationships dialog box

CustID field from the Customers table

CustID field from the Comments table

Enforce Referential Integrity check box

One-To-Many relationship, Customers to Comments

FIGURE A-13: Linking the Customers and Comments tables

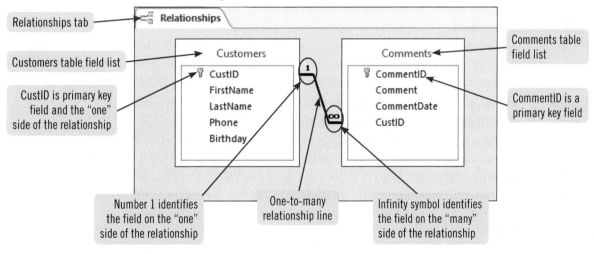

Relationships tab

Customers table field list

CustID is primary key field and the "one" side of the relationship

Comments table field list

CommentID is a primary key field

Number 1 identifies the field on the "one" side of the relationship

One-to-many relationship line

Infinity symbol identifies the field on the "many" side of the relationship

FIGURE A-14: Entering comments using the subdatasheet

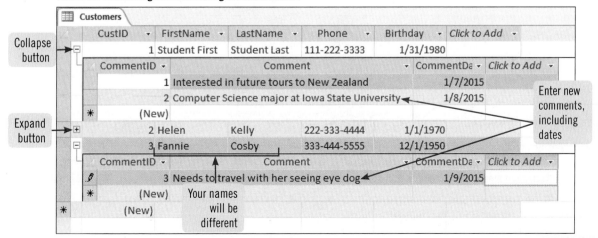

Collapse button

Expand button

Enter new comments, including dates

Your names will be different

Access 2013

Enter Data

Learning Outcomes
• Navigate records in a datasheet
• Enter records in a datasheet

Your skill in navigating and entering new records is a key to your success with a relational database. You can use many techniques to navigate through the records in the table's datasheet. **CASE** ▶ *Even though you have already successfully entered some records, Samantha Hooper asks you to master this essential skill by entering several more customers in the Quest database.*

STEPS

1. **Double-click the Customers table in the Navigation Pane to open it, press [Tab] three times, then press [Enter] three times**

   The Customers table reopens. The Comments subdatasheets are collapsed. Both the [Tab] and [Enter] keys move the focus to the next field. The **focus** refers to which data you would edit if you started typing. When you navigate to the last field of the record, pressing [Tab] or [Enter] advances the focus to the first field of the next record. You can also use the Next record ▶ and Previous record ◀ **navigation buttons** on the navigation bar in the lower-left corner of the datasheet to navigate through the records. The **Current record** text box on the navigation bar tells you the number of the current record as well as the total number of records in the datasheet.

   QUICK TIP
   Press [Tab] in the CustID AutoNumber field.

2. **Click the FirstName field of the fourth record to position the insertion point to enter a new record**

   You can also use the New (blank) record button ▶✱ on the navigation bar to move to a new record. You enter new records at the end of the datasheet. You learn how to sort and reorder records later. A complete list of navigation keystrokes is shown in **TABLE A-5**.

   QUICK TIP
   Access databases are multiuser with one important limitation: two users cannot edit the same *record* at the same time. In that case, a message explains that the second user must wait until the first user moves to a different record.

3. **At the end of the datasheet, enter the three records shown in FIGURE A-15**

   The **edit record symbol** ✎ appears to the left of the record you are currently editing. When you move to a different record, Access saves the data. Therefore, Access never prompts you to save *data* because it performs that task automatically. Saving data automatically allows Access databases to be **multiuser** databases, which means that more than one person can enter and edit data in the same database at the same time.

   Your CustID values might differ from those in **FIGURE A-15**. Because the CustID field is an **AutoNumber** field, Access automatically enters the next consecutive number into the field as it creates the record. If you delete a record or are interrupted when entering a record, Access discards the value in the AutoNumber field and does not reuse it. Therefore, AutoNumber values do not represent the number of records in your table. Instead, they provide a unique value per record, similar to check numbers.

Changing from Navigation mode to Edit mode

If you navigate to another area of the datasheet by clicking with the mouse pointer instead of pressing [Tab] or [Enter], you change from **Navigation mode** to Edit mode. In **Edit mode**, Access assumes that you are trying to make changes to the current field value, so keystrokes such as [Ctrl][End], [Ctrl][Home], [◀], and [▶] move the insertion point within the field. To return to Navigation mode, press [Tab] or [Enter] (thus moving the focus to the next field), or press [▲] or [▼] (thus moving the focus to a different record).

FIGURE A-15: New records in the Customers table

TABLE A-5: Navigation mode keyboard shortcuts

shortcut key	moves to the
[Tab], [Enter], or [→]	Next field of the current record
[Shift][Tab] or [←]	Previous field of the current record
[Home]	First field of the current record
[End]	Last field of the current record
[Ctrl][Home] or [F5]	First field of the first record
[Ctrl][End]	Last field of the last record
[↑]	Current field of the previous record
[↓]	Current field of the next record

© 2014 Cengage Learning

Cloud computing

Using SkyDrive, a free service from Microsoft, you can store files in the "cloud" and retrieve them anytime you are connected to the Internet. Saving your files to the SkyDrive is one example of cloud computing. **Cloud computing** means you are using an Internet resource to complete your work. You can find more information in the "Working in the Cloud" appendix.

Edit Data

Updating existing data in a database is another critical database task. To change the contents of an existing record, navigate to the field you want to change and type the new information. You can delete unwanted data by clicking the field and using [Backspace] or [Delete] to delete text to the left or right of the insertion point. Other data entry keystrokes are summarized in **TABLE A-6**. **CASE** *Samantha Hooper asks you to correct two records in the Customers table.*

STEPS

1. **Double-click the name in the FirstName field of the second record, type Kelsey, press [Enter], type Barker, press [Enter], type 111-222-4444, press [Enter], type 2/15/84, then press [Enter]**

   You changed the name, telephone number, and birth date of the second customer. When you entered the last two digits of the year value, Access inserted the first two digits after you pressed [Enter]. You'll also change the third customer.

2. **Press [Enter] to move to the FirstName field of the third record, type Joshua, press [Enter], type Lang, press [Enter], type 222-333-4444, then press [Esc]**

   Pressing [Esc] once removes the current field's editing changes, so the Phone value changes back to the previous entry. Pressing [Esc] twice removes all changes to the current record. When you move to another record, Access saves your edits, so you can no longer use [Esc] to remove editing changes to the current record. You can, however, click the Undo button ↩ on the Quick Access toolbar to undo changes to a previous record.

3. **Retype 222-333-4444, press [Enter], type 12/1/50 in the Birthday field, press [Enter], click the 12/1/50 date you just entered, click the Calendar icon 🗓, then click April 14, 1951, as shown in FIGURE A-16**

   When you are working in the Birthday field, which has a Date/Time data type, you can enter a date from the keyboard or use the **Calendar Picker**, a pop-up calendar to find and select a date.

4. **Click the record selector for the last record (Oscar Lee), click the Delete button in the Records group on the HOME tab, then click Yes**

   A message warns that you cannot undo a record deletion. The Undo button is dimmed, indicating that you cannot use it. The Customers table now has five records, as shown in **FIGURE A-17**. Keep in mind that your CustID values might differ from those in the figure because they are controlled by Access.

5. **Click the FILE tab, click Print, then click Print Preview to review the printout of the Customers table before printing**

6. **Click the Close Print Preview button, click the Close button in the upper-right corner of the window to close the Quest.accdb database and Access 2013, then click Yes if prompted to save design changes to the Customers table**

FIGURE A-16: Editing customer records

Quick Access toolbar; your buttons might be different

Record selector button for last record

Delete button

Calendar icon

April 14, 1951

Click the left or right arrow to change the month

FIGURE A-17: Final Customers datasheet

	CustID	FirstName	LastName	Phone	Birthday	Click to Add
⊞	1	Student First	Student Last	111-222-3333	1/31/1980	
⊞	2	Kelsey	Barker	111-222-4444	2/15/1984	
⊞	3	Joshua	Lang	222-333-4444	4/14/1951	
⊞	4	Renada	Champ	444-555-6666	4/1/1981	
⊞	5	Wilbur	Schafly	555-666-7777	5/1/1982	
✳	(New)					

Your name is entered in the first record

Oscar Lee record is deleted

TABLE A-6: Edit mode keyboard shortcuts

editing keystroke	action
[Backspace]	Deletes one character to the left of the insertion point
[Delete]	Deletes one character to the right of the insertion point
[F2]	Switches between Edit and Navigation mode
[Esc]	Undoes the change to the current field
[Esc][Esc]	Undoes all changes to the current record
[F7]	Starts the spell-check feature
[Ctrl][']	Inserts the value from the same field in the previous record into the current field
[Ctrl][;]	Inserts the current date in a Date field

Resizing and moving datasheet columns

You can resize the width of a field in a datasheet by dragging the column separator, the thin line that separates the field names to the left or right. The pointer changes to ↔ as you make the field wider or narrower. Release the mouse button when you have resized the field. To adjust the column width to accommodate the widest entry in the field, double-click the column separator. To move a column, click the field name to select the entire column, then drag the field name left or right.

Practice

Concepts Review

Label each element of the Access window shown in FIGURE A-18.

FIGURE A-18

Match each term with the statement that best describes it.

10. Field	**a.** A subset of data from one or more tables
11. Record	**b.** A collection of records for a single subject, such as all the customer records
12. Table	**c.** A professional printout of database information
13. Datasheet	**d.** A spreadsheet-like grid that displays fields as columns and records as rows
14. Query	**e.** A group of related fields for one item, such as all of the information for one
15. Form	customer
16. Report	**f.** A category of information in a table, such as a company name, city, or state
	g. An easy-to-use data entry screen

Select the best answer from the list of choices.

17. Which of the following is *not* a typical benefit of relational databases?

  a. Minimized duplicate data entry   **c.** Faster information retrieval

  b. More accurate data   **d.** More common than spreadsheets

18. **Which of the following is *not* an advantage of managing data with relational database software such as Access versus spreadsheet software such as Excel?**

    a. Allows multiple users to enter data simultaneously

    b. Uses a single table to store all data

    c. Provides data entry forms

    d. Reduces duplicate data entry

19. **When you create a new database, which object is created first?**

    a. Form   **c.** Module

    b. Query   **d.** Table

Skills Review

1. **Understand relational databases.**

    a. Write down five advantages of managing database information in Access versus using a spreadsheet.

    b. Write a sentence to explain how the terms *field, record, table*, and *relational database* relate to one another.

2. **Explore a database.**

    a. Start Access.

    b. Open the RealEstate-A.accdb database from the location where you store your Data Files. Click Enable Content if a yellow Security Warning message appears.

    c. Open each of the four tables to study the data they contain. Complete the following table:

table name	number of records	number of fields

    d. Double-click the ListingsByRealtor query in the Navigation Pane to open it. Change any occurrence of Gordon Bono to *your* name. Move to another record to save your changes.

    e. Double-click the RealtorsMainForm in the Navigation Pane to open it. Use the navigation buttons to navigate through the 11 realtors to observe each realtor's listings.

    f. Double-click the RealtorListingReport in the Navigation Pane to open it. The records are listed in ascending order by last name. Scroll through the report to make sure your name is positioned correctly.

    g. Close the RealEstate-A database, and then close Access 2013.

3. **Create a database.**

    a. Start Access, click the Blank desktop database icon, use the Browse button to navigate to the location where you store your Data Files, type **RealEstateMarketing** as the filename, click OK, and then click Create to create a new database named RealEstateMarketing.accdb.

Skills Review (continued)

b. Switch to Table Design View, name the table **Prospects**, then enter the following fields and data types:

field name	data type
ProspectID	AutoNumber
ProspectFirst	Short Text
ProspectLast	Short Text
Phone	Short Text
Email	Hyperlink
Street	Short Text
City	Short Text
State	Short Text
Zip	Short Text

c. Save the table, switch to Datasheet View, and enter two records using *your* name in the first record and your instructor's name in the second. Tab through the ProspectID field, an AutoNumber field.

d. Enter **TX** (Texas) as the value in the State field for both records. Use school or fictitious (rather than personal) data for all other field data, and be sure to fill out each record completely.

e. Widen each column in the Prospects table so that all data is visible, then save and close the Prospects table.

4. Create a table.

a. Click the CREATE tab on the Ribbon, click the Table Design button in the Tables group, then create a new table with the following two fields and data types:

field name	data type
StateAbbrev	Short Text
StateName	Short Text

b. Save the table with the name **States**. Click No when asked if you want Access to create the primary key field.

5. Create primary keys.

a. In Table Design View of the States table, set the StateAbbrev as the primary key field.

b. Save the States table and open it in Datasheet View.

c. Enter one state record, using **TX** for the StateAbbrev value and **Texas** for the StateName value to match the State value of TX that you entered for both records in the Prospects table.

d. Close the States table.

6. Relate two tables.

a. From the DATABASE TOOLS tab, open the Relationships window.

b. Add the States, then the Prospects table to the Relationships window.

c. Drag the bottom edge of the Prospects table to expand the field list to display all of the fields.

FIGURE A-19

d. Drag the StateAbbrev field from the States table to the State field of the Prospects table.

e. In the Edit Relationships dialog box, click the Enforce Referential Integrity check box, then click Create. Your Relationships window should look similar to **FIGURE A-19**. If you connect the wrong fields by mistake, right-click the line connecting the two fields, click Delete, then try again.

f. Close the Relationships window, and save changes when prompted.

Skills Review (continued)

7. Enter data.

a. Open the States table and enter the following records:

StateAbbrev field	StateName field
CO	Colorado
IA	Iowa
KS	Kansas
MO	Missouri
NE	Nebraska
OK	Oklahoma
WI	Wisconsin

b. Add three more state records of your choice for a total of 11 records in the States table using the correct two-character abbreviation for the state and the correctly spelled state name.

c. Close and reopen the States table. Notice that Access automatically sorts the records by the values in the primary key field, the StateAbbrev field.

8. Edit data.

a. Click the Expand button for the TX record to see the two related records from the Prospects table.

b. Enter two more prospects in the TX subdatasheet using any fictitious but realistic data, as shown in **FIGURE A-20**. Notice that you are not required to enter a value for the State field, the foreign key field in the subdatasheet.

FIGURE A-20

StateAbbrev	StateName	Click to Add
⊞ CO	Colorado	
⊞ FL	Florida	
⊞ GA	Georgia	
⊞ IA	Iowa	
⊞ KS	Kansas	
⊞ LA	Louisiana	
⊞ MO	Missouri	
⊞ NE	Nebraska	
⊞ OK	Oklahoma	
⊟ TX	Texas	

ProspectID	ProspectFirst	ProspectLast	Phone	Email	Street	City	Zip
1	Student First	Student Last	111-222-3333	student@state.edu	12345 College Blvd	Overland Park	66222
2	Instructor First	Instructor Last	222-333-4444	instructor@state.edu	12345 State Road	Lenexa	66111
3	George	Washington	333-444-5555	george@state.edu	12345 Wagon Wheel	Dallas	99888
4	Betsy	Ross	444-555-6666	betsy@state.edu	12345 Dirt Road	Austin	99777
* (New)							

StateAbbrev	StateName	
⊞ WI	Wisconsin	

c. If required by your instructor, print the States datasheet and the Prospects datasheet.

d. Click the Close button in the upper-right corner of the Access window to close all open objects as well as the RealEstateMarketing.accdb database and Access 2013. If prompted to save any design changes, click Yes.

Independent Challenge 1

Consider the following twelve subject areas:

- Telephone directory
- College course offerings
- Restaurant menu items
- Vehicles
- Movie listings

- Islands of the Caribbean
- Physical activities
- Shopping catalog items
- Conventions
- Party guest list

- Members of the U.S. House
- Ancient wonders of the world of Representatives

a. For each subject, build a Word table with 4–7 columns and three rows. In the first row, enter field names that you would expect to see in a table used to manage that subject.

b. In the second and third rows of each table, enter two realistic records. The first table, Telephone Directory, is completed as an example to follow.

TABLE: Telephone Directory

FirstName	LastName	Street	Zip	Phone
Marco	Lopez	100 Main Street	88715	555-612-3312
Christopher	Stafford	253 Maple Lane	77824	555-612-1179

Independent Challenge 2

You are working with several civic groups to coordinate a community-wide cleanup effort. You have started a database called Recycle-A, which tracks the clubs, their trash deposits, and the trash collection centers that are participating.

a. Start Access, then open the Recycle-A.accdb database from the location where you store your Data Files. Enable content if prompted.

b. Open each table's datasheet to study the number of fields and records per table. Notice that there are no expand buttons to the left of any records because relationships have not yet been established between these tables.

c. In a Word document, re-create the following table and fill in the blanks:

d. Close all table datasheets, then open the Relationships window and create the following one-to-many relationships. Drag the tables from the Navigation Pane to the Relationships window, and drag the title bars and borders of the field lists to position them as shown in **FIGURE A-21**.

table name	number of fields	number of records

field on the "one" side of the relationship	field on the "many" side of the relationship
ClubNumber in Clubs table	ClubNumber in Deposits table
CenterNumber in Centers table	CenterNumber in Deposits table

e. Be sure to enforce referential integrity on all relationships. If you create an incorrect relationship, right-click the line linking the fields, click Delete, and try again. Your final Relationships window should look like **FIGURE A-21**.

f. Click the Relationship Report button on the DESIGN tab, and if required by your instructor, click Print to print a copy of the Relationships for Recycle-A report. To close the report, right-click the Relationships for Recycle-A tab and click Close. Click Yes when prompted to save changes to the report with the name **Relationships for Recycle-A**. Save and close the Relationships window.

FIGURE A-21

g. Open the Clubs table and add a new record with fictitious but realistic data in all of the fields. Enter **8** as the ClubNumber value and *your* name in the FName (first name) and LName (last name) fields.

h. Expand the subdatasheets for each record in the Clubs table to see the related records from the Deposits table. Which club made the most deposits? Be ready to answer in class. Close the Clubs table.

i. Open the Centers table and add a new record with fictitious but realistic data in all of the fields. Enter *your* first and last names in the CenterName field and **5** as the CenterNumber.

j. Expand the subdatasheets for each record in the Centers table to see the related records from the Deposits table. Which center made the most deposits? Be ready to answer in class. Close the Centers table.

k. Close the Recycle-A.accdb database, then exit Access 2013.

Independent Challenge 3

You are working for an advertising agency that provides advertising media for small and large businesses in the midwestern United States. You have started a database called BusinessContacts-A, which tracks your company's customers. (*Note: To complete this Independent Challenge, make sure you are connected to the Internet.*)

a. Start Access and open the BusinessContacts-A.accdb database from the location where you store your Data Files. Enable content if prompted.

b. Add a new record to the Customers table, using any local business name, *your* first and last names, **$7,788.99** in the YTDSales field, and fictitious but reasonable entries for the rest of the fields.

c. Edit the Sprint Systems record (ID 1). The Company name should be changed to **MTB Mobile**, and the Street value should be changed to **4455 College St**.

d. Delete the record for St Luke's Hospital (ID 20), then close the Customers table.

e. Create a new table with two fields, **State2** and **StateName**. Assign both fields a Short Text data type. The State2 field will contain the two-letter abbreviation for state names. The StateName field will contain the full state name.

f. Set the State2 field as the primary key field, then save the table as **States**.

g. Enter at least three records into the States table, making sure that all of the states used in the Customers datasheet are entered in the States table. This includes **KS Kansas**, **MO Missouri**, and any other state you entered in Step b when you added a new record to the Customers table.

h. Close all open tables. Open the Relationships window, add both the States and Customers field lists to the window, then expand the size of the Customers field list so that all fields are visible.

i. Build a one-to-many relationship between the States and Customers tables by dragging the State2 field from the States table to the State field of the Customers table to create a one-to-many relationship between the two tables. Enforce referential integrity on the relationship. If you are unable to enforce referential integrity, it means that a value in the State field of the Customers table doesn't have a perfect match in the State2 field of the States table. Open both table datasheets, making sure every state in the State field of the Customers table is also represented in the State2 field of the States table, close all datasheets, then reestablish the one-to-many relationship between the two tables with referential integrity.

j. Click the Relationship Report button on the DESIGN tab, then if requested by your instructor, click Print to print the report.

k. Right-click the Relationships for BusinessContacts-A tab, then click Close. Click Yes when prompted to save the report with the name **Relationships for BusinessContacts-A**.

l. Close the Relationships window, saving changes as prompted.

m. Close BusinessContacts-A.accdb database, and exit Access 2013.

Independent Challenge 4: Explore

Now that you've learned about Microsoft Access and relational databases, brainstorm how you might use an Access database in your daily life or career. Start by visiting the Microsoft Web site, and explore what's new about Access 2013.

(*Note:* To complete this Independent Challenge, make sure you are connected to the Internet.)

a. Using your favorite search engine, look up the keywords *benefits of a relational database* or *benefits of Microsoft Access* to find articles that discuss the benefits of organizing data in a relational database.

b. Read several articles about the benefits of organizing data in a relational database such as Access, identifying three distinct benefits. Use a Word document to record those three benefits. Also, copy and paste the Web site address of the article you are referencing for each benefit you have identified.

c. In addition, as you read the articles that describe relational database benefits, list any terminology unfamiliar to you, identifying at least five new terms.

d. Using a search engine or a Web site that provides a computer glossary such as *www.whatis.com* or *www.webopedia.com*, look up the definition of the new terms, and enter both the term and the definition of the term in your document as well as the Web site address where your definition was found.

e. Finally, based on your research and growing understanding of Access 2013, list three ways you could use an Access database to organize, enhance, or support the activities and responsibilities of your daily life or career. Type your name at the top of the document, and submit it to your instructor as requested.

Visual Workshop

Open the Basketball-A.accdb database from the location where you store your Data Files, then enable content if prompted. Open the Offense query datasheet, which lists offensive statistics by player by game. Modify any of the Ellyse Howard records to contain *your* first and last names, then move to a different record, observing the power of a relational database to modify every occurrence of that name throughout the database. Close the Offense query, then open the Players table. Note that there are no expand buttons to the left of the records indicating that this table does not participate on the "one" side of a one-to-many relationship. Close the Players table and open the Relationships window. Drag the tables from the Navigation Pane and create the relationships with referential integrity, as shown in **FIGURE A-22**. Note the one-to-many relationship between the Players and Stats table. Print the Relationships report if requested by your instructor and save it with the name **Relationships for Basketball**-A. Close the report and close and save the Relationships window. Now reopen the Players table noting the expand buttons to the left of each record. Expand the subdatasheet for your name and for several other players to observe the "many" records from the Stats table that are now related to each record in the Players table.

FIGURE A-22

Building and Using Queries

CASE ▶ Samantha Hooper, tour developer for U.S. group travel at Quest Specialty Travel, has several questions about the customer and tour information in the Quest database. You'll develop queries to provide Samantha with up-to-date answers.

Unit Objectives

After completing this unit, you will be able to:

- Use the Query Wizard
- Work with data in a query
- Use Query Design View
- Sort and find data

- Filter data
- Apply AND criteria
- Apply OR criteria
- Format a datasheet

Files You Will Need

QuestTravel-B.accdb
Recycle-B.accdb
Membership-B.accdb
Congress-B.accdb
Vet-B.accdb
Baseball-B.accdb

©Tumanyan/Shutterstock

Use the Query Wizard

Learning Outcomes
- Describe the purpose for a query
- Create a query with the Simple Query Wizard

A **query** answers a question about the information in the database. A query allows you to select a subset of fields and records from one or more tables and then present the selected data as a single datasheet. A major benefit of working with data through a query is that you can focus on only the specific information you need to answer a question, rather than navigating through all the fields and records from many large tables. You can enter, edit, and navigate data in a query datasheet just like a table datasheet. However, keep in mind that Access data is physically stored only in tables, even though you can select, view, and edit it through other Access objects such as queries and forms. Because a query doesn't physically store the data, a query datasheet is sometimes called a **logical view** of the data. Technically, a query is a set of **SQL (Structured Query Language)** instructions, but because you can use Access query tools such as Query Design View to create and modify the query, you are not required to know SQL to build or use Access queries. **CASE** *You use the Simple Query Wizard to create a query that displays fields from the Tours and Customers tables in one datasheet.*

STEPS

1. **Start Access, open the QuestTravel-B.accdb database, enable content if prompted, then maximize the window**

   Access provides several tools to create a new query. One way is to use the **Simple Query Wizard**, which prompts you for the information it needs to create a new query.

2. **Click the CREATE tab on the Ribbon, click the Query Wizard button in the Queries group, then click OK to start the Simple Query Wizard**

   The Simple Query Wizard dialog box opens, prompting you to select the fields you want to view in the new query. You can select fields from one or more existing tables or queries.

3. **Click the Tables/Queries list arrow, click Table: Tours, double-click TourName, double-click City, double-click Category, then double-click Price**

   So far, you've selected four fields from the Tours table to display basic tour information in this query. You also want to add the first and last name information from the Customers table so you know which customers purchased each tour.

4. **Click the Tables/Queries list arrow, click Table: Customers, double-click FName, then double-click LName**

   You've selected four fields from the Tours table and two from the Customers table for your new query, as shown in **FIGURE B-1**.

5. **Click Next, click Next to select Detail, select Tours Query in the title text box, type TourCustomerList as the name of the query, then click Finish**

   The TourCustomerList datasheet opens, displaying four fields from the Tours table and two from the Customers table, as shown in **FIGURE B-2**. The query can show which customers have purchased which tours because of the one-to-many table relationships established in the Relationships window.

FIGURE B-1: Selecting fields using the Simple Query Wizard

Simple Query Wizard

Which fields do you want in your query?

You can choose from more than one table or query.

Tables/Queries

Table: Customers

> Tables/Queries list arrow

Available Fields:

CustNo
Street
City
State
Zip
Phone
FirstContact

Selected Fields:

TourName
City
Category
Price
FName
LName

> Selected Fields list

> Four fields from the Tours table

> Two fields from the Customers table

> Available Fields list

Cancel   < Back   Next >   Finish

FIGURE B-2: TourCustomerList datasheet

TourCustomerList

> Four fields from Tours table

> Two fields from Customers table

TourName	City	Category	Price	FName	LName
Stanley Bay Shelling	Captiva	Adventure	$750	Ralph	Hopper
Stanley Bay Shelling	Captiva	Adventure	$750	Lisa	Wilson
Ames Ski Club	Breckenridge	Adventure	$850	Kristen	Collins
Stanley Bay Shelling	Captiva	Adventure	$750	Kris	Goode
Stanley Bay Shelling	Captiva	Adventure	$750	Lois	Goode
Stanley Bay Shelling	Captiva	Adventure	$750	Naresh	Hubert
Piper-Heitman Wedding	Captiva	Family	$550	Julia	Bouchart
Ames Ski Club	Breckenridge	Adventure	$850	Tom	Camel
Golden Footsteps	Orlando	Site Seeing	$550	Shirley	Walker
Golden Footsteps	Orlando	Site Seeing	$550	Zohra	Vogue
Golden Footsteps	Orlando	Site Seeing	$550	Kathryn	Dotey
Golden Footsteps	Orlando	Site Seeing	$550	Jose	Hammer
Red Reef Scuba	Islamadora	Adventure	$1,500	Jane	Taylor
Stanley Bay Shelling	Captiva	Adventure	$750	Kori	Yode
American Heritage Tour	Philadelphia	Educational	$1,200	Sharol	Olingback
American Heritage Tour	Philadelphia	Educational	$1,200	Lois	Goode
American Heritage Tour	Philadelphia	Educational	$1,200	Tim	Taylor
American Heritage Tour	Philadelphia	Educational	$1,200	Frank	Houston
Yosemite National Park (	Sacramento	Service	$1,100	Tom	Camel
American Heritage Tour	Philadelphia	Educational	$1,200	Jane	Taylor
Yosemite National Park (	Sacramento	Service	$1,100	Kristen	Collins
American Heritage Tour	Philadelphia	Educational	$1,200	Kris	Goode
American Heritage Tour	Philadelphia	Educational	$1,200	Ralph	Hopper
American Heritage Tour	Philadelphia	Educational	$1,200	Nancy	Langguth
American Heritage Tour	Philadelphia	Educational	$1,200	Brad	Langguth

Record: 1 of 102   No Filter   Search

> 102 records

Work with Data in a Query

Learning
Outcomes
• Edit records in
  a query
• Delete records in
  a query

You enter and edit data in a query datasheet the same way you do in a table datasheet. Because all data is stored in tables, any edits you make to data in a query datasheet are actually stored in the underlying tables and are automatically updated in all views of the data in other queries, forms, and reports. **CASE** ▶ *You want to change the name of one tour and update a customer name. You can use the TourCustomerList query datasheet to make these edits.*

STEPS

1. **Double-click Stanley in the TourName field of the first or second record, type Breeze, then click any other record**

   All occurrences of Stanley Bay Shelling automatically update to Breeze Bay Shelling because this tour name value is stored only once in the Tours table. See **FIGURE B-3**. The tour name is selected from the Tours table and displayed in the TourCustomerList query for each customer who purchased this tour.

2. **Double-click Orlando in the City field of any record for the Golden Footsteps tour, type Kissimmee, then click any other record**

   All occurrences of Orlando automatically update to Kissimmee because this value is stored only once in the City field of the Tours table for the Golden Footsteps record. The Golden Footsteps tour is displayed in the TourCustomerList query for each customer who purchased the tour.

3. **Click the record selector button to the left of the first record, click the HOME tab, click the Delete button in the Records group, then click Yes**

   You can delete records from a query datasheet the same way you delete them from a table datasheet. Notice that the navigation bar now indicates you have 101 records in the datasheet, as shown in **FIGURE B-4**.

4. **Right-click the TourCustomerList query tab, then click Close**

   Each time a query is opened, it shows a current view of the data. This means that as new tours, customers, or sales are recorded in the database, the next time you open this query, the information will include all updates.

Record selector button for first record →

Updating Stanley to Breeze in one record updates all records →

TourName	City	Category	Price	FName	LName
Breeze Bay Shelling	Captiva	Adventure	$750	Ralph	Hopper
Breeze Bay Shelling	Captiva	Adventure	$750	Lisa	Wilson
Ames Ski Club	Breckenridge	Adventure	$850	Kristen	Collins
Breeze Bay Shelling	Captiva	Adventure	$750	Kris	Goode
Breeze Bay Shelling	Captiva	Adventure	$750	Lois	Goode
Breeze Bay Shelling	Captiva	Adventure	$750	Naresh	Hubert
Piper-Heitman Wedding	Captiva	Family	$550	Julia	Bouchart
Ames Ski Club	Breckenridge	Adventure	$850	Tom	Camel
Golden Footsteps	Orlando	Site Seeing	$550	Shirley	Walker
Golden Footsteps	Orlando	Site Seeing	$550	Zohra	Vogue
Golden Footsteps	Orlando	Site Seeing	$550	Kathryn	Dotey
Golden Footsteps	Orlando	Site Seeing	$550	Jose	Hammer
Red Reef Scuba	Islamadora	Adventure	$1,500	Jane	Taylor
Breeze Bay Shelling	Captiva	Adventure	$750	Kori	Yode
American Heritage Tour	Philadelphia	Educational	$1,200	Sharol	Olingback

FIGURE B-4: Final TourCustomerList datasheet

(Design) View button

Delete button

Updating Orlando to Kissimmee in one record updates all records

101 records in the datasheet

Hiding and unhiding fields in a datasheet

To hide a field in a datasheet, right-click the field name at the top of the datasheet and click the Hide Fields option on the shortcut menu. To unhide a field, right-click any field name, click Unhide

Fields, and check the hidden field's check box in the Unhide Columns dialog box.

Freezing and unfreezing fields in a datasheet

In large datasheets, you may want to freeze certain fields so that they remain on the screen at all times. To freeze a field, right-click its

field name in the datasheet, and then click Freeze Fields. To unfreeze a field, right-click any field name and click Unfreeze All Fields.

Use Query Design View

Learning
Outcomes
• Work in Query
  Design View
• Add criteria to
  a query

You use **Query Design View** to add, delete, or move the fields in an existing query; to specify sort orders; or to add **criteria** to limit the number of records shown in the resulting datasheet. You can also use Query Design View to create a new query from scratch. Query Design View presents the fields you can use for that query in small windows called **field lists**. If you use the fields of two or more related tables in the query, the relationship between two tables is displayed with a **join line** (also called a **link line**) identifying which fields are used to establish the relationship. **CASE** *Samantha Hooper asks you to produce a list of tours in Florida. You use Query Design View to modify the existing ToursByState query to meet her request.*

STEPS

1. **Double-click the ToursByState query in the Navigation Pane to review the datasheet**

   The ToursByState query contains the StateName field from the States table and the TourName, TourStartDate, and Price fields from the Tours table. This query contains two ascending sort orders: StateName and TourName. All records in California, for example, are further sorted by the TourName value.

   QUICK TIP
   Drag the lower edge of the field list to view more fields.

2. **Click the View button ⊠ on the HOME tab to switch to Query Design View**

   Query Design View displays the tables used in the query in the upper pane of the window. The link line shows that one record in the States table may be related to many records in the Tours table. The lower pane of the window, called the **query design grid** (or query grid for short), displays the field names, sort orders, and criteria used within the query.

   QUICK TIP
   Query criteria are not case sensitive, so Florida equals FLORIDA equals florida.

3. **Click the first Criteria cell for the StateName field, then type Florida as shown in FIGURE B-5**

   Criteria are limiting conditions you set in the query design grid. In this case, the condition limits the selected records to only those with "Florida" in the StateName field.

4. **Click the View button ▦ in the Results group to switch to Datasheet View**

   Now only nine records are selected, because only nine of the tours have "Florida" in the StateName field, as shown in **FIGURE B-6**. You want to save this query with a different name.

5. **Click the FILE tab, click Save As, click Save Object As, click the Save As button, type FloridaTours, then click OK**

   In Access, the **Save As command** on the FILE tab allows you to save the entire database (and all objects it contains) or just the current object with a new name. Recall that Access saves *data* automatically as you move from record to record.

6. **Right-click the FloridaTours query tab, then click Close**

FIGURE B-5: ToursByState query in Design View

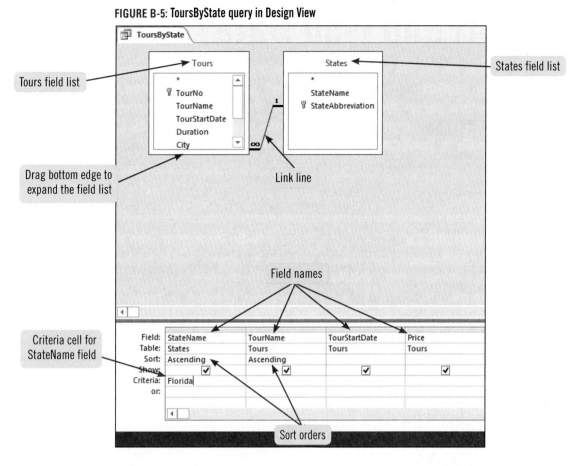

FIGURE B-6: ToursByState query with Florida criterion

StateName	TourName	TourStartDate	Price
Florida	Breeze Bay Shelling	07/06/2014	$750
Florida	Golden Footsteps	05/23/2014	$550
Florida	Gulfside Birdwatchers	06/29/2014	$700
Florida	High Adventurers	06/05/2014	$575
Florida	Hummer Trail	05/30/2014	$725
Florida	Patriot Debate Club	06/12/2014	$605
Florida	Piper-Heitman Wedding	05/30/2014	$550
Florida	Red Reef Scuba	07/06/2014	$1,500
Florida	Tropical Sailboats	06/19/2014	$655

TourName values are in ascending order

Only nine Florida records are selected

Adding or deleting a table in a query

You might want to add a table's field list to the upper pane of Query Design View to select fields from that table for the query. To add a new table to Query Design View, drag it from the Navigation Pane to Query Design View, or click the Show Table button on the Design tab, then add the desired table(s). To delete an unneeded table from Query Design View, click its title bar, then press [Delete].

Sort and Find Data

Learning Outcomes
- Apply sort orders to a query
- Find and replace data in a query
- Undo edits in a query

The Access sort and find features are handy tools that help you quickly organize and find data in a table or query datasheet. **TABLE B-1** describes the Sort and Find buttons on the HOME tab. Besides using these buttons, you can also click the list arrow on the field name in a datasheet, and then click a sorting option. **CASE** ▶ *Samantha asks you to provide a list of tours sorted by TourStartDate, and then by Price. You'll modify the ToursByCategory query to answer this query.*

STEPS

1. **Double-click the** ToursByCategory query **in the Navigation Pane to open its datasheet**

   The ToursByCategory query currently sorts tours by Category, then by TourName. You'll add the Duration field to this query, then change the sort order for the records.

QUICK TIP
Drag a selected field selector right or left to move the column to a new position in the query grid.

2. **Click the** View button **☑ in the Views group to switch to Design View, then double-click the** Duration field **in the Tours field list**

   When you double-click a field in a field list, Access inserts it in the next available column in the query grid. You can also drag a field from a field list to a specific column of the query grid. To select a field in the query grid, you click its field selector. The **field selector** is the thin gray bar above each field in the query grid. If you want to delete a field from a query, click its field selector, then press [Delete]. Deleting a field from a query does not delete it from the underlying table; the field is only deleted from the query's logical view.

   Currently, the ToursByCategory query is sorted by Category and then by TourName. Access evaluates sort orders from left to right. You want to change the sort order so that the records sort first by TourStartDate then by Price.

3. **Click** Ascending **in the Category Sort cell, click the** list arrow, **click** (not sorted), **click** Ascending **in the TourName Sort cell, click the** list arrow, **click** (not sorted), **double-click the** TourStartDate Sort cell **to specify an Ascending sort, then double-click the** Price Sort cell **to specify an Ascending sort**

   The records are now set to be sorted in ascending order, first by TourStartDate, then by the values in the Price field, as shown in **FIGURE B-7**. Because sort orders always work from left to right, you might need to rearrange the fields before applying a sort order that uses more than one field. To move a field in the query design grid, click its field selector, then drag it left or right.

4. **Click the** View button **▦ in the Results group**

   The new datasheet shows the Duration field in the fifth column. The records are now sorted in ascending order by the TourStartDate field. If two records have the same TourStartDate, they are further sorted by Price. Your next task is to replace all occurrences of "Site Seeing" with "Cultural" in the Category field.

5. **Click the** Find button **on the HOME tab, type** Site Seeing **in the Find What box, click the** Replace tab, **click in the** Replace With box, **then type** Cultural

   The Find and Replace dialog box is shown in **FIGURE B-8**.

TROUBLE
If your find-and-replace effort did not work correctly, click the Undo button ↺ and repeat Steps 5 and 6.

6. **Click the** Replace All button **in the Find and Replace dialog box, click** Yes **to continue, then click** Cancel **to close the Find and Replace dialog box**

   Access replaced all occurrences of "Site Seeing" with "Cultural" in the Category field, as shown in **FIGURE B-9**.

7. **Right-click the** ToursByCategory query tab, **click** Close, **then click** Yes **to save changes**

FIGURE B-7: Changing sort orders for the ToursByCategory query

Duration field in
Tours field list

Field selectors for Price
and Duration fields

Sort orders for Category
and TourName are removed

Ascending sort orders for
TourStartDate and Price are added

FIGURE B-8: Find and Replace dialog box

Site Seeing in the
Find What text box

Cultural in the
Replace With text box

Additional Find and
Replace options to
fine-tune the search

Replace All button

FIGURE B-9: Final ToursByCategory datasheet with new sort orders

Cultural replaces
Site Seeing in the
Category field

Find button

Records with the same
TourStartDate are further
sorted by the Price field

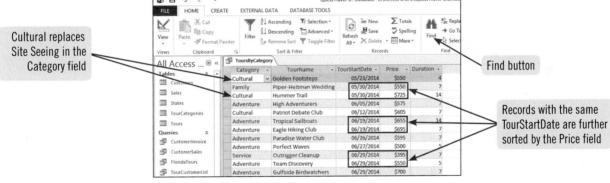

TABLE B-1: Sort and Find buttons

name	button	purpose
Ascending		Sorts records based on the selected field in ascending order (0 to 9, A to Z)
Descending		Sorts records based on the selected field in descending order (Z to A, 9 to 0)
Remove Sort		Removes the current sort order
Find		Opens the Find and Replace dialog box, which allows you to find data in a single field or in the entire datasheet
Replace		Opens the Find and Replace dialog box, which allows you to find and replace data
Go To		Helps you navigate to the first, previous, next, last, or new record
Select		Helps you select a single record or all records in a datasheet

Access 2013

Filter Data

Learning Outcomes
• Apply and remove filters in a query
• Use wildcards in criteria

Filtering a table or query datasheet *temporarily* displays only those records that match given criteria. Recall that criteria are limiting conditions you set. For example, you might want to show only tours in the state of California, or only tours with a duration of 14 days. Although filters provide a quick and easy way to display a temporary subset of records in the current datasheet, they are not as powerful or flexible as queries. Most important, a query is a saved object within the database, whereas filters are temporary because Access removes them when you close the datasheet. **TABLE B-2** compares filters and queries. **CASE** *Samantha asks you to find all Adventure tours offered in the month of July. You can filter the Tours table datasheet to provide this information.*

STEPS

QUICK TIP
You can also apply a sort or filter by clicking the Sort and filter arrow to the right of the field name and choosing the sort order or filter values you want.

1. **Double-click the Tours table to open it, click any occurrence of Adventure in the Category field, click the Selection button in the Sort & Filter group on the HOME tab, then click Equals "Adventure"**

   Eighteen records are selected, some of which are shown in **FIGURE B-10**. A filter icon appears to the right of the Category field. Filtering by the selected field value, called **Filter By Selection**, is a fast and easy way to filter the records for an exact match. To filter for comparative data (for example, where TourStartDate is *equal to* or *greater than* 7/1/2014), you must use the **Filter By Form** feature. Filter buttons are summarized in **TABLE B-3**.

2. **Click the Advanced button in the Sort & Filter group, then click Filter By Form**

   The Filter by Form window opens. The previous Filter By Selection criterion, "Adventure" in the Category field, is still in the grid. Access distinguishes between text and numeric entries by placing "quotation marks" around text criteria.

QUICK TIP
To clear previous criteria, click the Advanced button, then click Clear All Filters.

3. **Click the TourStartDate cell, then type 7/*/2014 as shown in FIGURE B-11**

   Filter By Form also allows you to apply two or more criteria at the same time. An asterisk (*) in the day position of the date criterion works as a wildcard, selecting any date in the month of July (the 7th month) in the year 2014.

QUICK TIP
Be sure to remove existing filters before applying a new filter, or the new filter will apply to the current subset of records instead of the entire datasheet.

4. **Click the Toggle Filter button in the Sort & Filter group**

   The datasheet selects two records that match both filter criteria, as shown in **FIGURE B-12**. Note that filter icons appear next to the TourStartDate and Category field names as both fields are involved in the filter.

5. **Close the Tours datasheet, then click Yes when prompted to save the changes**

   Saving changes to the datasheet saves the last sort order and column width changes. Filters are not saved.

Using wildcard characters

To search for a pattern, you can use a **wildcard** character to represent any character in the condition entry. Use a question mark (?) to search for any single character and an asterisk (*) to search for any number of characters. Wildcard characters are often used with the **Like** operator. For example, the criterion Like "12/*/13" would find all dates in December of 2013, and the criterion Like "F*" would find all entries that start with the letter F.

FIGURE B-10: Filtering the Tours table

Selection button

Advanced button

Sort and filter buttons

Filter icon

Adventure in the Category field

Toggle Filter button is selected, indicating the records are filtered

FIGURE B-11: Filtering By Form criteria

Tours: Filter by Form							
TourNo	TourName	TourStartDate	Duration	City	StateAb	Category	Price
		7/*/2014 ✓				"Adventure"	

TourStartDate criterion

Category criterion

FIGURE B-12: Results of filtering by form

Tours							
TourNo	TourName	TourStartDate	Duration	City	State	Category	Price
1	Breeze Bay Shelling	07/06/2014	3	Captiva	FL	Adventure	$750
2	Red Reef Scuba	07/06/2014	3	Islamadora	FL	Adventure	$1,500
*	(New)						

TourStartDate values are in July 2014

Filter icons

Category is equal to Adventure

TABLE B-2: Filters vs. queries

characteristics	filters	queries
Are saved as an object in the database		•
Can be used to select a subset of records in a datasheet	•	•
Can be used to select a subset of fields in a datasheet		•
Resulting datasheet used to enter and edit data	•	•
Resulting datasheet used to sort, filter, and find records	•	•
Commonly used as the source of data for a form or report		•
Can calculate sums, averages, counts, and other types of summary statistics across records		•
Can be used to create calculated fields		•

© 2014 Cengage Learning

TABLE B-3: Filter buttons

name	button	purpose
Filter	▼	Provides a list of values in the selected field that can be used to customize a filter
Selection	▼	Filters records that equal, do not equal, or are otherwise compared with the current value
Advanced	▣	Provides advanced filter features such as Filter By Form, Save As Query, and Clear All Filters
Toggle Filter	▼	Applies or removes the current filter

© 2014 Cengage Learning

Access 2013

Apply AND Criteria

Learning
Outcomes
• Enter AND criteria
  in a query
• Define criteria
  syntax
• Use comparison
  operators with
  criteria

You can limit the number of records that appear on a query datasheet by entering criteria in Query Design View. Criteria are tests, or limiting conditions, for which the record must be true to be selected for the query datasheet. To create **AND criteria**, which means that *all* criteria must be true to select the record, enter two or more criteria on the *same* Criteria row of the query design grid. **CASE** *Samantha Hooper asks you to provide a list of all Adventure tours in the state of Florida with a duration of 7 days or less. Use Query Design View to create the query with AND criteria to meet her request.*

STEPS

1. **Click the CREATE tab on the Ribbon, click the Query Design button, double-click Tours, then click Close in the Show Table dialog box**

   You want four fields from the Tours table in this query.

2. **Drag the bottom edge of the Tours field list down to display all of the fields, double-click TourName, double-click Duration, double-click StateAbbrev, then double-click Category to add these fields to the query grid**

   First add criteria to select only those records in Florida. Because you are using the StateAbbrev field, you need to use the two-letter state abbreviation for Florida, FL, as the Criteria entry.

3. **Click the first Criteria cell for the StateAbbrev field, type FL, then click the View button 🗒 to display the results**

   Querying for only those tours in the state of Florida selects nine records. Next, you add criteria to select only the tours in Florida in the Adventure category.

4. **Click the View button 📐, click the first Criteria cell for the Category field, type Adventure, then click the View button 🗒 in the Results group**

   Criteria added to the same line of the query design grid are AND criteria. When entered on the same line, each criterion must be true for the record to appear in the resulting datasheet. Querying for both FL and Adventure tours narrows the selection to five records. Every time you add AND criteria, you *narrow* the number of records that are selected because the record must be true for *all* criteria.

5. **Click the View button 📐, click the first Criteria cell for the Duration field, then type <=7, as shown in FIGURE B-13**

   Access assists you with **criteria syntax**, rules that specify how to enter criteria. Access automatically adds "quotation marks" around text criteria in Short Text and Long Text fields ("FL" and "Adventure") and pound signs (#) around date criteria in Date/Time fields. The criteria in Number, Currency, and Yes/No fields are not surrounded by any characters. See **TABLE B-4** for more information about comparison operators such as > (greater than).

TROUBLE
If your datasheet
doesn't match
FIGURE B-14, return
to Query Design View
and compare your
criteria with that of
FIGURE B-13.

6. **Click the View button 🗒**

   The third AND criterion further narrows the number of records selected to four, as shown in **FIGURE B-14**.

7. **Click the Save button 🖫 on the Quick Access toolbar, type AdventureFL as the query name, click OK, then close the query**

   The query is saved with the new name, AdventureFL, as a new object in the QuestTravel-B database. Criteria entered in Query Design View are permanently saved with the query (as compared with filters in the previous lesson, which are temporary and not saved with the object).

FIGURE B-13: Query Design View with AND criteria

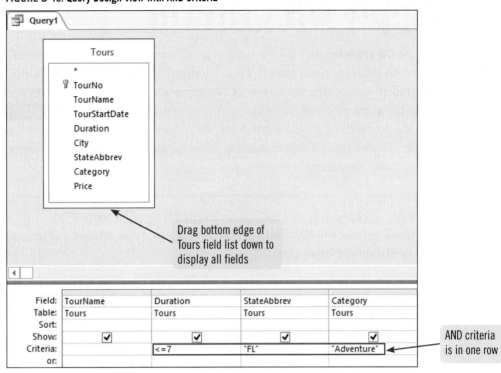

FIGURE B-14: Final datasheet of AdventureFL query

TourName	Duration	State	Category
Breeze Bay Shelling	3	FL	Adventure
Red Reef Scuba	3	FL	Adventure
High Adventurers	7	FL	Adventure
Gulfside Birdwatchers	7	FL	Adventure

Records meet all three criteria:
Duration <=7
State = "FL"
Category = "Adventure"

TABLE B-4: Comparison operators

operator	description	expression	meaning
>	Greater than	>500	Numbers greater than 500
>=	Greater than or equal to	>=500	Numbers greater than or equal to 500
<	Less than	<"Braveheart"	Names from A to Braveheart, but not Braveheart
<=	Less than or equal to	<="Bridgewater"	Names from A through Bridgewater, inclusive
<>	Not equal to	<>"Fontanelle"	Any name except for Fontanelle

Searching for blank fields

Is Null and Is Not Null are two other types of common criteria. The **Is Null** criterion finds all records where no entry has been made in the field. **Is Not Null** finds all records where there is any entry in the field, even if the entry is 0. Primary key fields cannot have a null entry.

Apply OR Criteria

Learning Outcomes
• Enter OR criteria in a query
• Rename a query

You use **OR criteria** when *any one* criterion must be true in order for the record to be selected. Enter OR criteria on *different* Criteria rows of the query design grid. As you add rows of OR criteria to the query design grid, you *increase* the number of records selected for the resulting datasheet because the record needs to match *only one* of the Criteria rows to be selected for the datasheet. **CASE** ► *Samantha Hooper asks you to add criteria to the previous query. She wants to include Cultural tours in the state of Florida that are shorter than or equal to 7 days in duration. To do this, you modify a copy of the AdventureFL query to use OR criteria to add the records.*

STEPS

1. **Right-click the AdventureFL query in the Navigation Pane, click Copy, right-click a blank spot in the Navigation Pane, click Paste, type AdventureCulturalFL in the Paste As dialog box, then click OK**

   By copying the AdventureFL query before starting your modifications, you avoid changing the AdventureFL query by mistake.

2. **Right-click the AdventureCulturalFL query in the Navigation Pane, click Design View, click the second Criteria cell in the Category field, type Cultural, then click the View button to display the query datasheet**

   The query selected 11 records including all of the tours with Cultural in the Category field. Note that some of the Duration values are greater than 7 and some of the StateAbbrev values are not FL. Because each row of the query grid is evaluated separately, all Cultural tours are selected regardless of criteria in any other row. In other words, the criteria in one row have no effect on the criteria of other rows. To make sure that the Cultural tours are also in Florida and have a duration of less than or equal to 7 days, you need to modify the second row of the query grid (the "or" row) to specify that criteria.

   QUICK TIP
   The Datasheet, Design, and other view buttons are also located in the lower-right corner of the Access window.

3. **Click the View button, click the second Criteria cell in the Duration field, type <=7, click the second Criteria cell in the StateAbbrev field, type FL, then click in any other cell of the grid**

   Query Design View should look like **FIGURE B-15**.

4. **Click the View button**

   Six records are selected that meet all three criteria as entered in row one *or* row two of the query grid, as shown in **FIGURE B-16**.

5. **Right-click the AdventureCulturalFL query tab, click Close, then click Yes to save and close the query datasheet**

FIGURE B-15: Query Design View with OR criteria

AdventureCulturalFL

Tours

*
🔑 TourNo
TourName
TourStartDate
Duration
City
StateAbbrev
Category
Price

Field:	TourName	Duration	StateAbbrev	Category
Table:	Tours	Tours	Tours	Tours
Sort:				
Show:	✓	✓	✓	✓
Criteria:		<=7	"FL"	"Adventure"
or:		<=7	"FL"	"Cultural"

OR criteria is on multiple rows

FIGURE B-16: Final datasheet of AdventureCulturalFL query

AdventureCulturalFL

TourName	Duration	State	Category
Breeze Bay Shelling	3	FL	Adventure
Red Reef Scuba	3	FL	Adventure
Golden Footsteps	4	FL	Cultural
High Adventurers	7	FL	Adventure
Patriot Debate Club	7	FL	Cultural
Gulfside Birdwatchers	7	FL	Adventure

Records meet all three criteria:
Duration <=7
State = "FL"
Category = "Adventure"
OR
Duration <=7
State = "FL"
Category = "Cultural"

Format a Datasheet

Learning Outcomes
• Zoom in print preview
• Format a datasheet
• Change page orientation

A report is the primary Access tool to create a professional printout, but you can print a datasheet as well. A datasheet allows you to apply some basic formatting modifications such as changing the font size, font face, colors, and gridlines. **CASE** *Samantha Hooper asks you to print a list of customers. You decide to format the Customers table datasheet before printing it for her.*

STEPS

1. **In the Navigation Pane, double-click the Customers table to open it in Datasheet View**

   Before applying new formatting enhancements, you preview the default printout.

2. **Click the FILE tab, click Print, click Print Preview, then click the header of the printout to zoom in**

   The preview window displays the layout of the printout, as shown in **FIGURE B-17**. By default, the printout of a datasheet contains the object name and current date in the header. The page number is in the footer.

3. **Click the Next Page button ▶ in the navigation bar to move to the next page of the printout**

   The last two fields print on the second page because the first is not wide enough to accommodate them. You decide to switch the report to landscape orientation so that all of the fields print on one page, and then increase the size of the font before printing to make the text easier to read.

4. **Click the Landscape button on the PRINT PREVIEW tab to switch the report to landscape orientation, then click the Close Print Preview button**

   You return to Datasheet View where you can make font face, font size, font color, gridline color, and background color choices.

5. **Click the Font list arrow Calibri (Body) ⌄ in the Text Formatting group, click Times New Roman, click the Font Size list arrow 11 ⌄, then click 12**

   With the larger font size applied, you need to resize some columns to accommodate the widest entries.

6. **Use the ↔ pointer to double-click the field separator between the Street and City field names, then double-click the field separator between the Phone and FirstContact field names**

   Double-clicking the field separators widens the columns as needed to display every entry in those fields, as shown in **FIGURE B-18**.

QUICK TIP
If you need a printout of this datasheet, click the Print button on the PRINT PREVIEW tab, then click OK.

7. **Click the FILE tab, click Print, click Print Preview, then click the preview to zoom in and out to review the information**

   All of the fields now fit across a page in landscape orientation. The preview of the printout is still two pages, but with the larger font size, it is easier to read.

8. **Right-click the Customers table tab, click Close, click Yes when prompted to save changes, then click the Close button on the title bar to close the QuestTravel-B.accdb database and Access 2013**

FIGURE B-17: Preview of Customers datasheet

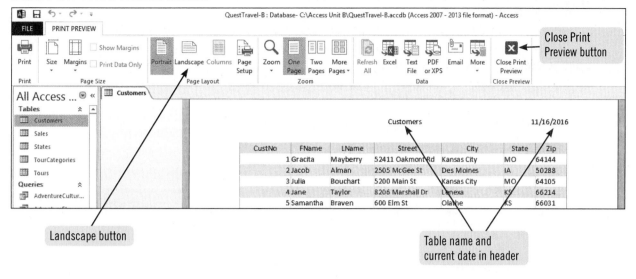

Landscape button

Close Print Preview button

Table name and current date in header

FIGURE B-18: Formatting the Customers datasheet

Font list arrow

Font Size list arrow

Field separator

Drag or double-click with this pointer to resize columns

Practice

Concepts Review

Label each element of the Access window shown in FIGURE B-19.

FIGURE B-19

AdventureCulturalFL

Tours

```
*
▢ TourNo
  TourName
  TourStartDate
  Duration
  City
  StateAbbrev
  Category
  Price
```

1 ───────→

2 ───────→

Field:	TourName	Duration	StateAbbrev	Category
Table:	Tours	Tours	Tours	Tours
Sort:				
Show:	☑	☑	☑	☑
Criteria:		<=7	"FL"	"Adventure"
or:		<=7	"FL"	"Cultural"

3

4

Match each term with the statement that best describes it.

5. **Query grid**
6. **Field selector**
7. **Filter**
8. **Filter By Selection**
9. **Field lists**
10. **Sorting**
11. **Join line**
12. **Is Null**
13. **Criteria**
14. **Syntax**
15. **Wildcard**

a. Putting records in ascending or descending order based on the values of a field
b. Limiting conditions used to restrict the number of records that are selected in a query
c. Creates a temporary subset of records
d. Small windows that display field names
e. Rules that determine how criteria are entered
f. Used to search for a pattern of characters
g. Criterion that finds all records where no entry has been made in the field
h. The lower pane in Query Design View
i. Identifies which fields are used to establish a relationship between two tables
j. A fast and easy way to filter the records for an exact match
k. The thin gray bar above each field in the query grid

Select the best answer from the list of choices.

16. AND criteria:

   a. Determine sort orders.

   b. Must all be true for the record to be selected.

   c. Determine fields selected for a query.

   d. Help set link lines between tables in a query.

17. SQL stands for which of the following?

   a. Structured Query Language

   b. Standard Query Language

   c. Special Query Listing

   d. Simple Query Listing

18. A query is sometimes called a logical view of data because:

   a. You can create queries with the Logical Query Wizard.

   b. Queries contain logical criteria.

   c. Query naming conventions are logical.

   d. Queries do not store data—they only display a view of data.

19. Which of the following describes OR criteria?

   a. Selecting a subset of fields and/or records to view as a datasheet from one or more tables

   b. Using two or more rows of the query grid to select only those records that meet given criteria

   c. Reorganizing the records in either ascending or descending order based on the contents of one or more fields

   d. Using multiple fields in the query design grid

20. Which of the following is *not* true about a query?

   a. A query is the same thing as a filter.

   b. A query can select fields from one or more tables in a relational database.

   c. A query can be created using different tools.

   d. An existing query can be modified in Query Design View.

Skills Review

1. Use the Query Wizard.

    a. Open the Recycle-B.accdb database from the location where you store your Data Files. Enable content if prompted.

    b. Create a new query using the Simple Query Wizard. Select the CenterName field from the Centers table, the DepositDate and Weight fields from the Deposits table, and the ClubName field from the Clubs table. Select Detail, and enter **CenterDeposits** as the name of the query.

    c. Open the query in Datasheet View, then change any record with the Barker Trash value to a center name that includes *your* last name.

2. Work with data in a query.

    a. Delete the first record (Hugo Trash Can with a DepositDate value of 2/4/2014).

    b. Change any occurrence of Lions of Fontanelle in the ClubName field to **Lions of Bridgewater**.

    c. Click any value in the DepositDate field, then click the Descending button on the HOME tab to sort the records in descending order on the DepositDate field.

    d. Use the Calendar Picker to choose the date of **12/16/2016** for the first record.

    e. Save and close the CenterDeposits query.

3. Use Query Design View.

    a. Click the CREATE tab, click the Query Design button, double-click Clubs, double-click Deposits, and then click Close to add the Clubs and Deposits tables to Query Design View.

    b. Drag the bottom edge of both field lists down to display all of the field names in both tables.

    c. Add the following fields from the Clubs table to the query design grid in the following order: FName, LName, ClubName. Add the following fields from the Deposits table in the following order: DepositDate, Weight. View the results in Datasheet View observing the number of records that are selected.

    d. In Design View, enter criteria to display only those records with a Weight value of **greater than or equal to 100**, then observe the number of records that are selected in Datasheet View.

    e. Save the query with the name **HeavyDeposits**.

4. Sort and find data.

    a. In Query Design View of the HeavyDeposits query, choose an ascending sort order for the ClubName field and a descending sort order for the Weight field.

    b. Display the query in Datasheet View noting how the records have been resorted.

    c. In the ClubName field, change any occurrence of Jaycees to **Dallas Jaycees**.

    d. In the FName field, change any occurrence of Tara to *your* initials.

5. Filter data.

    a. Filter the HeavyDeposits datasheet for only those records where the ClubName equals **Dallas Jaycees**.

    b. Apply an advanced Filter By Form and use the >= operator to further narrow the records so that only the deposits with a DepositDate value on or after 1/1/2015 are selected.

    c. Apply the filter to see the datasheet and if requested by your instructor, print the filtered HeavyDeposits datasheet.

    d. Save and close the HeavyDeposits query. Reopen the HeavyDeposits query to confirm that filters are temporary (not saved), and then close the HeavyDeposits query again.

Skills Review (continued)

6. Apply AND criteria.

a. Right-click the HeavyDeposits query, copy it, and then paste it as **Heavy2014Deposits**.

b. Open the Heavy2014Deposits query in Query Design View.

c. Modify the criteria to select all of the records with a DepositDate in **2014** and a Weight value **greater than or equal to 100**.

d. If requested by your instructor, print the Heavy2014Deposits datasheet, then save and close it.

7. Apply OR criteria.

a. Right-click the HeavyDeposits query, copy it, then paste it as **HeavyDeposits2Clubs**.

b. Open the HeavyDeposits2Clubs query in Design View, then add criteria to select the records with a ClubName of **Ice Kings** and a Weight value **greater than or equal to 100**.

c. Add criteria to also include the records with a ClubName of **Junior League** with a Weight value **greater than or equal to 100**. **FIGURE B-20** shows the results.

d. If requested by your instructor, print the HeavyDeposits2Clubs datasheet, then save and close it.

8. Format a datasheet.

a. In the Clubs table datasheet, apply an Arial Narrow font and a 14-point font size.

b. Resize all columns so that all data and field names are visible.

c. Display the Clubs datasheet in Print Preview, switch the orientation to landscape, click the Margins button in the Page Size group, then click Narrow to fit the printout on a single sheet of paper.

d. If requested by your instructor, print the Clubs datasheet.

e. Save and close the Clubs table, then close Access 2013.

FIGURE B-20

FName	LName	ClubName	DepositDate	Weight
SI	Jackson	Ice Kings	2/13/2014	200
SI	Jackson	Ice Kings	2/18/2015	185
SI	Jackson	Ice Kings	2/13/2015	185
SI	Jackson	Ice Kings	3/7/2015	145
SI	Jackson	Ice Kings	4/19/2015	115
SI	Jackson	Ice Kings	5/1/2015	105
SI	Jackson	Ice Kings	2/22/2016	100
SI	Jackson	Ice Kings	1/30/2015	100
SI	Jackson	Ice Kings	2/26/2014	100
Lottie	Moon	Junior League	9/24/2015	200
Lottie	Moon	Junior League	3/2/2015	150
Lottie	Moon	Junior League	2/8/2015	150
Lottie	Moon	Junior League	3/4/2014	150
Lottie	Moon	Junior League	3/1/2014	150
Lottie	Moon	Junior League	2/8/2014	150

Your initials in the FName field

Independent Challenge 1

You have built an Access database to track membership in a community service club. The database tracks member names and addresses as well as their community service hours.

a. Open the Membership-B.accdb database from the location where you store your Data Files, enable content if prompted, then open the Activities, Members, and Zips tables to review their datasheets.

b. In the Zips table, click the expand button to the left of the 64131, Overland Park, KS, record to display the two members linked to that zip code. Click the expand button to the left of the Gabriel Hammer record to display the three activity records linked to Gabriel.

c. Close all three datasheets, click the DATABASE TOOLS tab, then click the Relationships button. The Relationships window also shows you that one record in the Zips table is related to many records in the Members table through the common ZipCode field, and that one record in the Members table is related to many records in the Activities table through the common MemberNo field.

d. Click the Relationship Report button, then if requested by your instructor, print the Relationship report. Close and save the report with the default name **Relationships for Membership-B**. Close the Relationships window.

e. Using Query Design View, build a query with the following fields: FirstName and LastName from the Members table and ActivityDate and HoursWorked from the Activities table.

f. View the datasheet, observe the number of records selected, then return to Query Design View.

g. Add criteria to select only those records where the ActivityDate is in March of 2014.

h. In Query Design View, apply an ascending sort order to the LastName and ActivityDate fields, then view the datasheet.

i. Change the name Quentin Garden to *your* name, widen all columns so that all data and field names are visible, and save the query with the name **March2014**, as shown in FIGURE B-21.

j. If requested by your instructor, print the March2014 datasheet, then close the March2014 query and close Access 2013.

FIGURE B-21

FirstName	LastName	ActivityDate	HoursWorked
Bart	Bouchart	3/29/2014	4
Golga	Collins	3/31/2014	8
Martha	Duman	3/27/2014	4
Allie	Eahlie	3/29/2014	4
Jana	Eckert	3/29/2014	5
Student First	Student Last	3/29/2014	4
Student First	Student Last	3/30/2014	8
Loraine	Goode	3/29/2014	5
Gabriel	Hammer	3/29/2014	5
Jeremiah	Hopper	3/27/2014	4
Helen	Hubert	3/29/2014	5
Heidi	Kalvert	3/29/2014	4
Harvey	Mackintosh	3/30/2014	4
Jon	Maxim	3/30/2014	4
Micah	Mayberry	3/29/2014	4
Patch	Mullins	3/30/2014	8
Patch	Mullins	3/31/2014	8
Young	Nelson	3/30/2014	10
Mallory	Olson	3/31/2014	8
Su	Vogue	3/30/2014	8
Sherry	Walker	3/29/2014	4
Taney	Wilson	3/30/2014	8

Record: 7 of 22   No Filter   Search

Independent Challenge 2

You work for a nonprofit agency that tracks the voting patterns of Congress. You have developed an Access database with contact information for members of the House of Representatives. The director of the agency has asked you to create several state lists of representatives. You will use queries to extract this information.

a. Open the Congress-B.accdb database from the location where you store your Data Files, then enable content if prompted.

b. Open the Representatives and the States tables. Notice that one state is related to many representatives as evidenced by the expand buttons to the left of the records in the States tables.

c. Close both datasheets, then using Query Design View, create a query with the StateAbbrev, StateName, and Capital fields from the States table (in that order) as well as the LName field from the Representatives table.

d. Sort the records in ascending order on the StateName field, then in ascending order on the LName field.

e. Add criteria to select the representatives from Arizona or New Mexico. Use the StateAbbrev field to enter your criteria, using the two-character state abbreviations of **AZ** and **NM**.

f. Save the query with the name **ArizonaAndNewMexico** as shown in **FIGURE B-22**, view the results, then change the last name of Upton in the last record to *your* last name. Resize the columns as needed to view all the data and field names.

g. Print the ArizonaAndNewMexico datasheet if requested by your instructor, then close it and exit Access 2013.

FIGURE B-22

StateAbbrev	StateName	Capital	LName
AZ	Arizona	Phoenix	Christian
AZ	Arizona	Phoenix	Drake
AZ	Arizona	Phoenix	Gohmert
AZ	Arizona	Phoenix	Gonzalez
AZ	Arizona	Phoenix	Matheson
AZ	Arizona	Phoenix	McCaul
AZ	Arizona	Phoenix	Sanders
AZ	Arizona	Phoenix	Wolf
NM	New Mexico	Santa Fe	Miller
NM	New Mexico	Santa Fe	Student Last Name
NM	New Mexico	Santa Fe	Stupak

Independent Challenge 3

You have built an Access database to track the veterinarians and clinics in your area.

a. Open the Vet-B.accdb database from the location where you store your Data Files, then enable content if prompted.

b. Open the Vets table and then the Clinics table to review the data in both datasheets.

c. Click the expand button next to the Veterinary Specialists record in the Clinics table, then add *your* name as a new record to the Vets subdatasheet.

d. Close both datasheets.

e. Using the Simple Query Wizard, select the VetLast and VetFirst fields from the Vets table, and select the ClinicName and Phone fields from the Clinics table. Title the query **ClinicListing**, then view the datasheet.

f. Update any occurrence of Leawood Animal Clinic in the ClinicName field by changing Leawood to **Emergency** so the ClinicName is **Emergency Animal Clinic**.

g. In Query Design View, add criteria to select only **Emergency Animal Clinic** or **Veterinary Specialists** in the ClinicName field, then view the datasheet.

h. In Query Design View, move the ClinicName field to the first column, then add an ascending sort order on the ClinicName and VetLast fields.

i. Display the ClinicListing query in Datasheet View, resize the fields as shown in FIGURE B-23, then print the datasheet if requested by your instructor.

j. Save and close the ClinicListing datasheet, then exit Access 2013.

FIGURE B-23

ClinicName	VetLast	VetFirst	Phone
Emergency Animal Clinic	Ridwell	Kirk	(555) 555-1311
Emergency Animal Clinic	Rosenheim	Howard	(555) 555-1311
Emergency Animal Clinic	Salamander	Stephen	(555) 555-1311
Veterinary Specialists	Garver	Mark	(555) 555-4000
Veterinary Specialists	Major	Mark	(555) 555-4000
Veterinary Specialists	Manheim	Thomas	(555) 555-4000
Veterinary Specialists	Stewart	Frank	(555) 555-4000
Veterinary Specialists	Student Last	Student First	(555) 555-4000

Independent Challenge 4: Explore

An Access database is an excellent tool to help record and track job opportunities. For this exercise, you'll create a database from scratch that you can use to enter, edit, and query data in pursuit of a new job or career.

a. Create a new desktop database named **Jobs.accdb**.

b. Create a table named **Positions** with the following field names, data types, and descriptions:

Field name	Data type	Description
PositionID	AutoNumber	Primary key field
Title	Short Text	Title of position such as Accountant, Assistant Court Clerk, or Web Developer
CareerArea	Short Text	Area of the career field such as Accounting, Government, or Information Systems
AnnualSalary	Currency	Annual salary
Desirability	Number	Desirability rating of 1 = low to 5 = high to show how desirable the position is to you
EmployerID	Number	Foreign key field to the Employers table

c. Create a table named **Employers** with the following field names, data types, and descriptions:

Field name	Data type	Description
EmployerID	AutoNumber	Primary key field
CompanyName	Short Text	Company name of the employer
EmpStreet	Short Text	Employer's street address
EmpCity	Short Text	Employer's city
EmpState	Short Text	Employer's state
EmpZip	Short Text	Employer's zip code
EmpPhone	Short Text	Employer's phone, such as 913-555-8888

d. Be sure to set EmployerID as the primary key field in the Employers table and the PositionID as the primary key field in the Positions table.

e. Link the Employers and Positions tables together in a one-to-many relationship using the common EmployerID field. One employer record will be linked to many position records. Be sure to enforce referential integrity.

f. Using any valid source of potential employer data, enter five records into the Employers table.

g. Using any valid source of job information, enter five records into the Positions table by using the subdatasheets from within the Employers datasheet.
Because one employer may have many positions, all five of your Positions records may be linked to the same employer, you may have one position record per employer, or any other combination.

h. Build a query that selects CompanyName from the Employers table, and the Title, CareerArea, AnnualSalary, and Desirability fields from the Positions table. Sort the records in descending order based on Desirability. Save the query as **JobList**, and print it if requested by your instructor.

i. Close the JobList datasheet, then exit Access 2013.

Visual Workshop

Open the Baseball-B.accdb database from the location where you store your Data Files, and enable content if prompted. Create a query based on the Players and Teams tables, as shown in **FIGURE B-24**. Add criteria to select only those records where the PlayerPosition field values are equal to 1 or 2 (representing pitchers and catchers). In Query Design View, set an ascending sort order on the TeamName and PlayerPosition fields. In the results, change the name of Roy Campanella to *your* name. Save the query with the name **PitchersAndCatchers**, then compare the results with **FIGURE B-24**, making changes and widening columns to see all of the data. Print the datasheet if requested by your instructor. Save and close the query and the Baseball-B.accdb database, then exit Access 2013.

FIGURE B-24

TeamName	PlayerLast	PlayerFirst	Position
Brooklyn Beetles	Student Last Name	Student First Name	1
Brooklyn Beetles	Young	Cycylie	2
Mayfair Monarchs	Durocher	Luis	1
Mayfair Monarchs	Mathewson	Carl	2
Rocky's Rockets	Spalding	Andrew	1
Rocky's Rockets	Koufax	Sanford	2
Snapping Turtles	Ford	Charles	1
Snapping Turtles	Perry	Greg	2

Using Forms

CASE Samantha Hooper, a tour developer at Quest Specialty Travel, asks you to create forms to make tour information easier to access, enter, and update.

Unit Objectives

After completing this unit, you will be able to:

- Use the Form Wizard
- Create a split form
- Use Form Layout View
- Add fields to a form
- Modify form controls
- Create calculations
- Modify tab order
- Insert an image

Files You Will Need

QuestTravel-C.accdb	Membership-C.accdb
QuestLogo.bmp	People.jpg
RealEstate-C.accdb	Recycle-C.accdb
ForSale.bmp	Jobs-C.accdb
Dives-C.accdb	Baseball-C.accdb

Use the Form Wizard

Learning Outcomes
- Create a form with the Form Wizard
- Sort data in a form
- Describe form terminology and views

A **form** is an easy-to-use data entry and navigation screen. A form allows you to arrange the fields of a record in any layout so a **database user** can quickly and easily find, enter, edit, and analyze data. The **database designer** is the person responsible for building and maintaining tables, queries, forms, and reports for all of the database users. **CASE** ▸ *Samantha Hooper asks you to build a form to enter and maintain tour information.*

STEPS

1. **Start Access, open the QuestTravel-C.accdb database from the location where you store your Data Files, then enable content if prompted**

   You can use many methods to create a new form, but the Form Wizard is a fast and popular tool that helps you get started. The **Form Wizard** prompts you for information it needs to create a form, such as the fields, layout, and title for the form.

2. **Click the CREATE tab on the Ribbon, then click the Form Wizard button in the Forms group**

   The Form Wizard starts, prompting you to select the fields for this form. You want to create a form to enter and update data in the Tours table.

3. **Click the Tables/Queries list arrow, click Table: Tours, then click the Select All Fields button** `>>`

   You could now select fields from other tables, if necessary, but in this case, you have all of the fields you need.

4. **Click Next, click the Columnar option button, click Next, type Tours Entry Form as the title, then click Finish**

   The Tours Entry Form opens in **Form View**, as shown in **FIGURE C-1**. Access provides three different views of forms, as summarized in **TABLE C-1**. Each item on the form is called a **control**. A **label control** is used to *describe* the data shown in other controls such as text boxes. A label is also used for the title of the form, Tours Entry Form. A **text box** is used to *display* the data as well as enter, edit, find, sort, and also filter the data. A **combo box** is a combination of two controls: a text box and a list. The Category data is displayed in a combo box control. You click the arrow button on a combo box control to display a list of values, or you can edit data directly in the combo box itself.

QUICK TIP
Click in the text box of the field you want to sort *before* clicking a sort button.

5. **Click Breeze Bay Shelling in the TourName text box, click the Ascending button in the Sort & Filter group, then click the Next record button** ▶ **in the navigation bar to move to the second record**

   The Ames Ski Club is the second record when the records are sorted in ascending order on the TourName data. Information about the current record number and total number of records appears in the navigation bar, just as it does in a datasheet.

6. **Click the Previous record button** ◀ **in the navigation bar to move back to the first record, click the TourName text box, then change American Heritage Tour to Washington DC History Tour**

   Your screen should look like **FIGURE C-2**. Forms displayed in Form View are the primary tool for database users to enter, edit, and delete data in an Access database.

7. **Right-click the Tours Entry Form tab, then click Close**

   When a form is closed, Access automatically saves any edits made to the current record.

FIGURE C-1: Tours Entry Form in Form View

FIGURE C-2: Displaying the results of a calculation in Form View

TABLE C-1: Form views

view	primary purpose
Form	To find, sort, enter, and edit data
Layout	To modify the size, position, or formatting of controls; shows data as you modify the form, making it the tool of choice when you want to change the appearance and usability of the form while viewing live data
Design	To modify the Form Header, Detail, and Footer section, or to access the complete range of controls and form properties; Design View does not display data

Access 2013

Create a Split Form

**Learning
Outcomes**
• Create a split form
• Enter and edit
  data in a form

In addition to the Form Wizard, you should be familiar with several other form creation tools. **TABLE C-2** identifies those tools and the purpose for each. **CASE** ▶ *Samantha Hooper asks you to create another form to manage customer data. You'll work with the Split Form tool for this task.*

STEPS

QUICK TIP
Layout View allows you to view and filter the data, but not edit it.

1. **Click the Customers table in the Navigation Pane, click the CREATE tab, click the More Forms button, click Split Form, then click the Add Existing Fields button in the Tools group on the DESIGN tab to close the Field List if it opens**

   The Customers data appears in a split form with the top half in **Layout View**, as shown in **FIGURE C-3**. The benefit of a **split form** is that the upper pane allows you to display the fields of one record in any arrangement, and the lower pane maintains a datasheet view of the first few records. If you edit, sort, or filter records in the upper pane, the lower pane is automatically updated, and vice versa.

2. **Click MO in the State text box in the upper pane, click the HOME tab, click the Selection button in the Sort & Filter group, then click Does Not Equal "MO"**

   Thirty-seven records are filtered where the State field is not equal to MO. You also need to change a value in the Jacob Alman record.

TROUBLE
Make sure you edit the record in the datasheet in the lower pane.

3. **In the lower pane, select Des Moines in the City field of the first record, edit the entry to read Dallas Center, click any other record in the lower pane, then click Jacob in the first record of the lower pane**

   Moving from record to record automatically saves data. Note that "Dallas Center" is now the entry in the City field in both the upper and lower panes, as shown in **FIGURE C-4**.

4. **Click the record selector for the Kristen Collins record in the lower pane, then click the Delete button in the Records group on the HOME tab**

   You cannot delete this record because it contains related records in the Sales table. This is a benefit of referential integrity on the one-to-many relationship between the Customers and Sales tables. Referential integrity prevents the creation of **orphan records**, records on the *many* side of a relationship (in this case, the Sales table) that do not have a match on the *one* side (in this case, the Customers table).

5. **Click OK, right-click the Customers form tab, click Close, click Yes when prompted to save changes, then click OK to save the form with the name Customers**

TABLE C-2: Form creation tools

tool	icon	creates a form
Form	🖼	with one click based on the selected table or query
Form Design	🖼	from scratch in Form Design View
Blank Form	▢	from scratch in Form Layout View
Form Wizard	🖼	by answering a series of questions provided by the Form Wizard dialog boxes
Navigation	🖼	used to navigate or move between different areas of the database
More Forms	🖼	based on Multiple Items, Datasheet, Split Form, Modal Dialog, PivotChart, or PivotTable arrangements
Split Form	🖼	with two panes, the upper showing one record at a time and the lower displaying a datasheet of many records

FIGURE C-3: Customers table in a split form

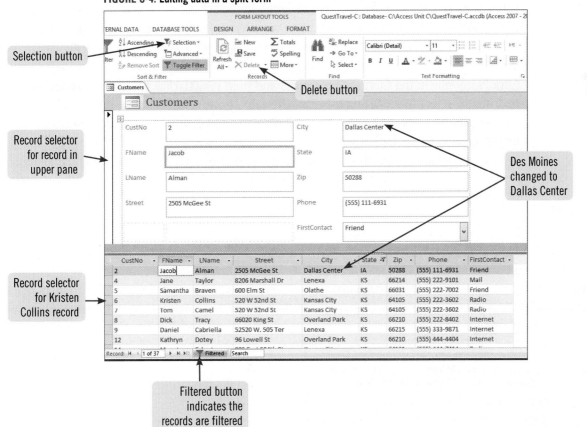

FIGURE C-4: Editing data in a split form

Use Form Layout View

Learning
Outcomes
• Resize controls in
Layout View
• Format controls in
Layout View

Layout View lets you make some design changes to a form while you are browsing the data. For example, you can move and resize controls, add or delete a field on the form, filter and sort data, or change formatting characteristics, such as fonts and colors. **CASE** *Samantha Hooper asks you to make several design changes to the Tours Entry Form. You can make these changes in Layout View.*

STEPS

1. **Right-click** Tours Entry Form **in the Navigation Pane, then click** Layout View

   In Layout View, you can move through the records, but you cannot enter or edit the data as you can in Form View.

   > **TROUBLE**
   > If your third record is not Bigfoot Rafting Club, sort the records in ascending order on the TourName field.

2. **Click the** Next record button **in the navigation bar twice to move to the third record, Bigfoot Rafting Club**

   You often use Layout View to make minor design changes, such as editing labels and changing formatting characteristics.

3. **Click the** TourNo label **to select it if it is not already selected, click between the words Tour and No, then press** [Spacebar]

   You also want to edit a few more labels.

   > **TROUBLE**
   > Be sure to modify the *labels in the left column* instead of the text boxes on the right.

4. **Continue editing the labels, as shown in** FIGURE C-5

   You also want to change the text color of the first two labels, Tour No and Tour Name, to red to make them more noticeable.

5. **Click the** Tour No label, **click the** HOME tab, **click the** Font Color button [A] **in the Text Formatting group, click the** Tour Name label, **then click** [A]

   Often, you want to apply the same formatting enhancement to multiple controls. For example, you decide to narrow the City and StateAbbrev text boxes. Select the text boxes at the same time to make the same change to both.

   > **TROUBLE**
   > Be sure to modify the *text boxes in the right column* instead of the labels on the left.

6. **Click** Placerville **in the City text box, press and hold** [Shift], **click** CA **in the StateAbbrev text box to select the two text boxes at the same time, release** [Shift], **then use the ↔ pointer to drag the** right edge of the selection **to the left to make the text boxes approximately half as wide**

   Layout View for the Tours Entry Form should look like **FIGURE C-6**. Mouse pointers in Form Layout and Form Design View are very important as they indicate what happens when you drag the mouse. Mouse pointers are described in **TABLE C-3**.

TABLE C-3: Mouse pointer shapes

shape	when does this shape appear?	action
⍣	When you point to any unselected control on the form (the default mouse pointer)	Single-clicking with this mouse pointer *selects* a control
✛	When you point to the upper-left corner or edge of a selected control in Form Design View or the middle of the control in Form Layout View	Dragging with this mouse pointer *moves* the selected control(s)
↕↔	When you point to any sizing handle (except the larger one in the upper-left corner in Form Design View)	Dragging with one of these mouse pointers *resizes* the control

Using Forms

FIGURE C-5: Using Layout View to modify form labels on the Tours Entry Form

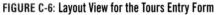

Edit these labels to include a space between the words

FIGURE C-6: Layout View for the Tours Entry Form

Labels are red

Resize mouse pointer

Table layouts

Layouts provide a way to group several controls together on a form or report to more quickly add, delete, rearrange, resize, or align controls. To insert a layout into a form or report, select the controls you want to group together, then choose the Stacked or Tabular button on the ARRANGE tab. Each option applies a table layout to the controls so that you can insert, delete, merge, or split the cells in the layout to quickly rearrange or edit the controls in the layout. To remove a layout, use the Remove Layout button on the ARRANGE tab in Form Design View.

Add Fields to a Form

Adding and deleting fields in an existing form is a common activity. You can add or delete fields in a form in either Layout View or Design View using the Field List. The **Field List** lists the database tables and the fields they contain. To add a field to the form, drag it from the Field List to the desired location on the form. To delete a field on a form, click the field to select it, then press the [Delete] key. Deleting a field from a form does not delete it from the underlying table or have any effect on the data contained in the field. You can toggle the Field List on and off using the Add Existing Fields button on the DESIGN tab. **CASE** *Samantha Hooper asks you to add the tour description from the TourCategories table to the Tours Entry Form. You can use Layout View and the Field List to accomplish this goal.*

STEPS

1. **Click the DESIGN tab on the Ribbon, click the Add Existing Fields button in the Tools group, then click the Show all tables link in the Field List**

   The Field List opens in Layout View, as shown in **FIGURE C-7**. Notice that the Field List is divided into sections. The upper section shows the tables currently used by the form, the middle section shows directly related tables, and the lower section shows other tables in the database. The expand/collapse button to the left of the table names allows you to expand (show) the fields within the table or collapse (hide) them. The Description field is in the TourCategories table in the middle section.

2. **Click the expand button ⊞ to the left of the TourCategories table, drag the Description field to the form, then use the ⁺ₖ pointer to drag the new Description text box and label below the Price label**

   When you add a new field to a form, two controls are usually created: a label and a text box. The label contains the field name and the text box displays the data in the field. The TourCategories table moved from the middle to the top section of the Field List. You also want to align and size the new controls with others already on the form. Form Design View works well for alignment activities.

3. **Right-click the Tours Entry Form tab, click Design View, click the Description label, press and hold [Shift], click the Price label to select both labels, release [Shift], click the ARRANGE tab, click the Align button in the Sizing & Ordering group, then click Left**

   Now resize the labels.

4. **With the two labels still selected, click the Size/Space button in the Sizing & Ordering group, then click To Widest**

   With the new controls in position, you want to enter a new record. You must switch to Form View to edit, enter, or delete data.

5. **Click the HOME tab, click the View button ▦ to switch to Form View, click the New (blank) record button ▶⁕ in the navigation bar, click the TourName text box, then enter a new record in the updated form, as shown in FIGURE C-8**

   Note that when you select a value in the Category combo box, the Description is automatically updated. This is due to the one-to-many relationship between the TourCategories and Tours tables in the Relationships window.

Using Forms

FIGURE C-7: Field List in Form Layout View

FIGURE C-8: Entering a record in the updated Tours Entry Form in Form View

Bound versus unbound controls

Controls are either bound or unbound. **Bound controls** display values from a field such as text boxes and combo boxes. **Unbound controls** do not display data; unbound controls describe data or enhance the appearance of the form. Labels are the most common type of unbound control, but other types include lines, images, tabs, and command buttons. Another way to distinguish bound from unbound controls is to observe the form as you move from record to record. Because bound controls display data, their contents change as you move through the records, displaying the entry in the field of the current record. Unbound controls such as labels and lines do not change as you move through the records in a form.

Learning Outcomes
• Modify control properties
• Define bound and unbound controls

Modify Form Controls

You have already made many modifications to form controls, such as changing the font color of labels and the size of text boxes. Labels and text boxes are the two most popular form controls. Other common controls are listed in **TABLE C-4**. When you modify controls, you change their **properties** (characteristics). All of the control characteristics you can modify are stored in the control's **Property Sheet**. **CASE** ▶ *Because Quest offers more Adventure tours than any other type of tour, you decide to use the Property Sheet of the Category field to modify the default value to be "Adventure." You also use the Property Sheet to make other control modifications to better size and align the controls.*

STEPS

1. **Click the** Layout View button ▦ **on the HOME tab, then click the** Property Sheet button **in the Tools group**

   The Property Sheet opens, showing you all of the properties for the selected item.

2. **Click the** Category combo box, **click the** Data tab **in the Property Sheet (if it is not already selected), click the** Default Value box, **type** Adventure, **then press** [Enter]

   The Property Sheet should look like **FIGURE C-9**. Access often helps you with the **syntax** (rules) of entering property values. In this case, Access added quotation marks around "Adventure" to indicate that the default entry is text. Properties are categorized in the Property Sheet with the Format, Data, Event, and Other tabs. The All tab is a complete list of all the control's properties. You can use the Property Sheet to make all control modifications, although you'll probably find that some changes are easier to make using the Ribbon. The property values change in the Property Sheet as you modify a control using the Ribbon.

   TROUBLE
   Be sure to click the Tour No label on the left, not the TourNo text box on the right.

3. **Click the** Format tab **in the Property Sheet, click the** Tour No label **in the form to select it, click the** HOME tab **on the Ribbon, then click the** Align Right button ≣ **in the Text Formatting group**

   Notice that the **Text Align property** on the Format tab in the Property Sheet is automatically updated from Left to Right even though you changed the property using the Ribbon instead of within the Property Sheet.

4. **Click the** Tour Name label, **press and hold** [Shift], **then click** each other label **in the first column on the form**

   With all the labels selected, you can modify their Text Align property at the same time.

   TROUBLE
   You may need to click ≣ twice.

5. **Click** ≣ **in the Text Formatting group**

   Don't be overwhelmed by the number of properties available for each control on the form or the number of ways to modify each property. Over time, you will learn about most of these properties. At this point, it's only important to know the purpose of the Property Sheet and understand that properties are modified in various ways.

   TROUBLE
   Don't worry if your Tour No value doesn't match **FIGURE C-10**. It is an AutoNumber value, controlled by Access.

6. **Click the** Save button ▦ **on the Quick Access toolbar, click the** Form View button ▦ **to switch to Form View, click the** New (blank) record button ▶▦ **in the navigation bar, then enter the record shown in FIGURE C-10**

   For new records, "Adventure" is provided as the default value for the Category combo box, but you can change it by typing a new value or selecting one from the list. With the labels right-aligned, they are much closer to the data in the text boxes that they describe.

FIGURE C-9: Using the Property Sheet

FIGURE C-10: Modified Tours Entry Form

TABLE C-4: Common form controls

name	used to	bound	unbound
Label	Provide consistent descriptive text as you navigate from record to record; the label is the most common type of unbound control and can also be used as a hyperlink to another database object, external file, or Web page		•
Text box	Display, edit, or enter data for each record from an underlying record source; the text box is the most common type of bound control	•	
List box	Display a list of possible data entries	•	
Combo box	Display a list of possible data entries for a field, and provide a text box for an entry from the keyboard; combines the list box and text box controls	•	
Tab control	Create a three-dimensional aspect on a form		•
Check box	Display "yes" or "no" answers for a field; if the box is checked, it means "yes"	•	
Toggle button	Display "yes" or "no" answers for a field; if the button is pressed, it means "yes"	•	
Option button	Display a choice for a field	•	
Option group	Display and organize choices (usually presented as option buttons) for a field	•	
Line and Rectangle	Draw lines and rectangles on the form		•
Command button	Provide an easy way to initiate a command or run a macro		•

Access 2013

Create Calculations

Learning Outcomes
• Build calculations on a form
• Move controls on a form

Text boxes are generally used to display data from underlying fields. The connection between the text box and field is defined by the **Control Source property** on the Data tab of the Property Sheet for that text box. A text box control can also display a calculation. To create a calculation in a text box, you enter an expression instead of a field name in the Control Source property. An **expression** is a combination of field names, operators (such as +, –, /, and *), and functions (such as Sum, Count, or Avg) that results in a single value. Sample expressions are shown in **TABLE C-5.** **CASE** Samantha Hooper asks you to add a text box to the Tours Entry Form to calculate the tour end date. You can add a text box in Form Design View to accomplish this.

STEPS

1. **Right-click the** Tours Entry Form tab, **then click** Design View

   You want to add the tour end date calculation just below the Duration text box. First, you'll resize the City and StateAbbrev fields.

2. **Click the** City label, **press and hold [Shift], click the** City text box, **click the** State Abbrev label, **click the** StateAbbrev text box **to select the four controls together, release [Shift], click the** ARRANGE tab, **click the** Size/Space button, **then click** To Shortest

   With the City and StateAbbrev fields resized, you're ready to move them to make room for the new control to calculate the tour end date.

3. **Click a blank spot on the form to deselect the four controls, click the** StateAbbrev text box, **use the** ⇱ **pointer to move it down, click the** City text box, **then use the** ⇱ **pointer to move it down**

   To add the calculation to determine the tour end date (the tour start date plus the duration), start by adding a new text box to the form between the Duration and City text boxes.

4. **Click the** DESIGN tab, **click the** Text Box button **ab|** **in the Controls group, then click between the Duration and City text boxes to insert the new text box**

   Adding a new text box automatically adds a new label to the left of the text box.

5. **Click the new** Text20 label **on the left, double-click** Text20, **type** Tour End Date, **then press [Enter]**

   With the label updated to correctly identify the text box to the right, you're ready to enter the expression to calculate the tour end date.

6. **Click the new text box to select it, click the** Data tab **in the Property Sheet, click the** Control Source property, **type** =[TourStartDate]+[Duration], **then press [Enter] to update the form, as shown in** FIGURE C-11

   All expressions entered in a control start with an equal sign (=). When referencing a field name within an expression, [square brackets]—(not parentheses) and not {curly braces}—surround the field name. In an expression, you must type the field name exactly as it was created in Table Design View, but you do not need to match the capitalization.

7. **Click the** View button **▦** **to switch to Form View, click the** value in the Tour Name text box, **click the** Ascending button, **select** 7 in the Duration text box, **type** 5, **then press [Enter]**

   Note that the tour end date, calculated by an expression, automatically changed to five days after the tour start date to reflect the new duration value. The updated Tours Entry Form with the tour date end calculation for the Ames Ski Club is shown in **FIGURE C-12.**

FIGURE C-11: Adding a text box to calculate a value

Modified label

New text box is selected

Expression entered in Control Source property

FIGURE C-12: Displaying the results of a calculation in Form View

Tours Entry Form

Tour No	3
Tour Name	Ames Ski Club
Tour Start Date	01/02/2015
Duration	5
Tour End Date	1/7/2015
City	Breckenridge
State Abbrev	CO
Category	Adventure
Price	$850
Description	Adventure tours include skiing, scul

Tour End Date recalculated to 5 days after the Tour Start Date =[TourStartDate]+[Duration]

TABLE C-5: Sample expressions

sample expression	description
=Sum([Salary])	Uses the **Sum function** to add the values in the Salary field
=[Price] * 1.05	Multiplies the Price field by 1.05 (adds 5% to the Price field)
=[Subtotal] + [Shipping]	Adds the value of the Subtotal field to the value of the Shipping field
=Avg([Freight])	Uses the **Avg function** to display an average of the values in the Freight field
=Date()	Uses the **Date function** to display the current date in the form of mm-dd-yy
="Page " &[Page]	Displays the word Page, a space, and the result of the [Page] field, an Access field that contains the current page number
=[FirstName]& " " &[LastName]	Displays the value of the FirstName and LastName fields in one control, separated by a space
=Left([ProductNumber],2)	Uses the **Left function** to display the first two characters in the ProductNumber field

© 2014 Cengage Learning

Learning
Outcomes
• Modify tab order
properties

Modify Tab Order

After positioning all of the controls on the form, you should check the tab order and tab stops. **Tab order** is the order the focus moves as you press [Tab] in Form View. A **tab stop** refers to whether a control can receive the focus in the first place. By default, the Tab Stop property for all text boxes and combo boxes is set to Yes, but some text boxes, such as those that contain expressions, will not be used for data entry. Therefore, the Tab Stop property for a text box that contains a calculation should be set to No. Unbound controls such as labels and lines do not have a Tab Stop property because they cannot be used to enter or edit data. **CASE** *You plan to check the tab order of the Tours Entry Form, then change tab stops and tab order as necessary.*

STEPS

1. **Press [Tab] enough times to move through several records, watching the focus move through the bound controls of the form**

   Because the Tour End Date text box is a calculated field, you don't want it to receive the focus. To prevent the Tour End Date text box from receiving the focus, you set its Tab Stop property to No using its Property Sheet. You can work with the Property Sheet in either Layout or Design View.

QUICK TIP
You can also switch between views using the View buttons in the lower-right corner of the window.

2. **Right-click the Tours Entry Form tab, click Design View, click the text box with the Tour End Date calculation if it is not selected, click the Other tab in the Property Sheet, double-click the Tab Stop property to toggle it from Yes to No, then change the Name property to TourEndDate, as shown in FIGURE C-13**

   The Other tab of the Property Sheet contains the properties you need to change the tab stop and tab order. The **Tab Stop property** determines whether the field accepts focus, and the **Tab Index property** indicates the numeric tab order for all controls on the form that have the Tab Stop property set to Yes. The **Name property** on the Other tab is also important as it identifies the name of the control, which is used in other areas of the database. To review your tab stop changes, return to Form View.

QUICK TIP
In Form Design View, press [Ctrl][.] to switch to Form View. In Form View, press [Ctrl][,] to switch to Form Design View.

3. **Click the View button to switch to Form View, then press [Tab] nine times to move to the next record**

   Now that the tab stop has been removed from the TourEndDate text box, the tab order flows correctly from the top to the bottom of the form, but skips the calculated field. To review the tab order for the entire form in one dialog box, you must switch to Form Design View.

TROUBLE
If the order of your fields does not match those in FIGURE C-14, move a field by clicking the field selector and then dragging the field up or down.

4. **Right-click the Tours Entry Form tab, click Design View, then click the Tab Order button in the Tools group to open the Tab Order dialog box, as shown in FIGURE C-14**

   The Tab Order dialog box allows you to view and change the tab order by dragging fields up or down using the **field selector** to the left of the field name. Moving fields up and down in this list also renumbers the Tab Index property for the controls in their respective Property Sheets. If you want Access to create a top-to-bottom and left-to-right tab order, click **Auto Order**.

5. **Click OK to close the Tab Order dialog box, click the Property Sheet button to toggle it off, then click the Save button on the Quick Access toolbar to save your work**

FIGURE C-13: Using the Property Sheet to set tab properties

FIGURE C-14: Tab Order dialog box

Layout positioning

If the controls on a form are organized in a layout, you can quickly modify that layout by modifying the margins, padding, and anchoring options of the layout. Each of these features is found in the Position group on the ARRANGE tab in Form Design View. **Margin** refers to the space between the outer edge of the control and the data displayed inside the control. **Padding** is the space between the controls. **Anchoring** allows you to tie controls together so you can work with them as a group.

Insert an Image

Learning Outcomes
• Insert an image on a form
• Modify form sections
• Print a selected record

Graphic images, such as pictures, logos, or clip art, can add style and professionalism to a form. The form section in which you place the images is significant. **Form sections** determine where controls are displayed and printed; they are described in **TABLE C-6**. For example, if you add a company logo to the Form Header section, the image appears at the top of the form in Form View as well as at the top of a printout. If you add the same image to the Detail section, it prints next to each record in the printout because the Detail section is printed for every record. **CASE** ▶ *Samantha Hooper suggests that you add the Quest logo to the top of the Tours Entry Form. You can add the control in either Layout or Design View, but if you want to place it in the Form Header section, you have to work in Design View.*

STEPS

1. **Click the** Form Header section bar, **click the** Insert Image button **in the Controls group, click** Browse, **then navigate to the location where you store your Data Files**
   The Insert Picture dialog box opens, prompting you for the location of the image.

2. **Double-click** QuestLogo.bmp, **then click in the Form Header section at about the 3" mark on the horizontal ruler**
   The QuestLogo image is added to the right side of the Form Header. You want to resize it to about 1" × 1".

TROUBLE
The lower-right corner of the image touches the top edge of the Detail section. To resize the Quest logo, click it to select it.

3. **With the QuestLogo image still selected, use the** ↖ **pointer to drag the** lower-right corner **of the image up and to the left so that the image is about 1" × 1", then drag the** top edge **of the Detail section up using the** ↕ **pointer, as shown in** FIGURE C-15
   When an image or control is selected in Design View, you can use **sizing handles**, which are small squares at the corners of the selection box. Drag a handle to resize the image or control. With the form completed, you open it in Form View to observe the changes.

4. **Click the** Save button 🖫 **on the Quick Access toolbar, then click the** View button 🖽 **to switch to Form View**
   You decide to add one more record with your final Tours Entry Form.

5. **Click the** New (blank) record button ▶✱ **in the navigation bar, then enter the new record shown in** FIGURE C-16, **using your last name in the TourName field**
   Now print only this single new record.

TROUBLE
If you do not click the Selected Record(s) option button, you will print *all* records, which creates a very long printout.

6. **Click the** FILE tab, **click** Print **in the navigation bar, click** Print, **click the** Selected Record(s) option button, **then click** OK

7. **Close the Tours Entry Form, click** Yes **if prompted to save it, close the QuestTravel-C.accdb database, then exit Access 2013**

TABLE C-6: Form sections

section	controls placed in this section print:
Form Header	Only once at the top of the first page of the printout
Detail	Once for every record
Form Footer	Only once at the end of the last page of the printout

© 2014 Cengage Learning

FIGURE C-15: Adding an image to the Form Header section

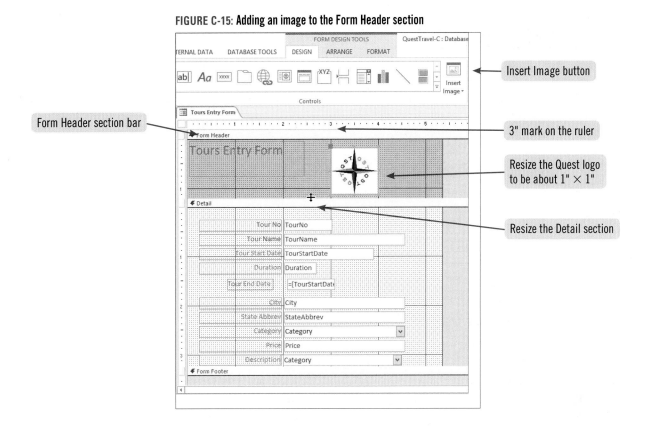

Form Header section bar

Insert Image button

3" mark on the ruler

Resize the Quest logo to be about 1" × 1"

Resize the Detail section

FIGURE C-16: Final Tours Entry Form with new record

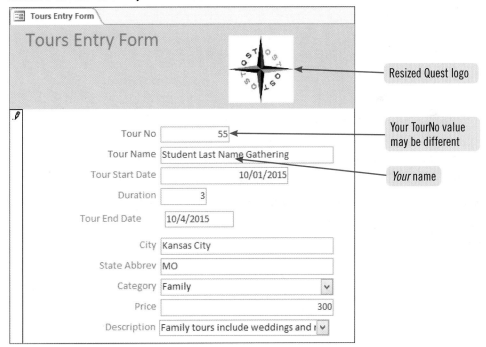

Resized Quest logo

Your TourNo value may be different

Your name

Applying a background image

A **background image** is an image that fills the entire form or report, appearing "behind" the other controls. A background image is sometimes called a watermark image. To add a background image, use the Picture property for the form or report to browse for the image that you want to use in the background.

Practice

Put your skills into practice with **SAM Projects!** SAM Projects for this unit can be found online. If you have a SAM account, go to www.cengage.com/sam2013 to download the most recent Project Instruction and Start Files.

Concepts Review

Label each element of Form Design View shown in FIGURE C-17.

FIGURE C-17

Match each term with the statement that best describes it.

10. **Bound control**
11. **Calculated control**
12. **Detail section**
13. **Database designer**
14. **Tab order**
15. **Form Footer section**

a. Created by entering an expression in a text box
b. Controls placed here print once for every record in the underlying record source
c. Used on a form to display data from a field
d. Controls placed here print only once at the end of the printout
e. The way the focus moves from one bound control to the next in Form View
f. Responsible for building and maintaining tables, queries, forms, and reports

Select the best answer from the list of choices.

16. **Every element on a form is called a(n):**
    a. Property.
    b. Control.
    c. Item.
    d. Tool.

17. **Which of the following is probably *not* a graphic image?**
    a. Logo
    b. Calculation
    c. Clip art
    d. Picture

18. **The most common bound control is the:**
   a. Text box.
   b. Label.
   c. Combo box.
   d. List box.

19. **The most common unbound control is the:**
   a. Combo box.
   b. Command button.
   c. Label.
   d. Text box.

20. **Which form view *cannot* be used to view data?**
   a. Datasheet
   b. Layout
   c. Preview
   d. Design

Skills Review

1. **Use the Form Wizard.**
   a. Start Access and open the RealEstate-C.accdb database from the location where you store your Data Files. Enable content if prompted.
   b. Click the CREATE tab, then use the Form Wizard to create a form based on all of the fields in the Realtors table. Use a Columnar layout and type **Realtor Entry Form** to title the form.
   c. Add a *new* record with *your* name in the RFirst and RLast text boxes. Note that the RealtorNo field is an AutoNumber field that is automatically incremented as you enter your first and last names. Enter your school's telephone number for the RPhone field value, and enter **4** as the AgencyNo field value.
   d. Save and close the Realtor Entry Form.

2. **Create a split form.**
   a. Click the Agencies table in the Navigation Pane, click the CREATE tab, click the More Forms button, then click Split Form.
   b. Switch to Form View and close the Property Sheet if it opens.
   c. Click the record selector in the lower pane for AgencyNo 3, Emerald Point Realtors, then click the Delete button in the Records group to delete this realtor. Click OK when prompted that you cannot delete this record because there are related records in the Realtors table.
   d. Navigate to the AgencyNo 4, Hollister Real Estate, record in either the upper or lower pane of the split form. Change 7744 Pokeberry Lane to **12345 Amanda Drive**.
   e. Right-click the Agencies form tab, click Close, click Yes when prompted to save changes, type **Agencies Split Form** as the name of the form, then click OK.

3. **Use Form Layout View.**
   a. Open the Realtor Entry Form in Layout View.
   b. Modify the labels on the left to read: **Realtor Number**, **Realtor First Name**, **Realtor Last Name**, **Realtor Phone**, **Agency Number**.
   c. Modify the text color of the labels to be black.
   d. Resize the RFirst, RLast, and RPhone text boxes on the right to be the same width as the RealtorNo and AgencyNo text boxes.
   e. Save the Realtor Entry Form.

4. **Add fields to a form.**
   a. Open the Field List, show all the tables, then expand the Agencies table to display its fields.
   b. Drag the AgencyName field to the form, then move the AgencyName label and combo box below the Agency Number controls.
   c. Modify the AgencyName label to read **Agency Name**.
   d. Modify the text color of the Agency Name label to black.
   e. Close the Field List and save and close the Realtor Entry Form.

Skills Review (continued)

5. **Modify form controls.**

   a. Reopen the Realtor Entry Form in Layout View, then use the Align Right button on the HOME tab to right-align each of the labels in the left column.

   b. Save the form, switch to Form View, then use the Agency Name combo box to change the Agency Name to **Marvin and Pam Realtors** for Realtor Number 1.

   c. If the combo box is not wide enough to display the entire entry for Marvin and Pam Realtors, switch back to Layout View and widen the combo box as much as needed to display the entire entry.

   d. In Layout View, resize and move all controls so that the labels are lined up on the left and the text boxes are lined up on the right, as shown in **FIGURE C-18**.

FIGURE C-18

6. **Create calculations.**

   a. Switch to Form Design View, then add a text box below the Realtor Entry Form label in the Form Header section. Delete the Text14 label that is created when you add a new text box. The number in your label is based on previous work done to the form, so it might vary.

   b. Widen the text box to be almost as wide as the entire form, then enter the following expression into the text box, which will add the words *Information for* to the realtor's first name, a space, and then the realtor's last name.
   ="Information for "&[RFirst]&" "&[RLast]

   c. Save the form, then view it in Form View. Be sure the new text box correctly displays spaces in the text. Return to Design View to edit the expression if #Name? appears, which indicates that the expression was entered incorrectly.

   d. In Form View, change the Realtor Last Name for Realtor Number 1 from West to **South**. Tab to the RPhone text box to observe how the expression in the Form Header automatically updates.

   e. Tab through several records, observing the expression in the Form Header section.

7. **Modify tab order.**

   a. Switch to Form Design View, then open the Property Sheet.

   b. Select the new text box with the expression in the Form Header section, then change the Tab Stop property from Yes to No.

   c. Select the RealtorNo text box in the Detail section, then change the Tab Stop property from Yes to No. (AutoNumber fields cannot be edited, so they do not need to have a tab stop.)

   d. Close the Property Sheet.

   e. Save the form and view it in Form View. Tab through the form to make sure that the tab order is sequential and skips the expression in the Form Header as well as the Realtor Number text box. Use the Tab Order button on the DESIGN tab in Form Design View to modify tab order, if necessary.

8. **Insert an image.**

   a. Switch to Design View, then click the Form Header section bar.

   b. Add the ForSale.bmp image to the right side of the Form Header, then resize the image to be about 1" × 1".

   c. Remove extra blank space in the Form Header section by dragging the top edge of the Detail section up as far as possible.

   d. Drag the right edge of the form as far as possible to the left.

   e. Save the form, then switch to Form View. Move through the records, observing the calculated field from record to record to make sure it is calculating correctly.

   f. Find the record with your name, as shown in **FIGURE C-18**, and if requested by your instructor, print only that record.

   g. Close the Realtor Entry Form, close the RealEstate-C.accdb database, then exit Access.

Independent Challenge 1

As the manager of the scuba divers branch of the Quest Specialty Travel tour company, you have developed a database to help manage scuba dives. In this exercise, you'll create a data entry form to manage the dive trips.

a. Start Access, then open the Dives-C.accdb database from the location where you store your Data Files. Enable content if prompted.

b. Using the Form Wizard, create a form that includes all the fields in the DiveTrips table and uses the Columnar layout, then type **Dive Trip Entry** as the title of the form.

c. Switch to Layout View, then delete the ID text box and label.

d. Using Form Design View, use the [Shift] key to select all of the text boxes except the last one for TripReport, then resize them to the shortest size using the To Shortest option on the Size/Space button on the ARRANGE tab.

e. Using Form Design View, resize the Location, City, State/Province, Country, and Lodging text boxes to be no wider than the Rating text box.

f. Using Form Design View, move and resize the controls, as shown in FIGURE C-19. Once the controls are resized, drag the top of the Form Footer section up to remove the extra blank space in the Detail section.

g. Using Form Layout View, modify the labels and alignment of the labels, as shown in FIGURE C-19. Note that there are spaces between the words in the labels, the labels are right-aligned, and the text boxes are left-aligned. Use a dark blue color for the labels and black for the text in the text boxes.

h. In Form View, find the Great Barrier Reef tour. Edit the State/Province, Certification Diving, and Trip Report fields, as shown in FIGURE C-19 for the TripReport field using *your* name.

i. Save the form, then if requested by your instructor, print only the record with your name.

j. Close the Dive Trip Entry form, close the Dives-C.accdb database, then exit Access 2013.

FIGURE C-19

Independent Challenge 2

You have built an Access database to track membership in a community service club. The database tracks member names and addresses as well as their status in the club, which moves from rank to rank as the members contribute increased hours of service to the community.

a. Start Access, then open the Membership-C.accdb database from the location where you store your Data Files. Enable content if prompted.

b. Using the Form Wizard, create a form based on all of the fields of the Members table and only the DuesOwed field in the Status table.

c. View the data by Members, use a Columnar layout, then enter **Member Information** as the title of the form.

d. Enter a new record with *your* name and the school name, address, and phone number of your school for the Company and address fields. Give yourself a StatusNo entry of **1**. In the DuesPaid field, enter **75**. DuesOwed automatically displays 100 because that value is pulled from the Status table and is based on the entry in the StatusNo field, which links the Members table to the Status table.

e. In Layout View, add a text box to the form and move it below the DuesOwed text box.

f. Open the Property Sheet for the new text box, display the Data tab, and in the Control Source property of the new text box, enter the expression that calculates the balance between DuesOwed and DuesPaid: **=[DuesOwed]-[DuesPaid]**.

g. Open the Property Sheet for the new label, and change the Caption property on the Format tab for the new label to **Balance**.

h. Right-align all of the labels in the first column.

i. Set the Tab Stop property for the text box that contains the calculated Balance to **No**, then close the Property Sheet.

j. In Layout or Design View, resize DuesPaid and DuesOwed text boxes to be the same width as the new Balance text box, then right-align all data within the three text boxes.

FIGURE C-20

Member Information

FName	Student First
LName	Student Last
Company	JCCC
Street	12345 College Blvd
City	Overland Park
State	KS
Zip	66213
Phone	(444) 850-5555
StatusNo	1
DuesPaid	$85.00
DuesOwed	$100.00
Balance	$15.00

Independent Challenge 2 (continued)

k. Open the Property Sheet for the text box that contains the expression, and change the Format property on the Format tab to Currency. Close the Property Sheet.

l. Switch to Form Design View, then drag the right edge of the form to the 7" mark on the horizontal ruler. The horizontal ruler is located just above the Form Header section.

m. Click a blank spot on the right edge of the form, click the Insert Image button on the DESIGN tab, browse for the People.jpg image, then insert it on the right side of the form in the Detail section. (*Hint*: You will need to change the Web-Ready Image Files list in the Insert Picture dialog box to All Files to find .jpg images.)

n. Resize the picture to be about 2" × 2", then drag the right edge of the form to the left as far as possible. Also drag the top edge of the Form Footer up as far as possible to eliminate blank space in the Detail section.

o. Save the form, find the record with your name, change the DuesPaid value to **85**, then move and resize controls as necessary to match **FIGURE C-20**.

p. If requested by your instructor, print only the record with your name.

q. Save and close the Member Information form, then close the Membership-C.accdb database and exit Access 2013.

Independent Challenge 3

You have built an Access database to organize the deposits at a recycling center. Various clubs regularly deposit recyclable material, which is measured in pounds when the deposits are made.

a. Open the Recycle-C.accdb database from the location where you store your Data Files. Enable content if prompted.

b. Using the Form Wizard, create a form based on all of the fields in the CenterDeposits query. View the data by Deposits, use the Columnar layout, and title the form **Deposit Listing**.

c. Switch to Layout View, then make each label bold.

d. Modify the labels so that CenterName is **Center Name**, DepositDate is **Deposit Date**, and ClubName is **Club Name**.

e. Switch to Form Design View and resize the CenterName and ClubName text boxes so they are the same height and width as the Weight text box, as shown in **FIGURE C-21**.

f. Switch to Form View, find and change any entry of Dallas Jaycees in the ClubName field to *your* last name, then print one record with your name if requested by your instructor.

g. Using Form View of the Deposit Listing form, filter for all records with your last name in the ClubName field.

h. Using Form View of the Deposit Listing form, sort the filtered records in descending order on the DepositDate field.

i. Preview the first record, as shown in **FIGURE C-21**. If requested by your instructor, print the first record.

j. Save and close the Deposit Listing form, close the Recycle-C.accdb database, then exit Access.

Access 2013

FIGURE C-21

Center Name	Hugo Trash Can
Deposit Date	10/31/2016
Weight	80
Club Name	Student Last Name

Independent Challenge 4: Explore

One way you can use an Access database on your own is to record and track your job search efforts. In this exercise, you will develop a form to help you enter data into your job-tracking database.

a. Start Access and open the Jobs-C.accdb database from the location where you store your Data Files. Enable content if prompted.

b. Click the CREATE tab, then use the Form Wizard to create a new form based on all the fields of both the Employers and Positions tables.

c. View the data by Employers, use a Datasheet layout for the subform, accept the default names for the form and subform, then open the form to view information.

d. Use Layout View and Design View to modify the form labels, text box positions, alignment, and sizes, as shown in **FIGURE C-22**. Note that the columns within the subform have been resized to display all of the data in the subform.

e. Change the CompanyName of IBM in the first record to **Your Last Name's Software**, and if instructed to create a printout, print only that record. Close the Employers form.

f. Click the Employers table in the Navigation Pane, then use the Split Form option on the More Forms button of the CREATE tab to create a split form on the Employers table. Close and save the split form with the name **Employers Split Form**.

FIGURE C-22

Employers

Employers

EmployerID	1		Phone	515-555-4444
Company	Your Last Name's Software			
Street	400 Locust St			
City State Zip	Des Moines	IA	51122	

Positions

PositionID ▾	Title ▾	CareerArea ▾	AnnualSalary ▾	Desirability ▾	EmployerID ▾
1	Marketing Representative	Computers	$35,000.00	5	1
2	Systems Engineer	Computers	$37,000.00	5	1
* (New)					1

Independent Challenge 4: Explore (continued)

g. Open the Employers Split Form in Form View, and change the address and phone number information for EmployerID 1 to *your* school's address and phone information, as shown in **FIGURE C-23**.

h. Navigate through all five records, then back to EmployerID 1, observing both the upper and lower panes of the split form as you move from record to record.

i. Open the Employers form and navigate forward and backward through all five records to study the difference between the Employers form, which uses a form/subform versus the Employers Split Form. Even though both the Employers form and Employers Split Form show datasheets in the bottom halves of the forms, they are fundamentally very different. The split form is displaying the records of only the Employers table, whereas the Employers form is using a subform to display related records from the Positions table in the lower datasheet. You will learn more about forms and subforms in later units.

j. Close the Jobs-C.accdb database, then exit Access.

FIGURE C-23

	Employers Split Form						

Employers

EmployerID	1	EmpCity	Your School's City
CompanyName	Your Last Name's Software	EmpState	IA
EmpStreet	Your School's Street	EmpZip	99999
		EmpPhone	999-999-9999

EmployerID ▾	CompanyName ▾	EmpStreet ▾	EmpCity ▾	EmpState ▾	EmpZip ▾	EmpPhone ▾
1	Your Last Name's Sc	Your School's S	Your School's C	IA	99999	999-999-9999
2	EDS	500 Cricket St	Ames	IA	50010	515-555-3333
3	Google	600 Crocker St	Omaha	NE	66000	616-555-2222
4	Apple	700 Beetle St	Lincoln	NE	66110	616-555-1111
5	Bass Pro Shops	800 Ladybug St	Sioux City	NE	66220	616-555-3333
* (New)						

Record: I◄ ◄ 1 of 5 ► ►I ►꘏ 🗑 No Filter | Search

Visual Workshop

Open the Baseball-C.accdb database, enable content if prompted, then use the Split Form tool to create a form named **Players**, as shown in FIGURE C-24, based on the Players table. Resize the PlayerLast text box as shown. Modify the labels as shown. View the data in Form View, and sort the records in ascending order by last name. Change the first, last, and nickname of the Henry Aaron record in the first record to *your* name, and if instructed to create a printout, print only that record. Save and close the Players form, close the Baseball-C.accdb database, then exit Access.

FIGURE C-24

Using Reports

CASE Samantha Hooper, a tour developer at Quest Specialty Travel, asks you to produce some reports to help her share and analyze data. A report is an Access object that creates a professional looking printout.

Unit Objectives

After completing this unit, you will be able to:

- Use the Report Wizard
- Use Report Layout View
- Review report sections
- Apply group and sort orders
- Add subtotals and counts
- Resize and align controls
- Format a report
- Create mailing labels

Files You Will Need

QuestTravel-D.accdb
RealEstate-D.accdb
Conventions-D.accdb
Membership-D.accdb
Recycle-D.accdb
JobSearch-D.accdb
Basketball-D.accdb

© Tumanyan/Shutterstock

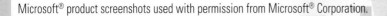

Use the Report Wizard

Learning
Outcomes
• Create a report
  with the Report
  Wizard
• Change page
  orientation

A **report** is the primary object you use to print database content because it provides the most formatting, layout, and summary options. A report may include various fonts and colors, clip art and lines, and multiple headers and footers. A report can also calculate subtotals, averages, counts, and other statistics for groups of records. You can create reports in Access by using the **Report Wizard**, a tool that asks questions to guide you through the initial development of the report. Your responses to the Report Wizard determine the record source, style, and layout of the report. The **record source** is the table or query that defines the fields and records displayed on the report. The Report Wizard also helps you sort, group, and analyze the records. CASE ▶ *You use the Report Wizard to create a report to display the tours within each state.*

STEPS

1. **Start Access, open the QuestTravel-D.accdb database, enable content if prompted, click the CREATE tab on the Ribbon, then click the Report Wizard button in the Reports group**

   The Report Wizard starts, prompting you to select the fields you want on the report. You can select fields from one or more tables or queries.

2. **Click the Tables/Queries list arrow, click Table: States, double-click the StateName field, click the Tables/Queries list arrow, click Table: Tours, click the Select All Fields button >> , click StateAbbrev in the Selected Fields list, then click the Remove Field button <**

   By selecting the StateName field from the States table, and all fields from the Tours table except the StateAbbrev field, you have all of the fields you need for the report, as shown in **FIGURE D-1**.

3. **Click Next, then click by States if it is not already selected**

   Choosing "by States" groups together the records for each state. In addition to record-grouping options, the Report Wizard later asks if you want to sort the records within each group. You can use the Report Wizard to specify up to four fields to sort in either ascending or descending order.

4. **Click Next, click Next again to include no additional grouping levels, click the first sort list arrow, click TourStartDate, then click Next**

   The last questions in the Report Wizard deal with report appearance and the report title.

5. **Click the Stepped option button, click the Landscape option button, click Next, type Tours by State for the report title, then click Finish**

   The Tours by State report opens in **Print Preview**, which displays the report as it appears when printed, as shown in **FIGURE D-2**. The records are grouped by state, the first state being California, and then sorted in ascending order by the TourStartDate field within each state. Reports are **read-only objects**, meaning you can use them to read and display data but not to change (write to) data. As you change data using tables, queries, or forms, reports constantly display those up-to-date edits just like all of the other Access objects.

6. **Scroll down to see the second grouping section on the report for the state of Colorado, then click the Next Page button ▶ in the navigation bar to see the second page of the report**

   Even in **landscape orientation** (11" wide by 8.5" tall as opposed to **portrait orientation**, which is 8.5" wide by 11" tall), the fields on the Tours by State report may not fit on one sheet of paper. The labels in the column headings and the data in the columns need to be resized to improve the layout. Depending on your monitor, you might need to scroll to the right to display all the fields on this page.

FIGURE D-1: Selecting fields for a report using the Report Wizard

Select All Fields button

Remove Field button

Tables/Queries list arrow

Selected fields

FIGURE D-2: Tours by State report in Print Preview

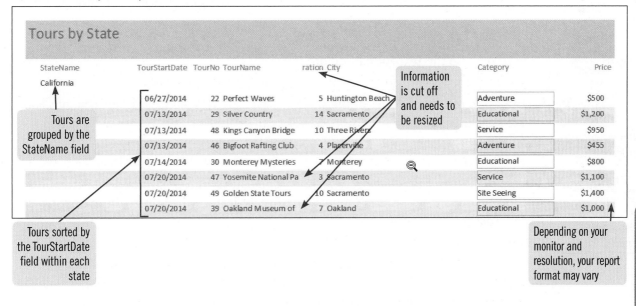

Tours are grouped by the StateName field

Information is cut off and needs to be resized

Tours sorted by the TourStartDate field within each state

Depending on your monitor and resolution, your report format may vary

Changing page orientation

To change page orientation from Portrait (8.5" wide by 11" tall) to Landscape (11" wide by 8.5" tall) and vice versa, click the Portrait or Landscape button on the PRINT PREVIEW tab when viewing the report in Print Preview. To switch to Print Preview, right-click the report in the Navigation Pane, and then choose Print Preview on the shortcut menu.

Use Report Layout View

Learning Outcomes
- Move and resize controls in Layout View
- Modify labels

Reports have multiple views that you use for various report-building and report-viewing activities. Although some tasks can be accomplished in more than one view, each view has a primary purpose to make your work with reports as easy and efficient as possible. The different report views are summarized in **TABLE D-1.** **CASE** *Samantha Hooper asks you to modify the Tours by State report so that all of the fields fit comfortably across one sheet of paper in landscape orientation.*

STEPS

TROUBLE
If the Field List window opens, close it.

1. **Right-click the** Tours by State report tab, **then click** Layout View
   Layout View opens and applies a grid to the report that helps you resize, move, and position controls. You decide to narrow the City column to make room for the Price data.

2. **Click** Huntington Beach **(or any value in the City column), then use the ↔ pointer to drag the right edge of the City column to the left to narrow it to about half of its current size, as shown in** FIGURE D-3
   By narrowing the City column, you create extra space in the report.

3. **Click** $500 **(or any value in the Price column), use the ⁺ᣟ pointer to drag the Price values to the left of the Category column, click the** Price label, **then use ⁺ᣟ to move the Price label to the left of the Category label**
   All the columns are now within the boundaries of a single sheet of paper in landscape orientation. You also notice that centering some data would make it easier to read.

4. **Click** 22 **(or any value in the TourNo column), click the** HOME **tab, then click the** Center **button** ≡ **in the Text Formatting group**
   The TourName column needs more space to completely display the tour names.

QUICK TIP
Resizing with ↔ instead of moving with ⁺ᣟ maintains the vertical alignment of the controls.

5. **Use ↔ to resize both sides of the** TourStartDate, TourNo, **and** TourName **columns and their labels to the left, then use ↔ to resize the** Category, Price, City, **and** Duration **columns and their labels to the right**
   Now the report has enough room to resize the TourName column and the Duration label.

QUICK TIP
You can use the Undo button arrow ↶ ▾ to undo many actions in Layout View.

6. **Resize the** TourName **column so that all of the data is visible, paying special attention to the longest value, Yosemite National Park Great Cleanup, then resize the** Duration label **to display the complete text**
   You can also rename labels in Report Layout View.

7. **Click the** StateName label, **click between the words** State **and** Name, **press the [Spacebar] so that the label reads State Name, then modify the** TourStartDate, TourNo, **and** TourName **labels to contain spaces as well**

8. **Continue resizing the columns so that all of the data is visible and your report looks like** FIGURE D-4

FIGURE D-3: Modifying the column width in Report Layout View

FIGURE D-4: Final Tours by State report in Report Layout View

TABLE D-1: Report views

view	primary purpose
Report View	To quickly review the report without page breaks
Print Preview	To review each page of an entire report as it will appear if printed
Layout View	To modify the size, position, or formatting of controls; shows live data as you modify the report, making it the tool of choice when you want to change the appearance and positioning of controls on a report while also reviewing live data
Design View	To work with report sections or to access the complete range of controls and report properties; Design View does not display data

Review Report Sections

Learning
Outcomes
• Navigate through
report sections
and pages
• Resize the width of
the report
• Work with error
indicators

Report **sections** determine where and how often controls in that section print in the final report. For example, controls in the Report Header section print only once at the beginning of the report, but controls in the Detail section print once for every record the report displays. **TABLE D-2** describes report sections. **CASE** You and Samantha Hooper preview the Tours by State report to review and understand report sections.

STEPS

1. **Right-click the** Tours by State tab, **click** Print Preview, **then scroll up and click the light blue bar at the top of the report if you need to zoom in to display the first page of the report, as shown in FIGURE D-5**

   The first page shows four sections: Report Header, Page Header, StateAbbreviation Header, and Detail.

2. **Click the** Next Page button ▶ **on the navigation bar to move to the second page of the report**

   If the second page of the report does not contain data, it means that the report may be too wide to fit on a single sheet of paper. You fix that problem in Report Design View.

3. **Right-click the** Tours by State tab, **click** Design View, **scroll to the far right using the bottom horizontal scroll bar, then use the ↔ pointer to drag the** right edge of the report **as far as you can to the left, as shown in FIGURE D-6**

   In Report Design View, you can work with the report sections and make modifications to the report that you cannot make in other views, such as narrowing the width. Report Design View does not display any data, though. For your report to fit on one page in landscape orientation, you need to move all of the controls within the 10.5" mark on the horizontal **ruler** using the default 0.25" left and right margins. You will practice fixing this problem by moving all controls within the 10" mark on the ruler to make sure they all fit on the landscape printout.

4. **Use the ⬚ pointer to drag the** page calculation **about 0.5" to the left, then use ↔ to drag the** right edge of the report **as far as you can to the left**

   To review your modifications, show the report in Print Preview.

5. **Right-click the** Tours by State tab, **click** Print Preview, **click** ▶ **to navigate to the last page of the report, then click the report to zoom in and out to examine the page, as shown in FIGURE D-7**

   Previewing each page of the report helps you confirm that no blank pages are created and allows you to examine how the different report sections print on each page.

TABLE D-2: Report sections

section	where does this section print?
Report Header	At the top of the first page
Page Header	At the top of every page (but below the Report Header on the first page)
Group Header	Before every group of records
Detail	Once for every record
Group Footer	After every group of records
Page Footer	At the bottom of every page
Report Footer	At the end of the report

FIGURE D-5: Tours by State in Print Preview

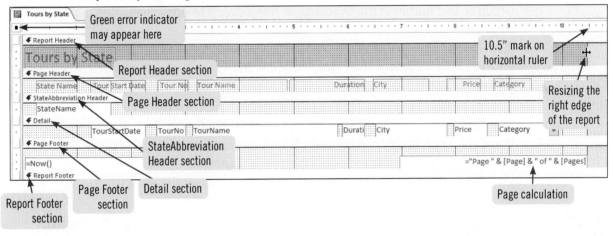

FIGURE D-6: Tours by State report in Design View

FIGURE D-7: Last page of Tours by State report in Print Preview

Using Reports

Apply Group and Sort Orders

Grouping means to sort records by a particular field *plus* provide a header and/or footer section before or after each group of sorted records. For example, if you group records by the StateName field, the Group Header is called the StateName Header and the Group Footer is called the StateName Footer. The StateName Header section appears once for each state in the report, immediately before the records in that state. The StateName Footer section also appears once for each state in the report, immediately after the records for that state. **CASE ►** *The records in the Tours by State report are currently grouped by the StateAbbreviation field. Samantha Hooper asks you to further group the records by the Category field (Adventure, Educational, and Family, for example) within each state.*

STEPS

1. **Click the Close Print Preview button to return to Report Design View, then click the Group & Sort button in the Grouping & Totals group to open the Group, Sort, and Total pane**

   Currently, the records are grouped by the StateAbbreviation field and further sorted by the TourStartDate field. To add the Category field as a grouping field within each state, you work with the Group, Sort, and Total pane in Report Design View.

2. **Click the Add a group button in the Group, Sort, and Total pane, click Category, then click the Move up button ⬆ on the right side of the Group, Sort, and Total pane so that Category is positioned between StateAbbreviation and TourStartDate**

   A Category Header section is added to Report Design View just below the StateAbbreviation Header section. You move the Category control from the Detail section to the Category Header section so it prints only once for each new Category instead of once for each record in the Detail section.

3. **Right-click the Category combo box in the Detail section, click Cut on the shortcut menu, right-click the Category Header section, click Paste, then use the ⬚ pointer to drag the Category combo box to the right to position it as shown in FIGURE D-8**

   Now that you've moved the Category combo box to the Category Header, it will print only once per category within each state. You no longer need the Category label in the Page Header section.

4. **Click the Category label in the Page Header section, press [Delete], then switch to Print Preview and zoom to 100%**

   The Tours by State report should look like **FIGURE D-9**. Notice that the records are now grouped by category within state. Detail records are further sorted in ascending order by the tour start date.

FIGURE D-8: Group, Sort, and Total pane and new Category Header section

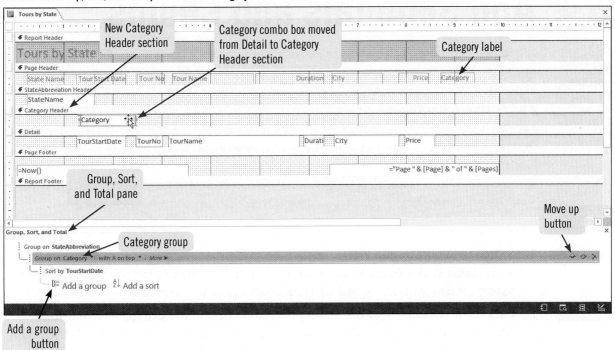

FIGURE D-9: Tours by State report grouped by category within state

Add Subtotals and Counts

Learning Outcomes
• Create calculations to subtotal and count records
• Cut and paste controls

In a report, you create a **calculation** by entering an expression into a text box. When a report is previewed or printed, the expression is evaluated and the resulting calculation is placed on the report. An **expression** is a combination of field names, operators (such as +, –, /, and *), and functions that results in a single value. A **function** is a built-in formula, such as Sum or Count, that helps you quickly create a calculation. Notice that every expression starts with an equal sign (=), and when it uses a function, the arguments for the function are placed in (parentheses). **Arguments** are the pieces of information that the function needs to create the final answer. When an argument is a field name, the field name must be surrounded by [square brackets]. **CASE** *Samantha Hooper asks you to add a calculation to the Tours by State report to sum the total number of tour days within each category and within each state.*

STEPS

1. **Switch to Report Design View**

   A logical place to add subtotals for each group is right after that group of records prints, in the Group Footer section. You use the Group, Sort, and Total pane to open Group Footer sections.

TROUBLE
Click Category in the Group, Sort, and Total pane to display the grouping options.

2. **Click the More button for the StateAbbreviation field in the Group, Sort, and Total pane, click the without a footer section list arrow, click with a footer section, then do the same for the Category field, as shown in FIGURE D-10**

   With the StateAbbreviation Footer and Category Footer sections open, you're ready to add controls to calculate the total number of tour days within each category and within each state. You use a text box control with an expression to make this calculation.

3. **Click the Text Box button [ab] in the Controls group, then click just below the Duration text box in the Category Footer section**

   Adding a new text box automatically adds a new label to its left. First, you modify the label to identify the information, then you modify the text box to contain the correct expression to sum the number of tour days for that category.

TROUBLE
Depending on your activity in Report Design View, you may see a different number in the Text##: label.

4. **Click the Text19 label to select it, double-click Text19, type Total days:, click the Unbound text box to select it, click Unbound again, type =Sum([Duration]), press [Enter], then widen the text box to view the entire expression**

   The expression =Sum([Duration]) uses the Sum function to add the days in the Duration field. Because the expression is entered in the Category Footer section, it will sum all Duration values for that category within that state. To sum the Duration values for each state, the expression needs to be inserted in the StateAbbreviation Footer.

QUICK TIP
Pasting the expression in the Report Footer section would subtotal the duration values for the entire report.

5. **Right-click the =Sum([Duration]) text box, click Copy, right-click the StateAbbreviation Footer section, click Paste, then press [→] enough times to position the controls in the StateAbbreviation Footer section just below those in the Category Footer section, as shown in FIGURE D-11**

   With the expression copied to the StateAbbreviation Footer section, you're ready to preview your work.

TROUBLE
Drag the top edge of all section bars up to eliminate extra blank space in the report.

6. **Switch to Print Preview, navigate to the last page of the report, then click to zoom so you can see all of the Washington tours**

   As shown in **FIGURE D-12**, 21 tour days are totaled for the Adventure category, and 3 for the Site Seeing category, which is a total of 24 tour days for the state of Washington. The summary data would look better if it were aligned more directly under the tour Duration values. You resize and align controls in the next lesson.

FIGURE D-10: Opening group footer sections

FIGURE D-11: Adding subtotals to group footer sections

FIGURE D-12: Previewing the new group footer calculations

Resize and Align Controls

After you add information to the appropriate section of a report, you might also want to align the data in precise columns and rows to make the information easier to read. To do so, you can use two different types of **alignment** commands. You can left-, right-, or center-align a control *within its own border* using the Align Left ▤, Center ▤, and Align Right ▤ buttons on the HOME tab. You can also align the edges of controls *with respect to one another* using the Left, Right, Top, and Bottom commands on the Align button of the ARRANGE tab in Report Design View. **CASE** ▶ *You decide to resize and align several controls to improve the readability of the Tours by State report. Layout View is a good choice for these tasks.*

STEPS

1. **Switch to Layout View, click the DESIGN tab on the Ribbon, then click the Group & Sort button to toggle off the Group, Sort, and Total pane**

   You decide to align the expressions that subtotal the number of tour days for each category within the Duration column.

2. **Click the Total days text box in the Category Footer, click the HOME tab, click the Align Right button ▤ in the Text Formatting group, then use the ↔ pointer to resize the text box so that the data is aligned in the Duration column, as shown in FIGURE D-13**

   With the calculation formatted as desired in the Category Footer, you can quickly apply those modifications to the calculation in the StateAbbreviation Footer as well.

3. **Scroll down the report far enough to find and then click the Total days text box in the StateAbbreviation Footer, click ▤, then use the ↔ pointer to resize the text box so that it is the same width as the text box in the Category Footer section**

   With both expressions right-aligned and resized so they line up under the Duration values in the Detail section, they are easier to read on the report.

4. **Scroll the report so you can see all of the Colorado tours, as shown in FIGURE D-14**

   You can apply resize, alignment, or formatting commands to more than one control at a time. **TABLE D-3** provides techniques for selecting more than one control at a time in Report Design View.

Precisely moving and resizing controls

You can move and resize controls using the mouse or other pointing device, but you can move controls more precisely using the keyboard. Pressing the arrow keys while holding [Ctrl] moves selected controls one **pixel (picture element)** at a time in the direction of the arrow. Pressing the arrow keys while holding [Shift] resizes selected controls one pixel at a time.

Using Reports

FIGURE D-13: Resizing controls in Layout View

FIGURE D-14: Reviewing the aligned and resized controls

TABLE D-3: Selecting more than one control at a time in Report Design View

technique	description
Click, [Shift]+click	Click a control, then press and hold [Shift] while clicking other controls; each one is selected
Drag a selection box	Drag a selection box (an outline box you create by dragging the pointer in Report Design View); every control that is in or is touched by the edges of the box is selected
Click in the ruler	Click in either the horizontal or vertical ruler to select all controls that intersect the selection line
Drag in the ruler	Drag through either the horizontal or vertical ruler to select all controls that intersect the selection line as it is dragged through the ruler

Access 2013

Format a Report

Learning
Outcomes
• Format controls
  and sections of a
  report
• Add labels to a
  report

Formatting refers to enhancing the appearance of the information. TABLE D-4 lists several of the most popular formatting commands found on the FORMAT tab when you are working in Layout or Report Design View. Although the Report Wizard automatically applies many formatting embellishments, you often want to change the appearance of the report to fit your particular needs. **CASE** *When reviewing the Tours by State report with Samantha, you decide to change the background color of some of the report sections to make the data easier to read. Your first change will be to shade each Category Header and Footer section (rather than alternating sections, the format initially provided by the Report Wizard). To make changes to entire report sections, you work in Report Design View.*

STEPS

QUICK TIP
The quick keystroke
for Undo is [Ctrl][Z].
The quick keystroke
for Redo is [Ctrl][Y].

1. **Switch to Design View, click the** Category Header section bar, **click the** FORMAT tab **on the Ribbon, click the** Alternate Row Color button arrow, **click** No Color, **click the** Shape Fill button, **then click the** Maroon 2 color square, **as shown in** FIGURE D-15

   Make a similar modification by applying a different fill color to the Category Footer section.

2. **Click the** Category Footer section bar, **click the** Alternate Row Color button arrow, **click** No Color, **click the** Shape Fill button, **then click the** Green 2 color square (just to the right of Maroon 2 in the Standard Colors section)

   When you use the Alternate Row Color and Shape Fill buttons, you're actually modifying the **Back Color** and **Alternate Back Color** properties in the Property Sheet of the section or control you selected. Background shades can help differentiate parts of the report, but be careful with dark colors as they may print as solid black on some printers and fax machines.

3. **Switch to Layout View to review your modifications**

   The category sections are clearer, but you decide to make one more modification to emphasize the report title.

4. **Click the** Tours by State label **in the Report Header section, click the** HOME tab, **then click the** Bold button B **in the Text Formatting group**

   The report in Layout View should look like FIGURE D-16. You also want to add a label to the Report Footer section to identify yourself.

5. **Switch to Report Design View, drag the** bottom edge of the Report Footer **down about 0.5", click the** Label button Aa **in the Controls group, click at the 1" mark in the Report Footer, type** Created by *your* name, **press [Enter], click the** HOME tab, **then click** B **in the Text Formatting group**

6. **Save and preview the Tours by State report**

7. **If required by your instructor, print the report, and then close it**

FIGURE D-15: Formatting section backgrounds

FIGURE D-16: Final formatted Tours by State report

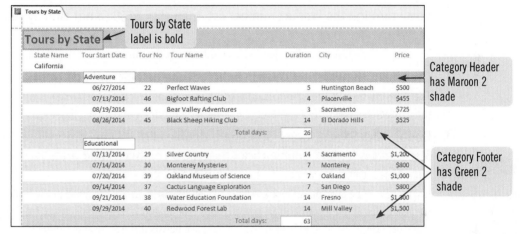

TABLE D-4: Useful formatting commands

button	button name	description
B	Bold	Toggles bold on or off for the selected control(s)
I	Italic	Toggles italic on or off for the selected control(s)
<u>U</u>	Underline	Toggles underline on or off for the selected control(s)
☰	Align Left	Left-aligns the selected control(s) within its own border
☰	Center	Centers the selected control(s) within its own border
☰	Align Right	Right-aligns the selected control(s) within its own border
🪣	Background Color or Shape Fill	Changes the background color of the selected control(s)
▦	Alternate Row Color	Changes the background color of alternate records in the selected section
A	Font Color	Changes the text color of the selected control(s)
✎	Shape Outline Line Thickness option Line Type option	Changes the border color of the selected control(s) Changes the border style of the selected control(s) Changes the special visual effect of the selected control(s)

Create Mailing Labels

Learning
Outcomes
• Create a report of
  labels
• Print specific
  pages of a report

Mailing labels are often created to apply to envelopes, postcards, or letters when assembling a mass mailing. They have many other business purposes too, such as applying them to paper file folders or name tags. Any data in your Access database can be converted into labels using the **Label Wizard**, a special report wizard that precisely positions and sizes information for hundreds of standard business labels. **CASE** ▶ *Samantha Hooper asks you to create mailing labels for all of the addresses in the Customers table. You use the Label Wizard to handle this request.*

STEPS

1. **Click the Customers table in the Navigation Pane, click the CREATE tab, then click the Labels button in the Reports group**

   The first Label Wizard dialog box opens. The Filter by manufacturer list box provides over 30 manufacturers of labels. Because Avery is the most common, it is the default choice. With the manufacturer selected, your next task is to choose the product number of the labels you will feed through the printer. The cover on the box of labels you are using provides this information. In this case, you'll be using Avery 5160 labels, a common type of sheet labels used for mailings and other purposes.

2. **Scroll through the Product number list, then click 5160 (if not already selected), as shown in FIGURE D-17**

   Note that by selecting a product number, you also specify the dimensions of the label and number of columns.

3. **Click Next, then click Next again to accept the default font and color choices**

   The third question of the Label Wizard asks how you want to construct your label. You'll add the fields from the Customers table with spaces and line breaks to pattern a standard mailing format.

4. **Double-click FName, press [Spacebar], double-click LName, press [Enter], double-click Street, press [Enter], double-click City, type a comma (,) and press [Spacebar], double-click State, press [Spacebar], then double-click Zip**

   If your prototype label doesn't look exactly like **FIGURE D-18**, delete the fields in the Prototype label box and try again. Be careful to put a space between the FName and LName fields in the first row, a comma and a space between the City and State fields, and a space between the State and Zip fields.

QUICK TIP

In this case, all data is displayed. This message reminds you to carefully preview the data to make sure long names and addresses fully display within the constraints of the 5160 label dimensions.

5. **Click Next, double-click LName to select it as a sorting field, click Next, click Finish to accept the name Labels Customers for the new report, then click OK if prompted that some data may not be displayed**

   A portion of the new report is shown in **FIGURE D-19**. It is generally a good idea to print the first page of the report on standard paper to make sure everything is aligned correctly before printing on labels.

6. **If requested by your instructor, click the Print button on the PRINT PREVIEW tab, click the From box, type 1, click the To box, type 1, then click OK to print the first page of the report**

QUICK TIP

To include your name on the printout, change Aaron Alito's name to *your* own name in the Customers table, then close and reopen the Labels Customers report.

7. **Close the Labels Customers report, close the QuestTravel-D.accdb database, then exit Access 2013**

FIGURE D-17: Label Wizard dialog box

Product number 5160, dimensions, and number of columns

Avery is the manufacturer

FIGURE D-18: Building a prototype label

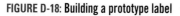

Prototype label box

Fields are arranged in three rows in a standard address format

FIGURE D-19: Labels Customers report

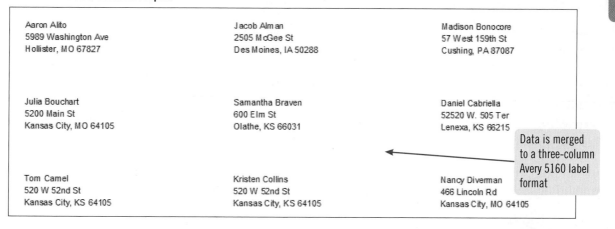

Aaron Alito	Jacob Alman	Madison Bonocore
5989 Washington Ave	2505 McGee St	57 West 159th St
Hollister, MO 67827	Des Moines, IA 50288	Cushing, PA 87087
Julia Bouchart	Samantha Braven	Daniel Cabriella
5200 Main St	600 Elm St	52520 W. 505 Ter
Kansas City, MO 64105	Olathe, KS 66031	Lenexa, KS 66215
Tom Camel	Kristen Collins	Nancy Diverman
520 W 52nd St	520 W 52nd St	466 Lincoln Rd
Kansas City, KS 64105	Kansas City, KS 64105	Kansas City, MO 64105

Data is merged to a three-column Avery 5160 label format

Practice

Concepts Review

Label each element of the Report Design View window shown in FIGURE D-20.

FIGURE D-20

Match each term with the statement that best describes it.

8. **Alignment**
9. **Expression**
10. **Grouping**
11. **Section**
12. **Detail section**
13. **Formatting**
14. **Record source**

a. Left, center, or right are common choices
b. Prints once for every record
c. Used to identify which fields and records are passed to the report
d. Sorting records *plus* providing a header or footer section
e. Determines how controls are positioned on the report
f. A combination of field names, operators, and functions that results in a single value
g. Enhancing the appearance of information displayed in the report

Select the best answer from the list of choices.

15. Which of the following is *not* a valid report view?
    a. Print Preview
    b. Section View
    c. Layout View
    d. Design View

16. Which type of control is most commonly placed in the Detail section?
    a. Image
    b. Line
    c. Text box
    d. Label

17. A title for a report would most commonly be placed in which report section?
    a. Group Footer
    b. Detail
    c. Report Header
    d. Report Footer

18. A calculated expression that presents page numbering information would probably be placed in which report section?
    a. Report Header
    b. Detail
    c. Group Footer
    d. Page Footer

19. Which of the following expressions counts the number of records using the FirstName field?
    a. =Count([FirstName])
    b. =Count[FirstName]
    c. =Count((FirstName))
    d. =Count{FirstName}

20. To align the edges of several controls with each other, you use the alignment commands on the:
    a. FORMATTING tab.
    b. DESIGN tab.
    c. PRINT PREVIEW tab.
    d. ARRANGE tab.

Skills Review

1. Use the Report Wizard.

  a. Start Access and open the RealEstate-D.accdb database from the location where you store your Data Files. Enable content if prompted.

  b. Use the Report Wizard to create a report based on the RLast and RPhone fields from the Realtors table, and the Type, SqFt, BR, Bath, and Asking fields from the Listings table.

  c. View the data by Realtors, do not add any more grouping levels, and sort the records in descending order by the Asking field. (*Hint*: Click the Ascending button to toggle it to Descending.)

  d. Use a Stepped layout and a Landscape orientation. Title the report **Realtor Listings**.

  e. Preview the first and second pages of the new report.

2. Use Report Layout View.

  a. Switch to Layout View and close the Field List and Property Sheet if they are open.

  b. Narrow the RLast, RPhone, and Bath columns enough so they are only as wide as needed to display all data.

  c. Modify the RLast label to read **Realtor**, the RPhone label to read **Phone**, the SqFt label to read **Square Feet**, the BR label to read **Bedrooms**, and the Bath label to read **Baths**.

  d. Switch to Print Preview to review your changes.

3. Review report sections.

  a. Switch to Report Design View.

  b. Drag the text box that contains the Page calculation in the lower-right corner of the Page Footer section to the left so that it is to the left of the 9" mark on the horizontal ruler.

  c. Drag the right edge of the entire report to the left so it ends within the 10" mark on the horizontal ruler. You may need to move or narrow the Baths label and Bath text box more than you did in Step 2b in order to accomplish this.

4. Apply group and sort orders.

  a. Open the Group, Sort, and Total pane.

  b. Add the Type field as a grouping field between the RealtorNo grouping field and Asking sort field. Make sure the sort order on the Asking field is in descending order (from largest to smallest).

  c. Cut and paste the Type combo box from its current position in the Detail section to the Type Header section.

  d. Move the Type combo box in the Type Header section so its left edge is at about the 1" mark on the horizontal ruler.

  e. Delete the Type label in the Page Header section.

  f. Switch to Layout View, and resize the Asking, Square Feet, Bedrooms, and Baths columns as needed so they are more evenly spaced across the page.

5. Add subtotals and counts.

  a. Switch to Report Design View, then open the RealtorNo Footer section.

  b. Add a text box control to the RealtorNo Footer section, just below the Asking text box in the Detail section. Change the label to read **Subtotal:**, and enter the expression **=Sum([Asking])** in the text box.

  c. Drag the bottom edge of the Report Footer down about 0.25" to add space to the Report Footer.

  d. Copy and paste the new expression in the RealtorNo Footer section to the Report Footer section. Position the new controls in the Report Footer section directly below the controls in the RealtorNo Footer section.

  e. Modify the Subtotal: label in the Report Footer section to read **Grand Total:**.

  f. Preview the last page of the report to view the new subtotals in the RealtorNo Footer and Report Footer sections.

6. Resize and align controls.

  a. Switch to Layout View, click the Group & Sort button on the DESIGN tab to close the Group, Sort, and Total pane if it is open, and move to the last page of the report to view the Subtotal and Grand Total calculations at the same time.

  b. Right-align the text within the Subtotal and Grand Total labels.

Skills Review (continued)

   c. Switch to Design View, click the Asking text box, press and hold [Shift], and then click the text box in the RealtorNo and also the Report Footer sections to select all three text boxes at the same time. Click the ARRANGE tab, click the Align button, then click Right to right-align the edges of the Subtotal and Grand Total text boxes.

   d. With all three text boxes still selected, click the FORMAT tab on the Ribbon, click the Apply Comma Number Format button, and click the Decrease Decimals button twice.

   e. Preview the report to view the alignment and format on the Asking data and subtotals.

7. Format a report.

   a. In Report Design View, change the Alternate Row Color of the Detail section to No Color.

   b. Change the Alternate Row Color of the Type Header section as well as the RealtorNo Header section to No Color.

   c. Change the Shape Fill color of the RealtorNo Header section to Green 2.

   d. Select the RLast text box in the RealtorNo Header section, and change the Shape Fill color to Green 2 to match the RealtorNo Header section. Apply the Green 2 background color to the RPhone text box as well.

FIGURE D-21

   e. Bold the title of the report, the **Realtor Listings** label in the Report Header, and resize it to make it a little wider to accommodate the bold text.

   f. Change the font color of each label in the Page Header section to black.

   g. Save and preview the report in Report View. It should look like **FIGURE D-21**. The report should fit on two pages and the grand total for all Asking values should be 7,771,513. If there are blank pages between printed pages, return to Report Design View and drag the right edge of the report to the left.

   h. In Report Design View, add a label to the left side of the Report Footer section with your name.

   i. Return to Print Preview, print the report if requested by your instructor, then save and close the Realtor Listings report.

8. Create mailing labels.

   a. Click the Agencies table in the Navigation Pane, then start the Label Wizard.

   b. Choose Avery 5160 labels and the default text appearance choices.

   c. Build a prototype label with the AgencyName on the first line, Street on the second line, and City, State, and Zip on the third line with a comma and space between City and State, and a space between State and Zip.

   d. Sort by AgencyName, and name the report **Labels Agencies**.

   e. Preview then save and close the report. Click OK if a warning dialog box appears regarding horizontal space. The data in your label report does not exceed the dimensions of the labels.

   f. If your instructor asks you to print the Labels Agencies report, open the Agencies table and change the name of Four Lakes Realtors to *Your* **LastName Realtors**. Close the Agencies table, reopen the Labels Agencies report, then print it.

   g. Close the Labels Agencies report, close the RealEstate-D.accdb database, then exit Access 2013.

Independent Challenge 1

As the office manager of an international convention planning company, you have created a database to track convention, enrollment, and company data. Your goal is to create a report of up-to-date attendee enrollments.

a. Start Access, then open the Conventions-D.accdb database from the location where you store your Data Files. Enable content if prompted.

b. Use the Report Wizard to create a report with the AttendeeFirst and AttendeeLast fields from the Attendees table, the CompanyName field from the Companies table, and the ConventionName and CountryName from the Conventions table.

c. View your data by Conventions, do not add any more grouping levels, and sort in ascending order by CompanyName, then AttendeeLast.

d. Use the Block layout and Portrait orientation, then name the report **Convention Listing**.

e. In Layout View, change the labels in the Page Header section from ConventionName to **Convention** and AttendeeLast to **Attendee**. Delete the CountryName, CompanyName, and AttendeeFirst labels in the Page Header section.

f. In Report Design View, open the Group, Sort, and Total pane, then open the CompanyName Header and CompanyName Footer sections.

g. In Report Design View, expand the ConventionNo Header section about 0.25", then use the Cut and Paste commands to move the ConventionName text box from the Detail section to the left edge of the ConventionNo Header section.

h. Cut and paste the CountryName text box from the Detail section to the ConventionNo Header section. Move it to the right of the ConventionName text box.

i. Drag the top edge of the CompanyName Header section up to remove any extra blank space in the ConventionNo Header section.

j. Cut and paste the CompanyName text box from the Detail section to the CompanyName Header section. Move it to the right of the ConventionName text box in the ConventionNo Header section and to the left of the AttendeeLast text box in the Detail section.

k. Remove any extra blank space in the CompanyName Header section by dragging the top edge of the Detail section up as far as possible. Close the Group, Sort, and Total pane.

l. In Layout View, scroll through the entire report and resize the ConventionName, CountryName, and CompanyName text boxes as needed to show all of the data. Be careful, however, to not expand the report beyond the width of the portrait orientation of the report.

m. In Design View, expand the CompanyName Footer about 0.5", and add a new text box positioned below the AttendeeLast text box in the Detail section. Modify the new label in the Company Name Footer to read **Count:**. Enter an expression in a new text box to count the values in the AttendeeLast field, **=Count([AttendeeLast])**.

n. Format the text color of the Count: label to black and right-align the text within the label.

o. Change the color of the report title and the labels in the Page Header section to black. Preview the report. The subtotal count for the first convention should be 21.

p. Add a label with your name to the right side of the Report Header section, then print the first page if required by your instructor.

q. Save and close the Convention Listing report, close the Conventions-D.accdb database, then exit Access 2013.

Independent Challenge 2

You have built an Access database to track membership in a community service club. The database tracks member names and addresses as well as their status and rank in the club, and their hours of service to the community.

a. Start Access and open the Membership-D.accdb database from the location where you store your Data Files. Enable content if prompted.

b. Open the Members table, find and change the name of Traci Kalvert to *your* name, then close the Members table.

c. Use the Report Wizard to create a report using the Status and DuesOwed fields from the Status table, and the FName, LName, and DuesPaid fields from the Members table.

d. View the data by Status. Do not add any more grouping fields, and sort the records in ascending order by LName then FName.

e. Use a Stepped layout and Portrait orientation, title the report **Dues Report**, then preview the report.

f. Switch to Report Design View, then use the Group, Sort, and Total pane to open the StatusNo Footer section.

g. Add a text box to the StatusNo Footer section, just below the DuesPaid text box in the Detail section. Change the label to **Count:** and the expression in the text box to **=Count([DuesPaid])**.

h. Expand the StatusNo Footer section to provide more space, and add a second text box to the StatusNo Footer section, just below the first. Change the label to **Subtotal:** and the expression in the text box to **=Sum([DuesPaid])**.

i. Expand the StatusNo Footer section to provide more space, and add a third text box to the StatusNo Footer section, just below the second. Change the accompanying label to **Balance:**.

j. Change the text box expression to **=Count([DuesPaid])*[DuesOwed]–Sum([DuesPaid])**. This expression counts the number of values in the DuesPaid field, and multiplies it by the DuesOwed field. From that value, the sum of the DuesPaid field is subtracted. This calculates the balance between dues owed and dues paid.

k. Open the Property Sheet for the =Sum([DuesPaid]) text box. On the Format tab, set the Format property to **Currency** and the Decimal Places property to **2**. Repeat these property changes for the text box with the balance calculation.

l. Select the DuesPaid text box in the Detail section, press and hold [Shift], then select all three text boxes in the StatusNo Footer section. Align the right edges of all four controls using the Align button, then Right command on the ARRANGE tab of the Ribbon. Also, right-align the contents within the text boxes of the StatusNo Footer section using the Align Right button on the HOME tab of the Ribbon. Right-align the right edges of the three new labels in the StatusNo Footer section.

m. Save, then preview the Dues Report. Make sure the report does not contain blank pages and fix that in Report Design View if needed. Print the first page of the Dues Report if requested by your instructor. The StatusNo Footer section for the first status, New, is shown in **FIGURE D-22**.

n. Close the Dues Report, close the Membership-D.accdb database, then exit Access.

FIGURE D-22

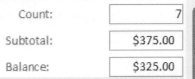

Independent Challenge 3

You have built an Access database to organize the deposits at a recycling center. Various clubs regularly deposit recyclable material, which is measured in pounds when the deposits are made.

a. Start Access and open the Recycle-D.accdb database from the location where you store your Data Files. Enable content if prompted.

b. Open the Centers table, change **Trash Can** to *Your* **Last Name Recycling**, then close the table.

c. Use the Report Wizard to create a report with the CenterName field from the Centers table, the DepositDate and Weight fields from the Deposits table, and the ClubName field from the Clubs table.

d. View the data by Centers, do not add any more grouping levels, and sort the records in ascending order by DepositDate.

e. Use a Stepped layout and a Portrait orientation, then title the report **Deposit Listing**.

f. In Layout View, center the Weight label and Weight data within their controls. Resize the DepositDate label and data by dragging the left edge of the control farther to the left so the label text and all dates are clearly displayed.

g. Add spaces to the labels so that CenterName becomes **Center Name**, DepositDate becomes **Deposit Date**, and ClubName becomes **Club Name**.

h. In Report Design View, open the Group, Sort, and Total pane and then open the CenterNumber Footer section.

i. Add a text box to the CenterNumber Footer section just below the Weight text box with the expression =**Sum([Weight])**.

j. Rename the new label to be **Total Center Weight** and move and resize it as needed so that it doesn't overlap the text box.

k. Resize the =Sum([Weight]) text box in the CenterNumber Footer section to be the same size as the Weight text box in the Detail section. Align the right edges of the Weight text box in the Detail section with the =Sum([Weight]) text box in the CenterNumber Footer section. Center the data in the =Sum([Weight]) text box.

l. Expand the Report Footer section, then copy and paste the =Sum([Weight]) text box from the CenterNumber Footer section to the Report Footer section.

m. Move and align the controls in the Report Footer section to be positioned directly under their counterparts in the CenterNumber Footer section.

n. Change the label in the Report Footer section to **Grand Total Weight**.

o. Remove extra blank space in the report by dragging the bottom of the report as well as the section bars up, then preview a portion of the last page of the report, as shown in FIGURE D-23. The last Total Center Weight and Grand Total Weight values on your report should match the figure.

p. Save and close the Deposit Listing report, close the Recycle-D.accdb database, then exit Access.

FIGURE D-23

6/4/2013	90	Lions
6/20/2013	85	Junior League
8/31/2013	50	Girl Scouts #11
10/2/2013	90	Lions
Total Center Weight	2720	
Grand Total Weight	9365	

Independent Challenge 4: Explore

One way you can use an Access database on your own is to record and track your job search efforts. In this exercise, you create a report to help read and analyze data into your job-tracking database.

    a. Start Access and open the JobSearch-D.accdb database from the location where you store your Data Files. Enable content if prompted.

    b. Open the Employers table, and enter five more records to identify five more potential employers.

    c. Use subdatasheets in the Employers table to enter five more potential jobs. You may enter all five jobs for one employer, one job for five different employers, or any combination thereof. Be sure to check the spelling of all data entered. For the Desirability field, enter a value from **1** to **5**, 1 being the least desirable and 5 the most desirable. Close the Employers table.

    d. Use the Report Wizard to create a report that lists the CompanyName, EmpCity, and EmpState fields from the Employers table, and the Title, AnnualSalary, and Desirability fields from the Positions table.

    e. View the data by Employers, do not add any more grouping levels, and sort the records in ascending order by Title.

    f. Use an Outline layout and a Landscape orientation, then title the report **Job Opportunities**.

    g. In Design View, revise the labels in the EmployerID Header section from CompanyName to **Company**, EmpCity to **City**, EmpState to **State**, and AnnualSalary to **Salary**.

    h. In Design View, right-align the text within the Company, City, and State labels so they are closer to the text boxes they describe.

    i. In Report Design View, move the Page expression in the Page Footer section and the right edge of the report to the left, within the 10.5" mark on the horizontal ruler, and then drag the right edge of the report to the left to make sure that the report fits within the margins of one sheet of paper in landscape orientation.

    j. Open the EmployerID Footer section and use the Line control in the Controls group on the DESIGN tab to add a horizontal line across the width of the report in the EmployerID Footer section. (*Hint*: The Line control may be on the second row of the Controls box. Also, press and hold [Shift] while dragging the line to create a perfectly horizontal line.)

    k. Click a green error indicator that appears on the labels in the EmployerID Header section, point to the warning button to read the ScreenTip, then click the drop-down arrow on the error indicator and click Ignore Error.

    l. Preview and save the Job Opportunities report making sure that the report fits within one page wide, then print the first page if requested by your instructor.

    m. Close the Job Opportunities report, close the JobSearch-D.accdb database, then exit Access 2013.

Visual Workshop

Open the Basketball-D.accdb database from the location where you store your Data Files and enable content if prompted. Open the Players table, enter *your* name instead of Kelsey Douglas, then close the table. Your goal is to create the report shown in **FIGURE D-24**. Use the Report Wizard, and select the PFirst, PLast, HomeTown, and HomeState fields from the Players table. Select the FieldGoals, 3Pointers, and FreeThrows fields from the Stats table. View the data by Players, do not add any more grouping levels, and do not add any more sorting levels. Use a Block layout and a Portrait orientation, then title the report **Scoring Report**. In Layout View, resize all of the columns so that they fit on a single piece of portrait paper, and change the labels in the Page Header section as shown. In Design View, open the PlayerNo Footer section and add text boxes with expressions to sum the FieldGoals, 3Pointers, and FreeThrow fields. Move, modify, align, and resize all controls as needed to match **FIGURE D-24**. Be sure to print preview the report to make sure that it fits within the width of one sheet of paper. Modify the report to narrow it in Report Design View if needed.

FIGURE D-24

Scoring Report

Player Name		Home Town	State	Field Goals	3 Pointers	Free Throws
Student First	Student Last	Linden	IA	4	1	3
				5	2	2
				5	3	3
				6	3	5
				4	1	1
				4	2	2
				3	2	1
				4	2	3
				4	2	3
				3	2	1
		Subtotals		42	20	24

Modifying the Database Structure

CASE Working with Samantha Hooper, the tour developer for U.S. group travel at Quest Specialty Travel, you are developing an Access database to track tours, customers, sales, and payments. The database consists of multiple tables that you link, modify, and enhance to create a relational database.

Unit Objectives

After completing this unit, you will be able to:

- Examine relational databases
- Design related tables
- Create one-to-many relationships
- Create Lookup fields
- Modify Short Text fields

- Modify Number and Currency fields
- Modify Date/Time fields
- Modify validation properties
- Create Attachment fields

Files You Will Need

QuestTravel-E.accdb   JobSearch-E.accdb
GMayberry.jpg   Training-E.accdb
Member1.jpg

Examine Relational Databases

Learning
Outcomes
• Design tables and
  fields
• Design primary
  and foreign key
  fields
• Analyze one-to-
  many relationships

The purpose of a relational database is to organize and store data in a way that minimizes redundancy and maximizes your flexibility when querying and analyzing data. To accomplish these goals, a relational database uses related tables rather than a single large table of data. **CASE** ▶ *At one time, the Sales Department at Quest Specialty Travel tracked information about their tour sales and payments using a single Access table called Sales, shown in* **FIGURE E-1**. *This created data redundancy problems because of the duplicate tour, customer, and payment information entered into a single table. You decide to study the principles of relational database design to help Quest Specialty Travel reorganize these fields into a correctly designed relational database.*

DETAILS

To redesign a list into a relational database, follow these principles:

- **Design each table to contain fields that describe only one subject**

  Currently, the table in **FIGURE E-1** contains four subjects—tours, sales, customers, and payments—which creates redundant data. For example, the tour name must be duplicated for each sale of that tour. The customer's name must be reentered every time that customer purchases a tour or makes a payment. The problems of redundant data include extra data entry work; more data entry inconsistencies and errors; larger physical storage requirements; and limitations on your ability to search for, analyze, and report on the data. You minimize these problems by implementing a properly designed relational database.

- **Identify a primary key field for each table**

  A **primary key field** is a field that contains unique information for each record. For example, in a customer table, the customer number field usually serves this purpose. Although using the customer's last name as the primary key field might work in a small database, names are generally a poor choice for a primary key field because the primary key could not accommodate two customers who have the same name.

- **Build one-to-many relationships**

  To tie the information from one table to another, a field must be common to each table. This linking field is the primary key field on the "one" side of the relationship and the **foreign key field** on the "many" side of the relationship. Recall that a primary key field stores unique information for each record in that table. For example, a CustomerNo field acting as the primary key field in the Customers table would link to a CustomerNo foreign key field in a Sales table to join one customer to many sales. You are not required to give the primary and foreign key fields the same name, although doing so does clarify which fields are used to link two tables in a one-to-many relationship.

  The revised design for the database is shown in **FIGURE E-2**. One customer can purchase many tours, so the Customers and Sales tables have a one-to-many relationship based on the linking CustNo field. One tour can be purchased many times, so the Tours and Sales tables have a one-to-many relationship (TourID in the Sales table and TourNo in the Tours table). One sale may have many payments, creating a one-to-many relationship between the Sales and Payments tables based on the common SalesNo field.

Enforcing referential integrity

Referential integrity is a set of rules that helps reduce invalid entries and orphan records. An **orphan record** is a record in the "many" table that doesn't have a matching entry in the linking field of the "one" table. With referential integrity enforced on a one-to-many relationship, you cannot enter a value in a foreign key field of the "many" table that does not have a match in the linking field of the "one" table. Referential integrity also prevents you from deleting a record in the "one" table if a matching entry exists in the foreign key field of the "many" table. You should enforce referential integrity on all one-to-many relationships if possible. If you are working with a database that already contains orphan records, you cannot enforce referential integrity on that relationship.

FIGURE E-1: Single Sales table results in duplicate data

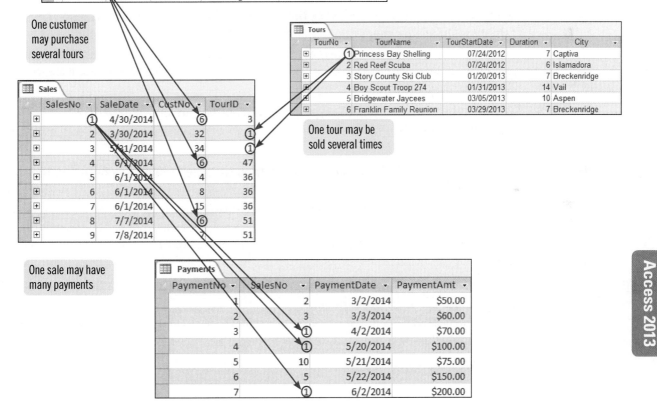

TourName	City	Price	SalesNo	SaleDate	FName	LName	PaymentDate	PaymentAmt
Princess Bay Shelling	Captiva	$750	2	3/30/2014	Lisa	Wilson	3/2/2014	$50.00
Princess Bay Shelling	Captiva	$750	3	5/31/2014	Kori	Yode	3/3/2014	$60.00
Story County Ski Club	Breckenridge	$850	1	4/30/2014	Kristen	Collins	4/2/2014	$70.00
Story County Ski Club	Breckenridge	$850	1	4/30/2014	Kristen	Collins	5/20/2014	$100.00
Bright Lights Expo	Branson	$200	10	7/9/2014	Mark	Custard	5/21/2014	$75.00
American Heritage Tour	Philadelphia	$1,200	5	6/1/2014	Kayla	Browning	5/22/2014	$150.00
Story County Ski Club	Breckenridge	$850	1	4/30/2014	Kristen	Collins	6/2/2014	$200.00

Tour information is duplicated for each sale or payment

Sales information is duplicated for each payment

Customer information is duplicated for each sale or payment

Payment fields

FIGURE E-2: Related tables reduce redundant data

Customers

CustNo	FName	LName	Street	City	State
1	Gracita	Mayberry	52411 Oakmont Rd	Kansas City	MO
2	Jacob	Alman	2505 McGee St	West Des Moines	IA
3	Julia	Bouchart	5200 Main St	Kansas City	MO
4	Kayla	Browning	8206 Marshall Dr	Lenexa	KS
5	Samantha	Braven	600 Elm St	Olathe	KS
6	Kristen	Collins	520 W 52nd St	Kansas City	KS
7	Tom	Camel	66020 King St	Overland Park	KS

One customer may purchase several tours

Tours

TourNo	TourName	TourStartDate	Duration	City
1	Princess Bay Shelling	07/24/2012	7	Captiva
2	Red Reef Scuba	07/24/2012	6	Islamadora
3	Story County Ski Club	01/20/2013	7	Breckenridge
4	Boy Scout Troop 274	01/31/2013	14	Vail
5	Bridgewater Jaycees	03/05/2013	10	Aspen
6	Franklin Family Reunion	03/29/2013	7	Breckenridge

Sales

SalesNo	SaleDate	CustNo	TourID
1	4/30/2014	6	3
2	3/30/2014	32	1
3	5/31/2014	34	1
4	6/1/2014	6	47
5	6/1/2014	4	36
6	6/1/2014	8	36
7	6/1/2014	15	36
8	7/7/2014	6	51
9	7/8/2014	7	51

One tour may be sold several times

One sale may have many payments

Payments

PaymentNo	SalesNo	PaymentDate	PaymentAmt
1	2	3/2/2014	$50.00
2	3	3/3/2014	$60.00
3	1	4/2/2014	$70.00
4	1	5/20/2014	$100.00
5	10	5/21/2014	$75.00
6	5	5/22/2014	$150.00
7	1	6/2/2014	$200.00

Using many-to-many relationships

As you design your database, you might find that two tables have a **many-to-many relationship**, which means that a record in one table may be related to many records in the other table and vice versa. To join them, you must establish a third table called a **junction table**, which contains two foreign key fields to serve on the "many" side of separate one-to-many relationships

with the two original tables. The Customers and Tours tables have a many-to-many relationship because one customer can purchase many tours and one tour can have many customers purchase it. The Sales table serves as the junction table to link the three tables together.

Design Related Tables

Learning Outcomes:
- Set field data types in Table Design View
- Set field descriptions in Table Design View

After you develop a valid relational database design, you are ready to create the tables in Access. Using **Table Design View**, you can specify all characteristics of a table, including field names, data types, field descriptions, field properties, Lookup properties, and primary key field designations. **CASE** ▶ *Using the new database design, you are ready to create the Payments table for Quest Specialty Travel.*

STEPS

1. **Start Access, open the QuestTravel-E.accdb database, then enable content if prompted**

   The Customers, Sales, and Tours tables have already been created in the database. You need to create the Payments table.

2. **Click the CREATE tab on the Ribbon, then click the Table Design button in the Tables group**

   Table Design View opens, where you can enter field names and specify data types and field properties for the new table. Field names should be as short as possible, but long enough to be descriptive. The field name you enter in Table Design View is used as the default name for the field in all later queries, forms, and reports.

   > **QUICK TIP**
   > When specifying field data types, you can type the first letter of the data type to quickly select it.

3. **Type PaymentNo, press [Enter], click the Data Type list arrow, click AutoNumber, press [Tab], type Unique payment number and primary key field, then press [Enter]**

   The AutoNumber data type automatically assigns the next available integer in the sequence to each new record. The AutoNumber data type is often used as the primary key field for a table because it always contains a unique value for each record.

4. **Type the other field names, data types, and descriptions, as shown in FIGURE E-3**

   Field descriptions entered in Table Design View are optional, but provide a way to add helpful information about the field.

   > **TROUBLE**
   > If you set the wrong field as the primary key field, click the Primary Key button again to toggle it off.

5. **Click PaymentNo in the Field Name column, then click the Primary Key button in the Tools group**

   A **key symbol** appears to the left of PaymentNo to indicate that this field is defined as the primary key field for this table. Primary key fields have two roles: They uniquely define each record, and they may also serve as the "one" side of a one-to-many relationship between two tables. **TABLE E-1** describes common examples of one-to-many relationships.

   > **QUICK TIP**
   > To delete or rename an existing table, right-click it in the Navigation Pane, then click Delete or Rename.

6. **Click the Save button 🖫 on the Quick Access toolbar, type Payments in the Table Name text box, click OK, then close the table**

   The Payments table is now displayed as a table object in the QuestTravel-E.accdb database Navigation Pane, as shown in **FIGURE E-4**.

FIGURE E-3: Table Design View for the new Payments table

Field Name	Data Type	Description (Optional)
PaymentNo	AutoNumber	Unique payment number and primary key field
PaymentDate	Date/Time	Date the payment is made
PaymentAmt	Currency	Amount of the payment
SalesNo	Number	Foreign key field to the Sales table

Field names → Field Name column
Data types → Data Type column
Descriptions → Description column

FIGURE E-4: Payments table in the Navigation Pane of the QuestTravel-E database

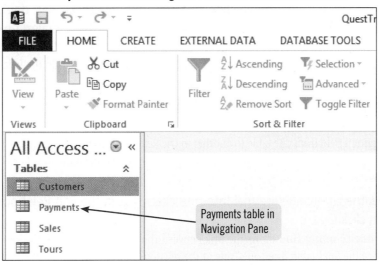

Payments table in Navigation Pane

TABLE E-1: Common one-to-many relationships

table on "one" side	table on "many" side	linking field	description
Products	Sales	ProductID	A ProductID field must have a unique entry in a Products table, but it is listed many times in a Sales table
Students	Enrollments	StudentID	A StudentID field must have a unique entry in a Students table, but it is listed many times in an Enrollments table as the student enrolls in multiple classes
Employees	Promotions	EmployeeID	An EmployeeID field must have a unique entry in an Employees table, but it is listed many times in a Promotions table as the employee is promoted over time

Specifying the foreign key field data type

A foreign key field in the "many" table must have the same data type (Short Text or Number) as the primary key it is related to in the "one" table. An exception to this rule is when the primary key field in the "one" table has an AutoNumber data type. In this case, the linking foreign key field in the "many" table must have a Number data type. Also note that a Number field used as a foreign key field must have a Long Integer Field Size property to match the Field Size property of the AutoNumber primary key field.

Create One-to-Many Relationships

After creating the tables you need, you link them together in appropriate one-to-many relationships using the primary key field in the "one" table and the foreign key field in the "many" table. To avoid time-consuming rework, be sure that your table relationships are finished before building queries, forms, or reports using fields from multiple tables. **CASE** ➤ *You are ready to define the one-to-many relationships between the tables of the QuestTravel-E.accdb database.*

STEPS

1. **Click the** DATABASE TOOLS **tab on the Ribbon, click the** Relationships button, **click the** Show Table button, **double-click** Customers, **double-click** Sales, **double-click** Tours, **double-click** Payments, **then click** Close **in the Show Table dialog box**

   The four table field lists appear in the Relationships window. The primary key fields are identified with a small key symbol to the left of the field name. With all of the field lists in the Relationships window, you're ready to link them in proper one-to-many relationships.

2. **Click** CustNo **in the Customers table field list, then drag it to the** CustNo **field in the Sales table field list**

   Dragging a field from one table to another in the Relationships window links the two tables by the selected fields and opens the Edit Relationships dialog box, as shown in **FIGURE E-5**. Recall that referential integrity helps ensure data accuracy.

3. **Click the** Enforce Referential Integrity check box **in the Edit Relationships dialog box, then click** Create

   The **one-to-many line** shows the link between the CustNo field of the Customers table and the CustNo field of the Sales table. The "one" side of the relationship is the unique CustNo value for each record in the Customers table. The "many" side of the relationship is identified by an infinity symbol pointing to the CustNo field in the Sales table. You also need to link the Tours table to the Sales table.

4. **Click** TourNo **in the Tours table field list, drag it to** TourNo **in the Sales table field list, click the** Enforce Referential Integrity check box, **then click** Create

   Finally, you need to link the Payments table to the Sales table.

5. **Click** SalesNo **in the Sales table field list, drag it to** SalesNo **in the Payments table field list, click the** Enforce Referential Integrity check box, **click** Create, **then drag the** Tours title bar **down so all links are clear**

   The updated Relationships window should look like **FIGURE E-6**.

6. **Click the** Relationship Report button **in the Tools group, click the** Print button **on the PRINT PREVIEW tab, then click** OK

   A printout of the Relationships window, called the **Relationship report**, shows how your relational database is designed and includes table names, field names, primary key fields, and one-to-many relationship lines. This printout is helpful as you later create queries, forms, and reports that use fields from multiple tables. Note that it is not necessary to directly link each table to every other table.

7. **Right-click the** Relationships for QuestTravel-E report tab, **click** Close, **click** Yes **to save the report, then click** OK **to accept the default report name**

   The Relationships for QuestTravel-E report is saved in your database, as shown in the Navigation Pane.

8. **Close the Relationships window, then click** Yes **if prompted to save changes**

Modifying the Database Structure

FIGURE E-5: Edit Relationships dialog box

CustNo from Customers table on the "one" side

Enforce Referential Integrity check box

CustNo from Sales table on the "many" side

"One-to-many" relationship

FIGURE E-6: Final Relationships window

Show Table button

Relationship Report button

Primary key field symbol

One-to-many link line

"One" symbol

"Many" (infinity) symbol

Tours title bar

More on enforcing referential integrity

Recall that referential integrity is a set of rules to help ensure that no orphan records are entered or created in the database. An orphan record is a record in the "many" table (also called the **child table**) that doesn't have a matching entry in the linking field of the "one" table (also called the **parent table**). Referential integrity prevents orphan records in multiple ways. Referential integrity will not allow you to make an entry in the foreign key field of the child table that does not have a matching value in the linking field of the parent table. (So you can't make a sale to a customer who doesn't first exist in the Customers table, for example.) Referential integrity also prevents you from deleting a record in the parent table that has related records in the child table. (So you can't delete a customer from the Customers table who already has related sales records in the Sales table, for example.) You should enforce referential integrity on all one-to-many relationships if possible. Unfortunately, if you are working with a database that already contains orphan records, you cannot enforce this powerful set of rules unless you find and fix the data so that orphan records no longer exist. The process of removing and fixing orphan records is commonly called **scrubbing the database**.

Create Lookup Fields

A **Lookup field** is a field that contains Lookup properties. **Lookup properties** are field properties that supply a drop-down list of values for a field. The values can be stored in another table or directly stored in the **Row Source** Lookup property of the field. Fields that are good candidates for Lookup properties are those that contain a defined set of appropriate values such as State, Gender, or Department. You can set Lookup properties for a field in Table Design View using the **Lookup Wizard**. **CASE** ▶ *The FirstContact field in the Customers table identifies how the customer first made contact with Quest Specialty Travel such as being referred by a friend (Friend), finding the company through the Internet (Internet), or responding to a radio advertisement (Radio). Because the FirstContact field has only a handful of valid entries, it is a good Lookup field candidate.*

STEPS

1. **Right-click the** Customers table **in the Navigation Pane, then click** Design View
   The Lookup Wizard is included in the Data Type list.

2. **Click the** Short Text data type **for the FirstContact field, click the** Data Type list arrow, **then click** Lookup Wizard
   The Lookup Wizard starts and prompts you for information about where the Lookup column will get its values.

3. **Click the** I will type in the values that I want option button, **click** Next, **click the** first cell **in the Col1 column, type** Friend, **press** [Tab], **then type the rest of the values, as shown in** FIGURE E-7
   These are the values for the drop-down list for the FirstContact field.

4. **Click** Next, **then click** Finish **to accept the default label and complete the Lookup Wizard**
   Note that the data type for the FirstContact field is still Short Text. The Lookup Wizard is a process for setting Lookup property values for a field, not a data type itself.

5. **Click the** Lookup tab **in the Field Properties pane to observe the new Lookup properties for the FirstContact field, as shown in** FIGURE E-8
   The Lookup Wizard helped you enter Lookup properties for the FirstContact field, but you can always enter or edit them directly, too. Some of the most important Lookup properties include Row Source, Limit To List, and Allow Value List Edits. The **Row Source** property stores the values that are provided in the drop-down list for a Lookup field. The **Limit To List** Lookup property determines whether you can enter a new value into a field with other Lookup properties, or whether the entries are limited to the drop-down list. The **Allow Value List Edits** property determines whether users can add or edit the list of items.

6. **Click the** View button 🔲 **to switch to Datasheet View, click** Yes **when prompted to save the table, press** [Tab] **eight times to move to the** FirstContact **field, then click the** FirstContact list arrow, **as shown in** FIGURE E-9
   The FirstContact field now provides a list of four values for this field. To edit the list in Datasheet View, click the **Edit List Items button** below the list.

7. **Close the Customers table**

FIGURE E-7: Entering a list of values in the Lookup Wizard

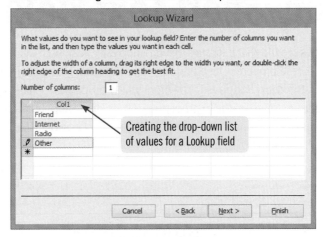

FIGURE E-8: Viewing Lookup properties

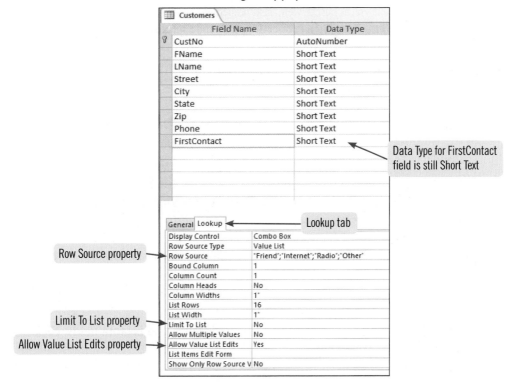

FIGURE E-9: Using a Lookup field in a datasheet

CustNo	FName	LName	Street	City	State	Zip	Phone	FirstContact	Click to Add
1	Gracita	Mayberry	52411 Oakmont Rd	Kansas City	MO	64144	(555) 444-1234	Friend	
2	Jacob	Alman	2505 McGee St	Des Moines	IA	50288	(555) 111-6931	Friend	
3	Julia	Bouchart	5200 Main St	Kansas City	MO	64105	(555) 111-3081	Internet	
4	Jane	Taylor	8206 Marshall Dr	Lenexa	KS	66214	(555) 222-9101	Radio	
5	Samantha	Braven	600 Elm St	Olathe	KS	66031	(555) 222-7002	Other	
6	Kristen	Collins	520 W 52nd St	Kansas City	KS	64105	(555) 222-3602	Radio	
7	Tom	Camel	520 W 52nd St	Kansas City	KS	64105	(555) 222-3602	Radio	

Drop-down list for Lookup field

Edit List Items button

Creating multivalued fields

Multivalued fields allow you to make more than one choice from a drop-down list for a field. As a database designer, multivalued fields allow you to select and store more than one choice without having to create a more advanced database design. To create a multivalued field, enter Yes in the **Allow Multiple Values** Lookup property.

Modify Short Text Fields

Learning
Outcomes
• Modify the Field
Size property for
Short Text fields
• Modify the Input
Mask property
• Enter data using
an input mask

Field properties are the characteristics that describe each field, such as Field Size, Default Value, Caption, or Row Source. These properties help ensure database accuracy and clarity because they restrict the way data is entered, stored, and displayed. You modify field properties in Table Design View. See **TABLE E-2** for more information on Short Text field properties. (*Note:* The "Short Text" data type was called the "Text" data type in previous versions of Access.) **CASE** ▶ *After reviewing the Customers table with Samantha Hooper, you decide to change field properties for several Short Text fields in that table.*

STEPS

1. **Right-click the Customers table in the Navigation Pane, then click Design View on the shortcut menu**

   The Customers table opens in Design View. Field properties appear on the General tab on the lower half of the Table Design View window, the **Field Properties pane**, and apply to the selected field. Field properties change depending on the field's data type. For example, when you select a field with a Short Text data type, you see the **Field Size property**, which determines the number of characters you can enter in the field. However, when you select a field with a Date/Time data type, Access controls the size of the data, so the Field Size property is not displayed. Many field properties are optional, but for those that require an entry, Access provides a default value.

2. **Press [▼] to move through each field while viewing the field properties in the lower half of the window**

   The **field selector button** to the left of the field indicates which field is currently selected.

3. **Click the FirstContact field name, double-click 255 in the Field Size property text box, type 8, click the Save button 🖫 on the Quick Access toolbar, then click Yes**

   The maximum and the default value for the Field Size property for a Short Text field is 255. In general, however, you want to make the Field Size property for Short Text fields only as large as needed to accommodate the longest entry. You can increase the size later if necessary. In some cases, shortening the Field Size property helps prevent typographical errors. For example, you should set the Field Size property for a State field that stores two-letter state abbreviations to 2 to prevent errors such as TXX. For the FirstContact field, your longest entry is "Internet"—8 characters.

4. **Change the Field Size property to 30 for the FName and LName fields, click 🖫, then click Yes**

   No existing entries are greater than 30 characters for either of these fields, so no data is lost. The **Input Mask** property provides a visual guide for users as they enter data. It also helps determine what types of values can be entered into a field.

   QUICK TIP

   If the Input Mask Wizard is not installed on your computer, type !(999) 000-0000;;_ for the Input Mask property for the Phone field.

5. **Click the Phone field name, click the Input Mask property text box, click the Build button 📖, click the Phone Number input mask, click Next, click Next, click Finish, then click to the right of the Input Mask property value so you can read it**

   Table Design View of the Customers table should look like **FIGURE E-10**, which shows the Input Mask property created for the Phone field by the Input Mask Wizard.

6. **Right-click the Customers table tab, click Datasheet View, click Yes to save the table, press [Tab] enough times to move to the Phone field for the first record, type 5552223333, then press [Enter]**

   The Phone Input Mask property creates an easy-to-use visual guide to facilitate accurate data entry.

7. **Close the Customers table**

FIGURE E-10: Changing Short Text field properties

TABLE E-2: Common Short Text field properties

property	description	sample field	sample property entry
Field Size	Controls how many characters can be entered into the field	State	2
Format	Controls how information will be displayed and printed	State	> (displays all characters in uppercase)
Input Mask	Provides a pattern for data to be entered	Phone	!(999) 000-0000;1;_
Caption	Describes the field in the first row of a datasheet, form, or report; if the Caption property is not entered, the field name is used to label the field	EmpNo	Employee Number
Default Value	Displays a value that is automatically entered in the given field for new records	City	Des Moines
Required	Determines if an entry is required for this field	LastName	Yes

Working with the Input Mask property

The Input Mask property provides a pattern for data to be entered, using three parts separated by semicolons. The first part provides a pattern for what type of data can be entered. For example, 9 represents an optional number, 0 a required number, ? an optional letter, and L a required letter. The second part determines whether all displayed characters (such as dashes in a phone number) are stored in the field. For the second part of the input mask, a 0 entry stores all characters such as 555-7722, and a 1 entry stores only the entered data, 5557722. The third part of the input mask determines which character Access uses to guide the user through the mask. Common choices are the asterisk (*), underscore (_), or pound sign (#).

Learning Outcomes
- Modify the Field Size property for Number fields
- Modify the Decimal Places property

Modify Number and Currency Fields

Although some properties for Number and Currency fields are the same as the properties of Short Text fields, each data type has its own list of valid properties. Number and Currency fields have similar properties because they both contain numeric values. Currency fields store values that represent money, and Number fields store values that represent values such as quantities, measurements, and scores. **CASE** ▶ *The Tours table contains both a Number field (Duration) and a Currency field (Price). You want to modify the properties of these two fields.*

STEPS

1. **Right-click the Tours table in the Navigation Pane, click Design View on the shortcut menu, then click the Duration field name**

   The default Field Size property for a Number field is **Long Integer**. See **TABLE E-3** for more information on the Field Size property and other common properties for a Number field. Access sets the size of Currency fields to control the way numbers are rounded in calculations, so the Field Size property isn't available for Currency fields.

   QUICK TIP
   The list arrow for each property is on the far right side of the property box.

2. **Click Long Integer in the Field Size property text box, click the Field Size list arrow, then click Byte**

   Choosing a **Byte** value for the Field Size property allows entries from 0 to 255, so it greatly restricts the possible values and the storage requirements for the Duration field.

   QUICK TIP
   Double-click a property name to toggle through the choices.

3. **Click the Price field name, click Auto in the Decimal Places property text box, click the Decimal Places list arrow, click 0, then press [Enter]**

   Your Table Design View should look like **FIGURE E-11**. Because all of Quest's tours are priced at a round dollar value, you do not need to display cents in the Price field.

   TROUBLE
   If values appear as #####, it means the column needs to be widened to see all of the data.

4. **Save the table, then switch to Datasheet View**

   You won't lose any data because none of the current entries in the Duration field is greater than 255, the maximum value allowed by a Number field with a Byte Field Size property. You want to test the new property changes.

5. **Press [Tab] three times to move to the Duration field for the first record, type 800, then press [Tab]**

   Because 800 is larger than what the Byte Field Size property allows (0–255), an Access error message appears indicating that the value isn't valid for this field.

6. **Press [Esc] twice to remove the inappropriate entry in the Duration field, then press [Tab] four times to move to the Price field**

   The Price field is set to display zero digits after the decimal point.

7. **Type 750.25 in the Price field of the first record, press [Tab], then click $750 in the Price field of the first record to see the full entry**

   Although the Decimal Places property for the Price field specifies that entries in the field are *formatted* to display zero digits after the decimal point, 750.25 is the actual value stored in the field. Modifying the Decimal Places property does not change the actual data. Rather, the Decimal Places property only changes the way the data is *presented*.

8. **Close the Tours table**

FIGURE E-11: Changing Currency and Number field properties

Price field is selected →

Decimal Places property →

Field Name	Data Type
TourNo	AutoNumber
TourName	Short Text
TourStartDate	Date/Time
Duration	Number
City	Short Text
StateAbbrev	Short Text
Category	Short Text
Price	Currency

General | Lookup

Format	Currency
Decimal Places	0
Input Mask	
Caption	
Default Value	
Validation Rule	
Validation Text	
Required	No
Indexed	No
Text Align	General

TABLE E-3: Common Number field properties

property	description
Field Size	Determines the largest number that can be entered in the field, as well as the type of data (e.g., integer or fraction)
Byte	Stores numbers from 0 to 255 (no fractions)
Integer	Stores numbers from –32,768 to 32,767 (no fractions)
Long Integer	Stores numbers from –2,147,483,648 to 2,147,483,647 (no fractions)
Single	Stores numbers (including fractions with six digits to the right of the decimal point) times 10 to the –38th to +38th power
Double	Stores numbers (including fractions with over 10 digits to the right of the decimal point) in the range of 10 to the –324th to +324th power
Decimal Places	The number of digits displayed to the right of the decimal point

Modifying fields in Datasheet View

When you work in Table *Datasheet* View, the FIELDS tab on the Ribbon provides many options to modify fields and field properties. For example, you can add and delete fields, change a field name or data type, and modify many field properties such as Caption, Default Value, and Format. Table *Design* View, however, gives you full access to *all* field properties such as all of the Lookup properties. In Datasheet View, an **Autofilter** arrow is displayed to the right of each field name. Click the Autofilter arrow to quickly sort or filter by that field.

Modify Date/Time Fields

Learning
Outcomes
• Modify the Format
  property for Date/
  Time fields

Many properties of the Date/Time field, such as Input Mask, Caption, and Default Value, work the same way as they do in fields with a Short Text or Number data type. One difference, however, is the **Format** property, which helps you format dates in various ways such as January 25, 2013; 25-Jan-13; or 01/25/2013. **CASE** ▶ *You want to change the format of Date/Time fields in the Tours table to display two digits for the month and day values and four digits for the year, as in 05/05/2015.*

STEPS

1. **Right-click the Tours table in the Navigation Pane, click Design View on the shortcut menu, then click the TourStartDate field name**

   You want the tour start dates to appear with two digits for the month and day, such as 07/05/2015, instead of the default presentation of dates, 7/5/2015.

   QUICK TIP
   Click any property box, then press [F1] to open a page on the Microsoft Web site where you can enter the property name in the Search box to display an explanation of how to use the property.

2. **Click the Format property box, then click the Format list arrow**

   Although several predefined Date/Time formats are available, none matches the format you want. To define a custom format, enter symbols that represent how you want the date to appear.

3. **Type mm/dd/yyyy then press [Enter]**

   The updated Format property for the TourStartDate field shown in **FIGURE E-12** sets the date to appear with two digits for the month, two digits for the day, and four digits for the year. The parts of the date are separated by forward slashes.

4. **Save the table, display the datasheet, then click the New (blank) record button ▶▦ on the navigation bar**

   To test the new Format property for the TourStartDate field, you can add a new record to the table.

   QUICK TIP
   Access assumes that years entered with two digits from 30 to 99 refer to the years 1930 through 1999, and 00 to 29 refers to the years 2000 through 2029. To enter a year before 1930 or after 2029, enter all four digits of the year.

5. **Press [Tab] to move to the TourName field, type Missouri Eagle Watchers, press [Tab], type 9/1/15, press [Tab], type 7, press [Tab], type Hollister, press [Tab], type MO, press [Tab], type Adventure, press [Tab], type 700, then press [Tab]**

   The new record you entered into the Tours table should look like **FIGURE E-13**. The Format property for the TourStartDate field makes the entry appear as 09/01/2015, as desired.

FIGURE E-12: Changing Date/Time field properties

TourStartDate field is selected →

Field Name	Data Type
TourNo	AutoNumber
TourName	Short Text
TourStartDate	Date/Time
Duration	Number
City	Short Text
StateAbbrev	Short Text
Category	Short Text
Price	Currency

General / Lookup

Format property →

Format	mm/dd/yyyy
Input Mask	
Caption	
Default Value	
Validation Rule	
Validation Text	
Required	No
Indexed	No
IME Mode	No Control
IME Sentence Mode	None
Text Align	General
Show Date Picker	For dates

Property Update Options button

FIGURE E-13: Testing the Format property

⊞	53	Salmon Run Fishing	05/05/2014	4	Seattle	WA	Adventure	$800
⊞	54	Northwest Passage	08/01/2014	10	Vancouver	WA	Adventure	$2,000
⊞	55	Space Needle Fireworks	07/04/2014	3	Seattle	WA	Site Seeing	$500
⊞	56	Missouri Eagle Watchers	09/01/2015	7	Hollister	MO	Adventure	$700
*	(New)							

Record: ◄ ◄ 52 of 52 ► ►I ►* ☒ No Filter   Search

Custom mm/dd/yyyy Format property applied to TourStartDate field

Access 2013

Using Smart Tags

Smart Tags are buttons that automatically appear in certain conditions. They provide a small menu of options to help you work with the task at hand. Access provides the **Property Update Options** 🖘 Smart Tag to help you quickly apply property changes to other objects of the database that use the field. The

Error Indicator ◈ Smart Tag helps identify potential design errors. For example, if you are working in Report Design View and the report is too wide for the paper, the Error Indicator appears in the upper-left corner by the report selector button to alert you to the problem.

Modify Validation Properties

Learning
Outcomes
• Modify the
Validation Rule
property
• Modify the
Validation Text
property
• Define Validation
Rule expressions

The **Validation Rule** property determines what entries a field can accept. For example, a validation rule for a Date/Time field might require date entries on or after a particular date. A validation rule for a Currency field might indicate that valid entries fall between a minimum and maximum value. You use the **Validation Text** property to display an explanatory message when a user tries to enter data that breaks the validation rule. Therefore, the Validation Rule and Validation Text field properties help you prevent unreasonable data from being entered into the database. **CASE** *Samantha Hooper reminds you that all new Quest tours start on or after May 1, 2014. You can use the validation properties to establish this rule for the TourStartDate field in the Tours table.*

STEPS

1. **Right-click the** Tours table tab, **click** Design View, **click the** TourStartDate field, **click the** Validation Rule property box, **then type** >=5/1/2014

   This entry forces all dates in the TourStartDate field to be greater than or equal to 5/1/2014. See **TABLE E-4** for more examples of Validation Rule expressions. The Validation Text property provides a helpful message to the user when the entry in the field breaks the rule entered in the Validation Rule property.

2. **Click the** Validation Text box, **then type** Date must be on or after 5/1/2014

   Design View of the Tours table should now look like **FIGURE E-14**. Access modifies a property to include additional syntax by changing the entry in the Validation Rule property to >=#5/1/2014#. Pound signs (#) are used to surround date criteria.

3. **Save the table, then click** Yes **when asked to test the existing data with new data integrity rules**

   Because no dates in the TourStartDate field are earlier than 5/1/2014, Access finds no date errors in the current data and saves the table. You now want to test that the Validation Rule and Validation Text properties work when entering data in the datasheet.

4. **Click the** View button ▦ **to display the datasheet, press [Tab] twice to move to the** TourStartDate field, **type** 5/1/13, **then press [Tab]**

   Because you tried to enter a date that was not true for the Validation Rule property for the TourStartDate field, a dialog box opens and displays the Validation Text entry, as shown in **FIGURE E-15**.

5. **Click** OK **to close the validation message**

   You now know that the Validation Rule and Validation Text properties work properly.

6. **Press [Esc] to reject the invalid date entry in the TourStartDate field**

7. **Close the Tours table**

FIGURE E-14: Entering Validation properties

TourStartDate field is selected

Field Name	Data Type
TourNo	AutoNumber
TourName	Short Text
TourStartDate	Date/Time
Duration	Number
City	Short Text
StateAbbrev	Short Text
Category	Short Text
Price	Currency

General | Lookup

Validation Rule property

Validation Text property

Format	mm/dd/yyyy
Input Mask	
Caption	
Default Value	
Validation Rule	>=#5/1/2014#
Validation Text	Date must be on or after 5/1/2014
Required	No
Indexed	No
IME Mode	No Control
IME Sentence Mode	None
Text Align	General
Show Date Picker	For dates

FIGURE E-15: Validation Text message

Tours

Entering a TourStartDate that breaks the Validation Rule

Validation Text message when Validation Rule is broken

TourNo	TourName	TourStartDate	Duration	City	State	Category	Price
1	Breeze Bay Shelling	5/1/13	3	Captiva	FL	Autofilter button	$750
2	Red Reef Scuba	07/06/2014	3	Islamadora	FL	Adventure	$1,500
3	Ames Ski Club	01/02/2015	7	Breckenridge	CO	Adventure	$850
4	Boy Scout Jamboree	01/13/2015	7	Vail	CO	Adventure	$1,900
5	Bridgewater Country	02/15/2015	10	Aspen	CO	Adventure	$1,200
6	Franklin Family Reunion	03/11/2015	3	Breckenridge	CO	Family	$700
7	Spare Tire Ski Club	03/13/2015	7	Monmouth	WA	Adventure	$600
8	Eagan Family Reunion	06/12/2015					$500
9	Gunnison Bikers	06/20/2015				ure	$250
10	Golden Footsteps	05/23/2014				eing	$550
11	Hummer Trail	05/30/2014				eing	$725
12	Piper-Heitman Wedding	05/30/2014					$550
13	High Adventurers	06/05/2014				ure	$575
15	Patriot Debate Club	06/12/2014	7	Orlando	FL	Site Seeing	$605

Microsoft Access

Date must be on or after 5/1/2014

OK   Help

TABLE E-4: Validation Rule expressions

data type	validation rule expression	description
Number or Currency	>0	The number must be positive
Number or Currency	>10 And <100	The number must be greater than 10 and less than 100
Number or Currency	10 Or 20 Or 30	The number must be 10, 20, or 30
Short Text	"IA" Or "NE" Or "MO"	The entry must be IA, NE, or MO
Date/Time	>=#7/1/93#	The date must be on or after 7/1/1993
Date/Time	>#1/1/10# And <#1/1/18#	The date must be greater than 1/1/2010 and less than 1/1/2018

© 2014 Cengage Learning

Modifying the Database Structure

Create Attachment Fields

An **Attachment field** allows you to attach an external file such as a picture, Word document, PowerPoint presentation, or Excel workbook to a record. Earlier versions of Access allowed you to link or embed external data using the **OLE** (object linking and embedding) data type. The Attachment data type stores more file formats such as JPEG images, requires no additional software to view the files from within Access, and allows you to attach more than one file to the Attachment field. **CASE** *Samantha Hooper asks you to incorporate images on forms and reports to help describe and market each tour. You can use an Attachment field to store JPEG images for customer photo identification.*

STEPS

1. **Right-click the** Customers table **in the Navigation Pane, then click** Design View

   You can insert a new field anywhere in the list.

2. **Click the** Street field selector, **click the** Insert Rows button **on the DESIGN tab, click the** Field Name cell, **type** Photo, **press [Tab], click the** Data Type list arrow, **then click** Attachment, **as shown in** FIGURE E-16

   Now that you've created the new Attachment field named Photo, you're ready to add data to it in Datasheet View.

3. **Click the** Save button 🖫 **on the Quick Access toolbar, click the** View button ▦ **on the DESIGN tab to switch to Datasheet View, then press [Tab] three times to move to the new Photo field**

   An Attachment field cell displays a small paper clip icon with the number of files attached to the field in parentheses. You have not attached any files to this field yet, so each record shows zero (0) file attachments. You can attach files to this field directly from Datasheet View.

4. **Double-click the** attachment icon 📎 **for the Gracita Mayberry record to open the Attachments dialog box, click** Add, **navigate to the location where you store your Data Files, double-click** GMayberry.jpg, **then click** OK

   The GMayberry.jpg file is now included with the first record, and the datasheet reflects that one (1) file is attached to the Photo field of the first record. You can add more than one file attachment and different types of files to the same field. You can view file attachments directly from the datasheet, form, or report.

5. **Double-click the** attachment icon 📎 **for the Gracita Mayberry record to open the Attachments dialog box shown in** FIGURE E-17, **then click** Open

   The image opens in the program that is associated with the .jpg extension on your computer such as Windows Photo Viewer. The **.jpg** file extension is short for **JPEG**, an acronym for **Joint Photographic Experts Group**. This group defines the standards for the compression algorithms that make JPEG files very efficient to use in databases and on Web pages.

6. **Close the window that displays the GMayberry.jpg image, click** Cancel **in the Attachments dialog box, close the Customers table, close the QuestTravel-E.accdb database, then exit Access**

FIGURE E-16: Adding an Attachment field

FIGURE E-17: Opening an attached file

Working with database file types

When you create a new database in Microsoft Access 2013, Access gives the file an **.accdb** extension, and saves it as an Access 2007-2013 database file type. Saving the database as an Access 2007-2013 file type allows users of Access 2007, 2010, and 2013 to share the same database. Access 2007 databases are *not* readable by earlier versions of Access such as Access 2000, Access 2002 (XP), or Access 2003. If you need to share your database with people using Access 2000, 2002, or 2003, you can use the Save As command on the FILE tab to save the database with an Access 2000 or 2002-2003 file type, which applies an **.mdb** file extension to the database. Databases with an Access 2000 file type can be used by any version of Access from Access 2000 through 2013, but some features such as multivalued fields and Attachment fields are only available when working with an Access 2007-2013 database.

Practice

Concepts Review

Identify each element of the Relationships window shown in FIGURE E-18**.**

FIGURE E-18

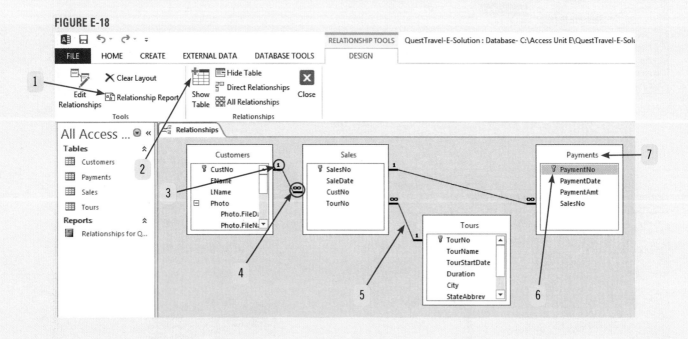

Match each term with the statement that best describes it.

8. **Validation Rule**
9. **Table Design View**
10. **Row Source**
11. **Attachment field**
12. **Limit To List**
13. **Input Mask**
14. **Lookup properties**
15. **Primary key field**
16. **Multivalued field**

a. Field that allows you to store external files such as a Word document, PowerPoint presentation, Excel workbook, or JPEG image

b. Field that holds unique information for each record in the table

c. Field that allows you to make more than one choice from a drop-down list

d. Determines whether you can enter a new value into a field

e. Field properties that allow you to supply a drop-down list of values for a field

f. Access window where all characteristics of a table, such as field names and field properties, are defined

g. Field property that provides a visual guide as you enter data

h. Field property that prevents unreasonable data entries for a field

i. Lookup property that determines where the Lookup field gets its list of values

Select the best answer from the list of choices.

17. Which of the following problems most clearly indicates that you need to redesign your database?
    a. Referential integrity is enforced on table relationships.
    b. The Input Mask Wizard has not been used.
    c. There is duplicated data in several records of a table.
    d. Not all fields have Validation Rule properties.

18. Which of the following is *not* done in Table Design View?
    a. Defining field data types
    b. Specifying the primary key field
    c. Setting Field Size properties
    d. Creating file attachments

19. What is the purpose of enforcing referential integrity?
    a. To require an entry for each field of each record
    b. To prevent incorrect entries in the primary key field
    c. To prevent orphan records from being created
    d. To force the application of meaningful validation rules

20. To create a many-to-many relationship between two tables, you must create:
    a. Foreign key fields in each table.
    b. A junction table.
    c. Two primary key fields in each table.
    d. Two one-to-one relationships between the two tables, with referential integrity enforced.

21. The linking field in the "many" table is called the:
    a. Attachment field.
    b. Child field.
    c. Foreign key field.
    d. Primary key field.

22. The default filename extension for a database created in Access 2013 is:
    a. .accdb.   c. .acc13.
    b. .mdb.   d. .mdb13.

23. If the primary key field in the "one" table is an AutoNumber data type, the linking field in the "many" table will have which data type?
    a. Number   c. Short Text
    b. AutoNumber   d. Attachment

24. Which symbol is used to identify the "many" field in a one-to-many relationship in the Relationships window?
    a. Arrow   c. Triangle
    b. Key   d. Infinity

25. The process of removing and fixing orphan records is commonly called:
    a. Relating tables.   c. Designing a relational database.
    b. Scrubbing the database.   d. Analyzing performance.

Skills Review

1. Examine relational databases.

a. List the fields needed to create an Access relational database to manage volunteer hours for the members of a philanthropic club or community service organization.

b. Identify fields that would contain duplicate values if all of the fields were stored in a single table.

c. Group the fields into subject matter tables, then identify the primary key field for each table.

d. Assume that your database contains two tables: Members and ServiceRecords. If you did not identify these two tables earlier, regroup the fields within these two table names, then identify the primary key field for each table, the foreign key field in the ServiceRecords table, and how the tables would be related using a one-to-many relationship.

2. Design related tables.

a. Start Access 2013, then create a new blank desktop database named **Service-E** in the location where you store your Data Files.

b. Use Table Design View to create a new table with the name **Members** and the field names, data types, descriptions, and primary key field, as shown in **FIGURE E-19**. Close the Members table.

FIGURE E-19

Field Name	Data Type	Description
MemberNo	AutoNumber	Member Number. Unique number for each member
FirstName	Short Text	Member's first name
LastName	Short Text	Member's last name
City	Short Text	Member's city
Phone	Short Text	Member's best phone number
Email	Short Text	Member's best email address
Birthdate	Date/Time	Member's birthdate
Gender	Short Text	Member's gender: male, female, unknown

c. Use Table Design View to create a new table named **ServiceHours** with the field names, data types, descriptions, and primary key field shown in **FIGURE E-20**. Close the ServiceHours table.

FIGURE E-20

Field Name	Data Type	Description (Optional)
ServiceNo	AutoNumber	Unique number to identify each ServiceHours record
MemberNo	Number	Foreign key field to Members table. One member may have many ServiceHours records
ServiceDate	Date/Time	Date that the service occurred
Location	Short Text	Location where the service occurred
Description	Short Text	Description of the service activity
ServiceHours	Number	Number of hours spent on service activity
ServiceValue	Currency	Monetary value of the service activity

3. Create one-to-many relationships.

a. Open the Relationships window, double-click Members, then double-click ServiceHours to add the two tables to the Relationships window. Close the Show Table dialog box.

b. Resize all field lists by dragging the bottom border down so that all fields are visible, then drag the MemberNo field from the Members table to the MemberNo field in the ServiceHours table.

Skills Review (continued)

c. Enforce referential integrity, and create the one-to-many relationship between Members and ServiceHours. See **FIGURE E-21**.

d. Create a Relationship report for the Service-E database, add your name as a label to the Report Header section of the report in Report Design View, save the Relationship report with the default name, **Relationships for Service-E**, then preview it.

e. Print the report if requested by your instructor, close the Relationship report, then save and close the Relationships window.

FIGURE E-21

4. Create Lookup fields.

a. Open the Members table in Design View, then start the Lookup Wizard for the Gender field.

b. Select the option that allows you to enter your own values, then enter **Female, Male,** and **Unknown** as the values for the Lookup column in the Col1 list.

c. Use the default **Gender** label, click the Limit To List check box, then click Finish to finish the Lookup Wizard.

d. Save the Members table, display it in Datasheet View, and enter *your* name in the FirstName and LastName fields for the first record. Enter your school's city, **5556667777** in the Phone field, *your* school email address in the Email field, **1/1/1990** in the Birthdate field, and any valid choice in the Gender field.

e. Type **Test** in the Gender field, then press [Tab] to test the Limit To List property. If it worked properly, you should receive an error message that states that the text you entered isn't an item on the list. Click OK in that dialog box, make a choice from the Gender drop-down list, then press [Tab] to finish the record. (*Hint*: If you were allowed to enter Test in the Gender field, it means that the Limit To List property is set to No instead of Yes. If that's the case, delete the Test entry, then switch to Table Design View. Modify the Limit To List Lookup property in the Lookup properties for the Gender field from No to Yes, save the table, then switch back to Datasheet View. Retest the property change by repeating Step e.)

f. Resize fields in Datasheet View as needed to clearly see all entries.

5. Modify Short Text fields.

a. Open the Members table in Design View.

b. Use the Input Mask Wizard to create an Input Mask property for the Phone field. Choose the Phone Number Input Mask. Accept the other default options provided by the Input Mask Wizard. (*Hint*: If the Input Mask Wizard is not installed on your computer, type **!(999) 000-0000;;_** for the Input Mask property for the Phone field.)

c. Change the Field Size property of the FirstName, LastName, and City fields to **30**. Change the Field Size property of the Phone field to **10**. Change the Field Size property of the Gender field to **7**. Save the Members table. None of these fields has data greater in length than the new Field Size properties, so click OK when prompted that some data may be lost.

d. Open the Members table in Datasheet View, and enter a new record with *your* instructor's name in the FirstName and LastName fields and *your* school's City and Phone field values. Enter *your* instructor's email address, **1/1/1980** for the Birthdate field, and an appropriate choice for the Gender field. Close the Members table.

Skills Review (continued)

6. **Modify Number and Currency fields.**

   a. Open the ServiceHours table in Design View.

   b. Change the Decimal Places property of the ServiceHours field to **0**.

   c. Change the Decimal Places property of the ServiceValue field to **2**.

   d. Save and close the ServiceHours table.

7. **Modify Date/Time fields.**

   a. Open the ServiceHours table in Design View.

   b. Change the Format property of the ServiceDate field to **mm/dd/yyyy**.

   c. Save and close the ServiceHours table.

   d. Open the Members table in Design View.

   e. Change the Format property of the Birthdate field to **mm/dd/yyyy**.

   f. Save and close the Members table.

8. **Modify validation properties.**

   a. Open the Members table in Design View.

   b. Click the Birthdate field name, click the Validation Rule text box, then type **<1/1/2000**. (Note that Access automatically adds pound signs around date criteria in the Validation Rule property.)

   c. Click the Validation Text box, then type **Birthdate must be before 1/1/2000**.

   d. Save and accept the changes, then open the Members table in Datasheet View.

   e. Test the Validation Text and Validation Rule properties by tabbing to the Birthdate field and entering a date after 1/1/2000 such as **1/1/2001**. Click OK when prompted with the Validation Text message, press [Esc] to remove the invalid Birthdate field entry, then close the Members table. (*Note*: Be sure your Validation Text message is spelled properly. If not, correct it in Table Design View.)

9. **Create Attachment fields.**

   a. Open the Members table in Design View, then add a new field after the Gender field with the field name **Picture** and an Attachment data type. Enter **Member's picture** for the Description. Save the Members table.

   b. Display the Members table in Datasheet View, then attach a .jpg file of yourself to the record. If you do not have a .jpg file of yourself, use the **Member1.jpg** file provided in the location where you store your Data Files.

   c. Close the Members table.

   d. Use the Form Wizard to create a form based on all of the fields in the Members table. Use a Columnar layout, and title the form **Member Entry Form**.

   e. If requested by your instructor, print the first record in the Members Entry Form that shows the picture you just entered in the Picture field, then close the form.

   f. Close the Service-E.accdb database, then exit Access.

Independent Challenge 1

As the manager of a music store's instrument rental program, you decide to create a database to track rentals to school-children. The fields you need to track are organized with four tables: Instruments, Rentals, Customers, and Schools.

a. Start Access, then create a new blank desktop database called **Music-E** in the location where you store your Data Files.

b. Use Table Design View or the FIELDS tab on the Ribbon of Table Datasheet View to create the four tables in the MusicStore-E database using the field names, data types, descriptions, and primary keys shown in FIGURES E-22, E-23, E-24, and E-25.

FIGURE E-22

Schools

Field Name	Data Type	Description (Optional)
SchoolName	Short Text	Full name of school
SchoolCode	Short Text	Unique three character code for each school

FIGURE E-23

Customers

Field Name	Data Type	Description (Optional)
FirstName	Short Text	Customer's first name
LastName	Short Text	Customer's last name
Street	Short Text	Customer's street
City	Short Text	Customer's city
State	Short Text	Customer's state
Zip	Short Text	Customer's zip code
CustNo	AutoNumber	Unique number to identify each customer
SchoolCode	Short Text	Three character school code for that customer

FIGURE E-24

Instruments

Field Name	Data Type	Description (Optional)
Description	Short Text	Description of the instrument
SerialNo	Short Text	Unique serial number on each instrument
MonthlyFee	Currency	Monthly rental fee

FIGURE E-25

Rentals

Field Name	Data Type	Description (Optional)
RentalNo	AutoNumber	Unique rental number for each record
CustNo	Number	Foreign key field to Customers table. One customer can be linked to many rental records
SerialNo	Short Text	Foreign key field to Instruments table. One instrument can be linked to many rental records
RentalStartDate	Date/Time	Date the rental starts

Independent Challenge 1 (continued)

c. In Design View of the Rentals table, enter **>1/1/2014** as the Validation Rule property for the RentalStartDate field. This change allows only dates later than 1/1/2014, the start date for this business, to be entered into this field.

d. Enter **Rental start dates must be after January 1, 2014** as the Validation Text property to the RentalStartDate field of the Rentals table. Note that Access adds pound signs (#) to the date criteria entered in the Validation Rule as soon as you tab out of the Validation Text property.

e. Save and close the Rentals table.

f. Open the Relationships window, then add the Schools, Customers, Rentals, and Instruments tables to the window. Expand the Customers field list to view all fields. Create one-to-many relationships, as shown in **FIGURE E-26**. Be sure to enforce referential integrity on each relationship.

FIGURE E-26

g. Preview the Relationship report, add *your* name as a label to the Report Header section, then save the report with the default name **Relationships for Music-E**. If requested by your instructor, print the report then close it.

h. Save and close the Relationships window.

i. Close the Music-E.accdb database, then exit Access.

Independent Challenge 2

You want to create a database that documents blood bank donations by the employees of your company. You want to track information such as employee name, blood type, date of donation, and the hospital where the employee chooses to make the donation. You also want to track basic hospital information, such as the hospital name and address.

a. Start Access, then create a new, blank desktop database called **BloodDrive-E** in the location where you store your Data Files.

b. Create an **Employees** table with appropriate field names, data types, and descriptions to record the automatic employee ID, employee first name, employee last name, and blood type. Make the EmployeeID field the primary key field. Use **FIGURE E-27** as a guide for appropriate field names.

c. Add Lookup properties to the blood type field in the Employees table to provide only valid blood type entries of **A+, A–, B+, B–, O+, O–, AB+,** and **AB–** for this field.

d. Create a **Donations** table with appropriate field names, data types, and descriptions to record an automatic donation ID, date of the donation, employee ID field, and hospital code field. Make the donation ID the primary key field. Use **FIGURE E-27** as a guide for appropriate field names.

e. Create a **Hospitals** table with fields and appropriate field names, data types, and descriptions to record a hospital code, hospital name, street, city, state, and zip. Make the hospital code field the primary key field. Use **FIGURE E-27** as a guide for appropriate field names.

f. In the Relationships window, create one-to-many relationships with referential integrity between the tables in the database, as shown in **FIGURE E-27**. One employee may make several donations over time. Each donation is marked for a particular hospital so each hospital may receive many donations over time.

FIGURE E-27

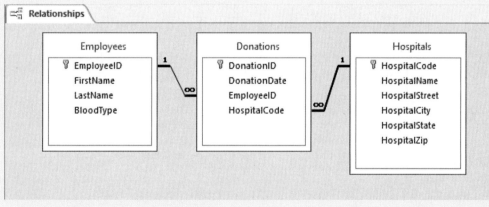

g. Preview the Relationship report, add *your* name as a label to the Report Header section, then save the report with the default name **Relationships for BloodDrive-E**. If requested by your instructor, print the report then close it.

h. Save and close the Relationships window.

i. Close the BloodDrive-E.accdb database, then exit Access.

Independent Challenge 3

You're a member and manager of a recreational baseball team and decide to create an Access database to manage player information, games, and batting statistics.

a. Start Access, then create a new, blank desktop database called **Baseball-E** in the location where you store your Data Files.

b. Create a **Players** table with appropriate field names, data types, and descriptions to record the player first name, last name, and uniform number. Make the uniform number field the primary key field. Use **FIGURE E-28** as a guide for appropriate field names.

c. Create a **Games** table with appropriate field names, data types, and descriptions to record an automatic game number, date of the game, opponent's name, home score, and visitor score. Make the game number field the primary key field. Use **FIGURE E-28** as a guide for appropriate field names.

d. Create an **AtBats** table with appropriate field names, data types, and descriptions to record hits, at bats, the game number, and the uniform number of each player. The game number and uniform number fields will both be foreign key fields. This table does not need a primary key field. Use **FIGURE E-28** as a guide for appropriate field names.

e. In the Relationships window, create one-to-many relationships with referential integrity between the tables shown in **FIGURE E-28**. The AtBats table contains one record for each player that plays in each game to record his hitting statistics, hits and at bats, for each game. Therefore, one player record is related to many records in the AtBats table and one game record is related to many records in the AtBats table.

f. Preview the Relationship report, add *your* name as a label to the Report Header section, then save the report with the default name **Relationships for Baseball-E**. If requested by your instructor, print the report then close it.

g. Save and close the Relationships window.

h. Close the Baseball-E.accdb database, then exit Access.

FIGURE E-28

Independent Challenge 4: Explore

An Access database can help record and track your job search efforts. In this exercise, you will modify two fields in the Positions table in your JobSearch database with Lookup properties to make data entry easier, more efficient, and more accurate.

a. Start Access, open the JobSearch-E.accdb database from the location where you store your Data Files, then enable content if prompted.

b. Open the Positions table in Design View. Click the EmployerID field, then start the Lookup Wizard.

c. In this situation, you want the EmployerID field in the Positions table to look up both the EmployerID and the CompanyName fields from the Employers table, so leave the "I want the lookup field to get the values from another table or query" option button selected.

d. The Employers table contains the fields you want to display in this Lookup field. Select both the EmployerID field and the CompanyName fields. Sort the records in ascending order by the CompanyName field.

e. Deselect the "Hide key column" check box so that you can see the data in both the EmployerID and CompanyName fields.

f. Choose EmployerID as the field in which to store values, **EmployerID** as the label for the Lookup field, click the Enable Data Integrity check box, then click Finish to finish the Lookup Wizard. Click Yes when prompted to save the table.

g. Switch to Datasheet View of the Positions table and tab to the EmployerID field for the first record. Click the EmployerID list arrow. You should see both the EmployerID value as well as the CompanyName in the drop-down list, as shown in **FIGURE E-29**.

FIGURE E-29

h. Return to Design View of the Positions table, click the Desirability field, and start the Lookup Wizard. This field stores the values 1 through 5 as a desirability rating. You will manually enter those values, so choose the "I will type in the values that I want" option button.

i. Enter **1**, **2**, **3**, **4**, and **5** in the Col1 column; accept the Desirability label for the Lookup field; click the Limit To List check box; then click Finish to finish the Lookup Wizard.

Access 2013

Independent Challenge 4: Explore (continued)

j. Save the table, and test the Desirability field for the first record in Datasheet View. You should see a drop-down list with the values 1, 2, 3, 4, and 5 in the list, as shown in **FIGURE E-30**.

FIGURE E-30

Title	CareerArea	AnnualSalar	Desirability	EmployerID	PositionID	Click to Add
Marketing Representative	Computers	$35,000.00	5	1	1	
Systems Engineer	Computers	$37,000.00	1	1	2	
Office Specialist	Computers	$32,000.00	2	2	3	
Customer Service Rep	Computers	$31,000.00	3	2	4	
Technician	Computers	$30,500.00	4	2	5	
Professor	CSIT	$50,000.00	5	6	6	
Professor	CIS	$55,000.00	5	7	7	
Customer Service	CS	$30,000.00	3	8	8	
Analyst	HR	$35,000.00	4	9	9	
Advisor	Finance	$60,000.00	4	10	10	
*					(New)	

k. Save the table, and test the Desirability and EmployerID fields. You should not be able to make any entries in those fields that are not presented in the list.

l. Close the Positions table, and open the Relationships window. Your Relationships window should look like **FIGURE E-31**. The Lookup Wizard created the relationship between the Employers and Positions table when you completed Step f. Save and close the Relationships window.

FIGURE E-31

Independent Challenge 4: Explore (continued)

m. Use the Form Wizard and select all of the fields from both the Employers and Positions tables. View the data by Employers, and use a Datasheet layout for the subform.

n. Title the form **Employers Entry Form** and the subform **Positions Subform**. View the form in Form View.

o. In Form Design View, use your skills to move, resize, align, and edit the controls, as shown in **FIGURE E-32**.

p. Add a new record to the subform for the first company, IBM. Use realistic but fictitious data. Note that the EmployerID and PositionID values are automatically entered.

q. Save and close the Employers Entry Form, close the JobSearch-E.accdb database, and exit Access.

FIGURE E-32

Visual Workshop

Open the Training-E.accdb database from the location where you store your Data Files, then enable content if prompted. Create a new table called **Vendors** using the Table Design View shown in FIGURE E-33 to determine field names, data types, and descriptions. Make the following property changes: Change the Field Size property of the VState field to **2**, the VZip field to **9**, and VPhone field to **10**. Change the Field Size property of the VendorName, VStreet, and VCity fields to **30**. Apply a Phone Number Input Mask to the VPhone field. Be sure to specify that the VendorID field is the primary key field. Relate the tables in the Training-E database, as shown in FIGURE E-34, then view the Relationship report in landscape orientation. Add *your* name as a label to the Report Header section to document the Relationship report, then print it if requested by your instructor. Save the Relationship report with the default name of **Relationships for Training-E**, close the report, save and close the Relationships window, close the Training-E database, and exit Access.

FIGURE E-33

Field Name	Data Type	
⚷ VendorID	AutoNumber	Unique vendor identification number
VendorName	Short Text	Vendor full name
VStreet	Short Text	Vendor street address
VCity	Short Text	Vendor city
VState	Short Text	Vendor State
VZip	Short Text	Vendor Zip code
VPhone	Short Text	Vendor phone

FIGURE E-34

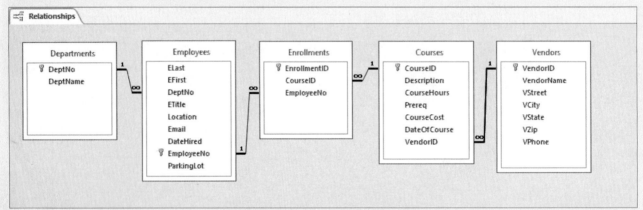

Improving Queries

CASE ▶ The Quest database has been updated to contain more customers, tours, and sales. You help Samantha Hooper, a Quest tour developer for U.S. travel, create queries to analyze this information.

Unit Objectives

After completing this unit, you will be able to:

- Create multitable queries
- Apply sorts and view SQL
- Develop AND criteria
- Develop OR criteria
- Create calculated fields
- Build summary queries
- Build crosstab queries
- Create a report on a query

Files You Will Need

QuestTravel-F.accdb   RealEstate-F.accdb

Service-F.accdb   Scholarships-F.accdb

MusicStore-F.accdb   Training-F.accdb

© Tumanyan/Shutterstock

Create Multitable Queries

Learning Outcomes
- Create a multitable query in Query Design View
- Add and delete fields in Query Design View

A **select query**, the most common type of query, selects fields from related tables and displays records in a datasheet where you can view, enter, edit, or delete data. You can create select queries by using the Simple Query Wizard, or you can start from scratch in Query Design View. **Query Design View** gives you more options for selecting and presenting information. When you open (or **run**) a query, the fields and records that you selected for the query are presented in **Query Datasheet View**, also called a **logical view** of the data. **CASE** Samantha Hooper asks you to create a query to analyze customer payments. You select fields from the Customers, Tours, Sales, and Payments tables to complete this analysis.

STEPS

1. **Start Access, open the QuestTravel-F.accdb database from the location where you store your Data Files, then enable content if prompted**

2. **Click the CREATE tab on the Ribbon, then click the Query Design button in the Queries group**

   The Show Table dialog box opens and lists all the tables in the database.

3. **Double-click Customers, double-click Sales, double-click Tours, double-click Payments, then click Close**

   Recall that the upper pane of Query Design View displays the fields for each of the selected tables in field lists. The name of the table is shown in the field list title bar. Primary key fields are identified with a small key icon. Relationships between tables are displayed with **one-to-many join lines** that connect the linking fields. You select the fields you want by adding them to the query design grid.

4. **Double-click the FName field in the Customers table field list to add this field to the first column of the query design grid, double-click LName, double-click TourName in the Tours field list, scroll then double-click Price in the Tours field list, double-click PaymentDate in the Payments field list, then double-click PaymentAmt, as shown in FIGURE F-1**

   When you *double-click* a field in a field list, it is automatically added as the next field in the query grid. When you *drag* a field to the query design grid, any existing fields move to the right to accommodate the new field.

5. **Click the View button [⊞] in the Results group to run the query and display the query datasheet**

   The resulting datasheet looks like **FIGURE F-2**. The datasheet shows the six fields selected in Query Design View: FName and LName from the Customers table, TourName and Price from the Tours table, and PaymentDate and PaymentAmt from the Payments table. The datasheet displays 78 records because 78 different payments have been made. Some of the payments are from the same customer. For example, Kristen Collins has made payments on multiple tours (records 2 and 20). Kristen's last name has changed to Bayes.

6. **Double-click Collins in the LName field of the second record, type Bayes, then click any other record**

   Because Kristen's data is physically stored in only one record in the Customers table (but selected multiple times in this query because Kristen has made more than one payment), changing any occurrence of her last name automatically updates all other selections of that data in this query and throughout all other queries, forms, and reports in the database, too. Note that Kristen's name has been updated to Kristen Bayes in record 20, as shown in **FIGURE F-2**.

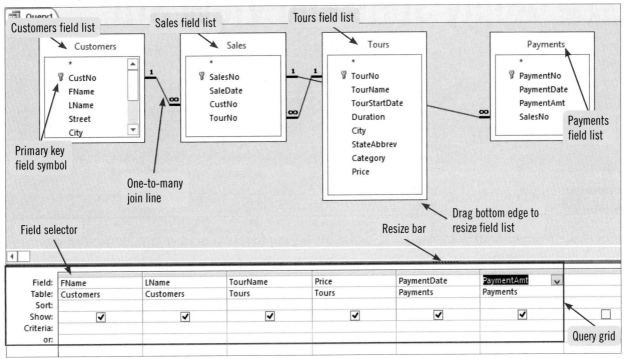

FIGURE F-2: Query datasheet

Deleting a field from the query grid

If you add the wrong field to the query design grid, you can delete it by clicking the **field selector**, the thin gray bar above each field name, then pressing [Delete]. Deleting a field from the query design grid removes it from the logical view of this query's data-sheet, but does not delete the field from the database. A field is defined and the field's contents are stored in a table object only.

Apply Sorts and View SQL

Learning
Outcomes
• Apply sort orders
  in Query Design
  View
• View Structured
  Query Language
• Define SQL
  keywords

Sorting refers to reordering records in either ascending or descending order based on the values in a field. You can specify more than one sort field in Query Design View. Sort orders are evaluated from left to right, meaning that the sort field on the far left is the primary sort field. Sort orders defined in Query Design View are saved with the query object. **CASE** *You want to list the records in alphabetical order based on the customer's last name. If the customer has made more than one payment, you further sort the records by the payment date.*

STEPS

1. **Click the View button** ⟋ **on the HOME tab to return to Query Design View**

   To sort the records by last name then by payment date, the LName field must be the primary sort field, and the PaymentDate field must be the secondary sort field.

2. **Click the LName field Sort cell in the query design grid, click the Sort list arrow, click Ascending, click the PaymentDate field Sort cell in the query design grid, click the Sort list arrow, then click Ascending**

   The resulting query design grid should look like **FIGURE F-3**.

QUICK TIP
You can resize the columns of a datasheet by pointing to the right column border that separates the field names, then dragging left or right to resize the columns. Double-click ⟷ to automatically adjust the column width to fit the widest entry.

3. **Click the View button** ▦ **in the Results group to display the query datasheet**

   The records of the datasheet are now listed in ascending order based on the values in the LName field. When the same value appears in the LName field, the records are further sorted by the secondary sort field, PaymentDate, as shown in **FIGURE F-4**. Jacob Alman made two payments, one on 7/26/2014 and the next on 9/1/2014. Kristen Bayes made many payments.

4. **Click the Save button** 🖫 **on the Quick Access toolbar, type CustomerPayments in the Save As dialog box, then click OK**

   When you save a query, you save a logical view of the data, a selection of fields and records from underlying tables. Technically, when you save a query, you are saving a set of instructions written in **Structured Query Language (SQL)**. You can view the SQL code for any query by switching to **SQL View**.

QUICK TIP
SQL keywords such as SELECT, FROM, or ORDER BY should not be used as field names.

5. **Click the View button list arrow, click SQL View, then click in the lower part of the SQL window to deselect the code**

   The SQL statements shown in **FIGURE F-5** start with the **SELECT** keyword. Field names follow SELECT, and how the tables are joined follow the **FROM** keyword. The **ORDER BY** keyword determines how records are sorted. Fortunately, you do not have to write or understand SQL to use Access or select data from multiple tables. The easy-to-use Query Design View gives you a way to select and sort data from underlying tables without being an SQL programmer.

6. **Close the CustomerPayments query**

FIGURE F-3: Specifying multiple sort orders in Query Design View

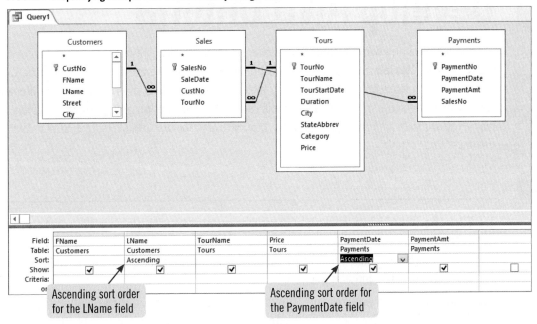

FIGURE F-4: Records sorted by LName, then by PaymentDate

FName	LName	TourName	Price	PaymentDat	PaymentAm
Jacob	Alman	Red Reef Scuba	$1,500	7/26/2014	$300.00
Jacob	Alman	Red Reef Scuba	$1,500	9/1/2014	$100.00
Kristen	Bayes	Ames Ski Club	$850	4/30/2014	$750.00
Kristen	Bayes	Yosemite National Park (	$1,100	7/13/2014	$450.00
Kristen	Bayes	ge Tour	$1,200	7/20/2014	$400.00
Kristen	Bayes	American Heritage Tour	$1,200	8/20/2014	$100.00

Primary sort order

Secondary sort order

FIGURE F-5: SQL View

SELECT keyword

```
SELECT Customers.FName, Customers.LName, Tours.TourName, Tours.Price, Payments.PaymentDate, Payments.PaymentAmt
FROM Tours INNER JOIN (Customers INNER JOIN Sales ON Customers.CustNo = Sales.CustNo) ON Tours.TourNo = Sales.TourNo) INNER JOIN Payments ON Sales.SalesNo = Payments.SalesNo
ORDER BY Customers.LName, Payments.PaymentDate;
```

FROM keyword

ORDER BY keyword

Specifying a sort order different from the field order in the datasheet

If your database has several customers with the same last name, you can include a secondary sort on the first name field to distinguish the customers. If you want to display the fields in a different order from which they are sorted, you can use the solution shown in **FIGURE F-6**. Add a field to the query design grid twice, once to select for the datasheet, and once to use as a sort order. Use the Show check box to deselect the field used as a sort order.

FIGURE F-6: Sorting on a field that is not displayed

Show check box is unchecked

Primary sort order

Access 2013

Develop AND Criteria

You can limit the number of records that appear on the resulting datasheet by entering criteria in Query Design View. **Criteria** are tests, or limiting conditions, that must be true for the record to be selected for a datasheet. To create **AND criteria**, which means the query selects a record only if *all* criteria are true, enter two or more criteria on the *same* Criteria row of the query design grid. **CASE** ▶ *Samantha Hooper predicts strong sales for family tours that start in or after July. She asks you to create a list of the existing tours that meet those criteria.*

STEPS

1. **Click the CREATE tab, click the Query Design button, double-click Tours, then click Close in the Show Table dialog box**

   To query for family tours, you need to add the Category field to the query grid. In addition, you want to know the tour name and start date.

2. **Drag the bottom edge of the Tours field list down to resize it to display all fields, double-click the TourName field, double-click the TourStartDate field, then double-click the Category field**

   To find tours in the Family category, you need to add a criterion for this field in the query grid.

3. **Click the first Criteria cell for the Category field, then type Family**

   To find all tours that start after July 1st, use the > (greater than) operator.

4. **Click the first Criteria cell for the TourStartDate field, type >7/1/2014, then press [↓]**

   As shown in **FIGURE F-7**, Access assists you with criteria syntax, rules by which criteria need to be entered. Access automatically adds quotation marks around text criteria in Short Text fields, such as "Family" in the Category field, and pound signs around date criteria in Date/Time fields, such as #7/1/2014# in the TourStartDate field. The criteria in Number, Currency, and Yes/No fields are not surrounded by any characters. See **TABLE F-1** for more information on common Access comparison operators and criteria syntax.

5. **Click the Save button 🖫 on the Quick Access toolbar, type FamilyJuly in the Save As dialog box, click OK, then click the View button ▦ to view the query results**

   The query results are shown in **FIGURE F-8**.

6. **Close the FamilyJuly datasheet**

FIGURE F-7: Entering AND criteria on the same row

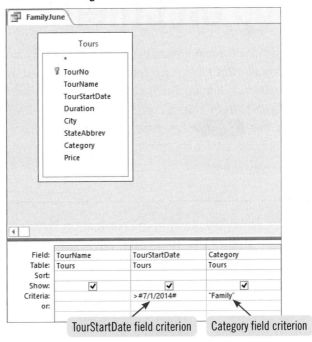

FamilyJune

Tours

*
🔑 TourNo
TourName
TourStartDate
Duration
City
StateAbbrev
Category
Price

Field:	TourName	TourStartDate	Category
Table:	Tours	Tours	Tours
Sort:			
Show:	✓	✓	✓
Criteria:		>#7/1/2014#	"Family"
or:			

TourStartDate field criterion   Category field criterion

FIGURE F-8: Datasheet for FamilyJuly records

FamilyJuly

TourName	TourStartDate	Category
Franklin Family Reunion	03/11/2015	Family
Eagan Family Reunion	06/12/2015	Family
Dalgren-Smith Wedding	07/02/2014	Family
Lang Reunion	07/02/2014	Family
Buehler Reunion	07/02/2014	Family

All records have a
TourStartDate after 7/1/2014
AND are in the Family category

TABLE F-1: Common comparison operators

operator	description	example	result
>	Greater than	>50	Value exceeds 50
>=	Greater than or equal to	>=50	Value is 50 or greater
<	Less than	<50	Value is less than 50
<=	Less than or equal to	<=50	Value is 50 or less
<>	Not equal to	<>50	Value is any number other than 50
Between...And	Finds values between two numbers or dates	Between #2/2/2014# And #2/2/2015#	Dates between 2/2/2014 and 2/2/2015, inclusive
In	Finds a value that is one of a list	In ("IA","KS","NE")	Value equals IA or KS or NE
Null	Finds records that have no entry in a particular field	Null	No value has been entered in a field
Is Not Null	Finds records that have any entry in a particular field	Is Not Null	Any value has been entered in a field
Like	Finds records that match the criterion, used with the * (asterisk) wildcard character	Like "A*"	Value starts with A
Not	Finds records that do not match the criterion	Not 2	Numbers other than 2

Develop OR Criteria

Learning Outcomes
• Use AND and OR criteria in the same query
• Define advanced wildcard characters

As you experienced in the previous lesson, AND criteria *narrow* the number of records in the datasheet by requiring that a record be true for multiple criteria. You also learned that AND criteria are entered on the *same* row. OR criteria work in the opposite way. **OR criteria** *expand* the number of records in the datasheet because a record needs to be true for *only one* of the criteria. You enter OR criteria in the query design grid on *different* criteria rows. **CASE** *Samantha Hooper asks you to modify the FamilyJuly query to expand the number of records to include tours in the Adventure category that start after 7/1/2014 as well.*

STEPS

1. **Right-click the** FamilyJuly query **in the Navigation Pane, click** Copy, **right-click a blank spot in the** Navigation Pane, **click** Paste, **type** FamilyAdventureJuly **in the Paste As dialog box, then click** OK

   By making a copy of the FamilyJuly query before modifying it, you won't change the FamilyJuly query by mistake. To add OR criteria, you have to enter criteria in the next available "or" row of the query design grid. By default, the query grid displays eight rows for additional OR criteria, but you can add even more rows using the Insert Rows button on the DESIGN tab.

2. **Right-click the** FamilyAdventureJuly query, **click** Design View, **type** Adventure **in the next row (the "or" row) of the Category column, then click the** View button ▦ **to display the datasheet**

   The datasheet expands from 5 to 26 records because 21 tours with a Category of Adventure were added to the datasheet. But notice that many of the TourStartDate values for the Adventure records are prior to 7/1/2014. To select only those Adventure tours with a TourStartDate after 7/1/2014, you need to add more criteria to Query Design View.

QUICK TIP
To include a TourStartDate that starts *on* 7/1/2014, use the criterion >=7/1/2014 versus >7/1/2014.

3. **Click the** View button ⊠ **to return to Query Design View, click the next** TourStartDate **Criteria cell, type** >7/1/2014, **then click elsewhere in the grid, as shown in FIGURE F-9**

   Criteria in one row do not affect criteria in another row. Therefore, to select only those tours that start after 7/1/2014, you must put the same TourStartDate criterion in *both* rows of the query design grid.

4. **Click** ▦ **to return to Datasheet View**

   The resulting datasheet selects 18 records, as shown in **FIGURE F-10**. When no sort order is applied, the records are sorted by the primary key field of the first table in the query (in this case, TourNo, which is not selected for this query). All of the records have a Category of Family or Adventure and a TourStartDate value greater than 7/1/2014.

5. **Save and close the FamilyAdventureJuly query**

   The QuestTravel-F.accdb Navigation Pane displays the three queries you created plus the StateAnalysis query that was already in the database.

FIGURE F-9: Entering OR criteria on different rows

Field:	TourName	TourStartDate	Category
Table:	Tours	Tours	Tours
Sort:			
Show:	☑	☑	☑
Criteria:		>#7/1/2014#	"Family"
or:		>#7/1/2014#	"Adventure"

"or" row → or:

OR criteria is entered on different rows

FIGURE F-10: Datasheet for FamilyAdventureJuly query

FamilyAdventureJuly

TourName	TourStartDate	Category
Breeze Bay Shelling	07/06/2014	Adventure
Red Reef Scuba	07/06/2014	Adventure
Ames Ski Club	01/02/2015	Adventure
Boy Scout Jamboree	01/13/2015	Adventure
Bridgewater Country	02/15/2015	Adventure
Franklin Family Reunion	03/11/2015	Family
Spare Tire Ski Club	03/13/2015	Adventure
Eagan Family Reunion	06/12/2015	Family
Gunnison Bikers	06/20/2015	Adventure
Dalgren-Smith Wedding	07/02/2014	Family
Lang Reunion	07/02/2014	Family
Buehler Reunion	07/02/2014	Family
Bear Valley Adventures	08/19/2014	Adventure
Black Sheep Hiking Club	08/26/2014	Adventure
Bigfoot Rafting Club	07/13/2014	Adventure
Missouri Bald Eagle Watc	08/13/2014	Adventure
Northwest Passage	08/01/2014	Adventure
Missouri Eagle Watchers	09/01/2015	Adventure

All records have a TourStartDate after 7/1/2014 AND are in the Family or Adventure category

Record: 1 of 18   No Filter   Search

Using wildcard characters in query criteria

To search for a pattern, use a **wildcard character** to represent any character in the criteria entry. Use a **question mark (?)** to search for any single character, and an **asterisk (*)** to search for any number of characters. Wildcard characters are often used with the Like operator. For example, the criterion Like "10/*/2015" finds all dates in October of 2015, and the criterion Like "F*" finds all entries that start with the letter F.

Create Calculated Fields

Learning Outcomes
- Create calculated fields in queries
- Define functions and expressions

A **calculated field** is a field of data that can be created based on the values of other fields. For example, you can calculate the value for a Tax field by multiplying the value of the Sales field by a percentage. To create a calculated field, define it in Query Design View using an expression that describes the calculation. An **expression** is a combination of field names, operators (such as +, −, /, and *), and functions that result in a single value. A **function** is a predefined formula that returns a value such as a subtotal, count, or the current date. See TABLE F-2 for more information on arithmetic operators and TABLE F-3 for more information on functions. **CASE** *Samantha Hooper asks you to find the number of days between the sale date and the tour start date. To determine this information, you create a calculated field called LeadTime that subtracts the SaleDate from the TourStartDate. You create another calculated field to determine the commission on each tour sale.*

STEPS

1. **Click the CREATE tab on the Ribbon, click the Query Design button, double-click Tours, double-click Sales, then click Close in the Show Table dialog box**

   First, you add the fields to the grid that you want to display in the query.

   QUICK TIP
   Drag the bottom edge of the Tours field list down to display all fields.

2. **Double-click the TourName field, double-click the TourStartDate field, double-click the Price field, then double-click the SaleDate field**

   You create a calculated field in the Field cell of the design grid by entering a new descriptive field name followed by a colon, followed by an expression. Field names used in an expression must be surrounded by square brackets.

   QUICK TIP
   To display a long entry in a field cell, right-click the cell, then click Zoom.

3. **Click the blank Field cell in the fifth column, type LeadTime:[TourStartDate]-[SaleDate], then drag the ↔ pointer on the right edge of the fifth column selector to the right to display the entire entry**

   You create another calculated field to determine the commission paid on each sale, which is calculated as 11% of the Price field.

   TROUBLE
   Field names in expressions are surrounded by [square brackets] not {curly braces} and not (parentheses).

4. **Click the blank Field cell in the sixth column, type Commission:[Price]*0.11, then widen the column, as shown in FIGURE F-11**

   You view the datasheet to see the resulting calculated fields.

5. **Click the View button ▦, press [Tab], type 8/1/14 in the TourStartDate field for the first record, press [Tab], type 1000 in the Price field for the first record, then press [↓]**

   A portion of the resulting datasheet, with two calculated fields, is shown in FIGURE F-12. The LeadTime field is automatically recalculated, showing the number of days between the SaleDate and the TourStartDate. The Commission field is also automatically recalculated, multiplying the Price value by 11%.

6. **Click the Save button 🖫 on the Quick Access toolbar, type LeadTimesAndCommissions in the Save As dialog box, click OK, then close the datasheet**

FIGURE F-11: Creating calculated fields

Calculated field names are followed by a colon

Field:	TourName	TourStartDate	Price	SaleDate	LeadTime: [TourStartDate]-[SaleDate]	Commission: [Price]*0.11
Table:	Tours	Tours	Tours	Sales		
Sort:						
Show:	✓	✓	✓	✓	✓	✓
Criteria:						
or:						

Calculations are determined by expressions that follow the colon

Drag the column separator to widen the column

FIGURE F-12: Viewing and testing calculated fields

Query1

TourName	TourStartDate	Price	SaleDate	LeadTime	Commission
Breeze Bay Shelling	08/01/2014	$1,000	4/30/2014	93	110
Breeze Bay Shelling	08/01/2014	$1,000	4/30/2014	93	110
Breeze Bay Shelling	08/01/2014	$1,000	4/30/2014	93	110
Breeze Bay Shelling	08/01/2014	$1,000	4/30/2014	93	110
Breeze Bay Shelling	08/01/2014	$1,000	5/31/2014	62	110
Breeze Bay Shelling	08/01/2014	$1,000	6/30/2014	32	110
Red Reef Scuba	07/06/2014	$1,500	5/11/2014	56	165
Red Reef Scuba	07/06/2014	$1,500	7/1/2014	5	165
Red Reef Scuba	07/06/2014	$1,500	7/1/2014	5	165
Red Reef Scuba	07/06/2014	$1,500	7/1/2014	5	165
Red Reef Scuba	07/06/2014	$1,500	7/1/2014	5	165
Red Reef Scuba	07/06/2014	$1,500	7/1/2014	5	165
Red Reef Scuba	07/06/2014	$1,500	7/1/2014	5	165
Red Reef Scuba	07/06/2014	$1,500	7/2/2014	4	165
Red Reef Scuba	07/06/2014	$1,500	7/2/2014	4	165
Ames Ski Club	01/02/2015	$850	4/30/2014	247	93.5
Ames Ski Club	01/02/2015	$850	5/1/2014	246	93.5
Ames Ski Club	01/02/2015	$850	7/11/2014	175	93.5

Commission equals Price * 11%

LeadTime equals the days between the SaleDate and TourStartDate

TABLE F-2: Arithmetic operators

operator	description
+	Addition
–	Subtraction
*	Multiplication
/	Division
^	Exponentiation

TABLE F-3: Common functions

function	sample expression and description
DATE	DATE()-[BirthDate] Calculates the number of days between today and the date in the BirthDate field; Access expressions are not case sensitive, so DATE()-[BirthDate] is equivalent to date()-[birthdate] and DATE()-[BIRTHDATE]; therefore, use capitalization in expressions in any way that makes the expression easier to read
PMT	PMT([Rate],[Term],[Loan]) Calculates the monthly payment on a loan where the Rate field contains the monthly interest rate, the Term field contains the number of monthly payments, and the Loan field contains the total amount financed
LEFT	LEFT([LastName],2) Returns the first two characters of the entry in the LastName field
RIGHT	RIGHT([PartNo],3) Returns the last three characters of the entry in the PartNo field
LEN	LEN([Description]) Returns the number of characters in the Description field

Build Summary Queries

Learning Outcomes
• Create a summary query
• Define aggregate functions

A **summary query** calculates statistics for groups of records. To create a summary query, you add the **Total row** to the query design grid to specify how you want to group and calculate the records using aggregate functions. **Aggregate functions** calculate a statistic such as a subtotal, count, or average on a field in a group of records. Some aggregate functions, such as Sum or Avg (Average), only work on fields with Number or Currency data types. Other functions, such as Min (Minimum), Max (Maximum), or Count, also work on Short Text fields. **TABLE F-4** provides more information on aggregate functions. A key difference between the statistics displayed by a summary query and those displayed by calculated fields is that summary queries provide calculations that describe a *group of records*, whereas calculated fields provide a new field of information for *each record*. **CASE** Samantha Hooper asks you to calculate total sales for each tour category. You build a summary query to provide this information.

STEPS

1. **Click the CREATE tab on the Ribbon, click the Query Design button, double-click Sales, double-click Tours, then click Close in the Show Table dialog box**

   It doesn't matter in what order you add the field lists to Query Design View, but it's important to move and resize the field lists as necessary to clearly see all field names and relationships.

2. **Double-click the SalesNo field in the Sales field list, double-click the Category field in the Tours field list, double-click the Price field in the Tours field list, then click the View button to view the datasheet**

   One hundred and one records are displayed, representing all 101 records in the Sales table. You can add a Total row to any datasheet to calculate grand total statistics for that datasheet.

3. **Click the Totals button in the Records group, click the Total cell below the Price field, click the Total list arrow, click Sum, then use ╁ to widen the Price column to display the entire total**

   The Total row is added to the bottom of the datasheet and displays the sum total of the Price field, $85,510. Other Total row statistics you can select include Average, Count, Maximum, Minimum, Standard Deviation, and Variance. To create subtotals per Category, you need to modify the query in Query Design View.

4. **Click the View button to return to Query Design View, click the Totals button in the Show/Hide group, click Group By in the SalesNo column, click the list arrow, click Count, click Group By in the Price column, click the list arrow, then click Sum**

   The Total row is added to the query grid below the Table row. To calculate summary statistics for each category, the Category field is the Group By field, as shown in **FIGURE F-13**. With the records grouped together by Category, you will subtotal the Price field using the Sum operator to calculate a subtotal of revenue for each Category of tour sales.

5. **Click to display the datasheet, widen each column as necessary to view all field names, click in the Total row for the SumOfPrice field, click the list arrow, click Sum, then click another row in the datasheet to remove the selection**

   The Adventure category leads all others with a count of 55 sales totaling $52,560. The total revenue for all sales is $85,510, as shown in **FIGURE F-14**.

6. **Click the Save button on the Quick Access toolbar, type CategorySummary, click OK, then close the datasheet**

FIGURE F-13: Summary query in Design View

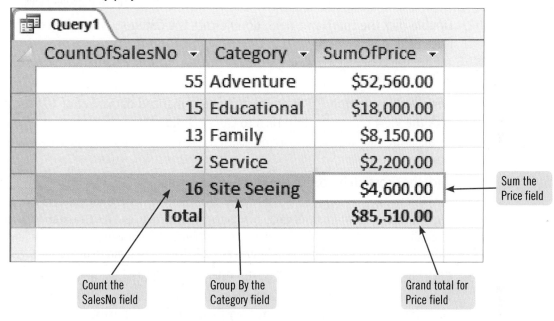

Total row is added to query grid

Field:	SalesNo	Category	Price	
Table:	Sales	Tours	Tours	
Total:	Count	Group By	Sum ⌄	
Sort:				
Show:	☑	☑	☑	
Criteria:				
or:				

Count the SalesNo field

Group By the Category field

Sum the Price field

FIGURE F-14: Summary query datasheet

Query1

CountOfSalesNo ▾	Category ▾	SumOfPrice ▾
55	Adventure	$52,560.00
15	Educational	$18,000.00
13	Family	$8,150.00
2	Service	$2,200.00
16	Site Seeing	$4,600.00
Total		$85,510.00

Sum the Price field

Count the SalesNo field

Group By the Category field

Grand total for Price field

TABLE F-4: Aggregate functions

aggregate function	used to find the
Sum	Total of values in a field
Avg	Average of values in a field
Min	Minimum value in a field
Max	Maximum value in a field
Count	Number of values in a field (not counting null values)
StDev	Standard deviation of values in a field
Var	Variance of values in a field
First	Field value from the first record in a table or query
Last	Field value from the last record in a table or query

Build Crosstab Queries

Learning Outcomes
• Create a crosstab query
• Describe the Find Duplicates and Find Unmatched Query Wizards

A **crosstab query** subtotals one field by grouping records using two other fields that are placed in the column heading and row heading positions. You can use the **Crosstab Query Wizard** to guide you through the steps of creating a crosstab query, or you can build the crosstab query from scratch using Query Design View. **CASE** *Samantha Hooper asks you to continue your analysis of prices per category by summarizing the price values for each tour within each category. A crosstab query works well for this request because you want to subtotal the Price field as summarized by two other fields, TourName and Category.*

STEPS

1. **Click the CREATE tab on the Ribbon, click the Query Design button, double-click Tours, double-click Sales, then click Close in the Show Table dialog box**

   The fields you need for your crosstab query come from the Tours table, but you also need to include the Sales table in this query to select tour information for each record (sale) in the Sales table.

2. **Double-click the TourName field, double-click the Category field, then double-click the Price field**

   The first step in creating a crosstab query is to create a select query with the three fields you want to use in the crosstabular report.

3. **Click the View button 📋 to review the unsummarized datasheet of 101 records, then click the View button 📐 to return to Query Design View**

   To summarize these 101 records in a crosstabular report, you need to change the current select query into a crosstab query.

4. **Click the Crosstab button in the Query Type group**

   Note that two new rows are added to the query grid—the Total row and the Crosstab row. The **Total row** helps you determine which fields group or summarize the records, and the **Crosstab row** identifies which of the three positions each field takes in the crosstab report: Row Heading, Column Heading, or Value. The **Value field** is typically a numeric field, such as Price, that can be summed or averaged.

5. **Click Group By in the Total cell of the Price field, click the list arrow, click Sum, click the Crosstab cell for the TourName field, click the list arrow, click Row Heading, click the Crosstab cell for the Category field, click the list arrow, click Column Heading, click the Crosstab cell for the Price field, click the list arrow, then click Value**

   The completed Query Design View should look like **FIGURE F-15**. Note the choices made in the Total and Crosstab rows of the query grid.

6. **Click 📋 to review the crosstab datasheet**

   The final crosstab datasheet is shown in **FIGURE F-16**. The datasheet summarizes all 101 sales records by the Category field used as the column headings and by the TourName field used in the row heading position. Although you can switch the row and column heading fields without changing the numeric information on the crosstab datasheet, you should generally place the field with the most entries (in this case, TourName has more values than Category) in the row heading position so that the printout is taller than it is wide.

7. **Click the Save button 💾 on the Quick Access toolbar, type TourCrosstab as the query name, click OK, then close the datasheet**

   Crosstab queries appear with a crosstab icon to the left of the query name in the Navigation Pane.

FIGURE F-15: Query Design View of crosstab query

Total row

Crosstab row

Field: TourName — Tours — Group By — Row Heading
Category — Tours — Group By — Column Heading
Price — Tours — Sum — Value

Sum

Row Heading   Column Heading   Value

FIGURE F-16: Crosstab query datasheet

TourName	Adventure	Educational	Family	Service	Site Seeing
American Heritage Tour		$18,000.00			
Ames Ski Club	$11,050.00				
Bear Valley Adventures	$1,450.00				
Bigfoot Rafting Club	$910.00				
Black Sheep Hiking Club	$1,050.00				
Boy Scout Jamboree	$3,800.00				
Breeze Bay Shelling	$6,000.00				
Bridgewater Country	$9,600.00				
Bright Lights Expo					$2,400.00
Eagan Family Reunion			$2,000.00		
Franklin Family Reunion			$5,600.00		
Golden Footsteps					$2,200.00
Gunnison Bikers	$1,000.00				
Piper-Heitman Wedding			$550.00		
Red Reef Scuba	$13,500.00				
Spare Tire Ski Club	$4,200.00				
Yosemite National Park (				$2,200.00	

Category field values are column headings

TourName field values are row headings

Price field values are subtotaled

Using query wizards

Four query wizards are available to help you build queries including the Simple (which creates a select query), Crosstab, Find Duplicates, and Find Unmatched Query Wizards. Use the **Find Duplicates Query Wizard** to determine whether a table contains duplicate values in one or more fields. Use the **Find Unmatched Query Wizard** to find records in one table that do not have related records in another table. To use the query wizards, click the Query Wizard button on the CREATE tab.

Create a Report on a Query

**Learning
Outcomes**
• Create a report on
  a query
• Modify a report's
  Record Source
  property

When you want a more professional printout of the information than can be provided by a query datasheet, you use a report object. By first selecting the fields and records you want in a query and then basing the report on that query, you can easily add new fields and calculations to the report by adding them to the underlying query. When you base a report on a query, the query name is identified in the **Record Source** property of the report. **CASE** *Samantha Hooper asks you to create a report to subtotal the revenue for each tour.*

STEPS

1. **Double-click the** StateAnalysis query **in the Navigation Pane to open its datasheet**

   The StateAnalysis query contains the customer state, tour name, and price of each tour sold. Analyzing which tours are the most popular in various states will help focus marketing expenses. Creating a query to select the fields and records needed on a report is the first step in creating a report that can be easily modified later.

2. **Close the** StateAnalysis query, **click the** CREATE tab **on the Ribbon, click the** Report Wizard button, **click the** Tables/Queries list arrow, **click** Query: StateAnalysis, **click the** Select All button >> , **then click** Next

   The Report Wizard wants to group the records by the State field. This is also how you want to analyze the data.

3. **Click** Next, **click** TourName, **then click the** Select Field button > **to add the TourName field as a second grouping level, click** Next, **click** Next **to not choose any sort orders, click** Next **to accept a Stepped layout and Portrait orientation, type** State Revenue Report **as the title for the report, then click** Finish

   The report lists each tour sold within each state as many times as it has been sold. You decide to add the name of the customers who have purchased these tours to the report. First, you will need to add them to the StateAnalysis query. Given that the State Revenue Report is based on the StateAnalysis query, you can access the StateAnalysis query from Report Design View of the State Revenue Report.

4. **Right-click the** State Revenue Report tab, **click** Design View, **close the Field List if it is open, then click the** Property Sheet button **in the Tools group on the DESIGN tab**

   The Property Sheet for the State Revenue Report opens.

5. **Click the** Data tab, **click** StateAnalysis **in the Record Source property, then click the** Build button ··· , **as shown in** FIGURE F-17

   The StateAnalysis query opens in Query Design View.

6. **Close the Property Sheet, double-click the** FName field, **double-click the** LName field, **click the** Close button **on the DESIGN tab, then click** Yes **when prompted to save the changes**

   Now that the FName and LName fields have been added to the StateAnalysis query, they are available to the report.

7. **Click the** DESIGN tab, **click the** Text Box button ab , **click to the** left of the Price text box **in the Detail section, click the** Text13 label, **press** [Delete], **click** Unbound **in the text box, type** =[FName] &" "&[LName], **then press** [Enter]

   You could have added the FName and LName fields directly to the report but the information looks a little more professional as the result of one expression that calculates the entire name.

8. **Switch to Layout View, resize the new text box as shown in** FIGURE F-18 **to see the entire name, save and close the State Revenue Report, close the QuestTravel-F.accdb database, then exit Access**

FIGURE F-17: Modifying a query from the Record Source property

State Revenue Report

Report Header

Report selector button

Data tab

Page Header

State

Record Source property

State Header

State

TourName Header

Detail

Page Footer

=Now()

Report Footer

Property Sheet

Selection type: Report

Property Sheet Selection type: Report

Report

Format | Data | Event | Other | All

Record Source	StateAnalysis
Filter	
Filter On Load	No
Order By	
Order By On Load	Yes
Allow Filters	Yes

Build button

Price

Price

e " & [Page] & " of " & [Pages]

FIGURE F-18: Final State Revenue Report

State Revenue Report

State Revenue Report

State		TourName		Price
IA				
		American Heritage Tour		
		Ralph Hopper		$1,200
		Kris Goode		$1,200
		Brad Langguth		$1,200
		Lois Goode		$1,200
		Nancy Langguth		$1,200
		Ames Ski Club		
		Lois Goode		$850
		Toby Lang		$850
		Kris Goode		$850
		Elsie Lang		$850
		Brandon Larson		$850

Resize the text box as needed

Practice

Put your skills into practice with **SAM Projects**! SAM Projects for this unit can be found online. If you have a SAM account, go to www.cengage.com/sam2013 to download the most recent Project Instruction and Start Files.

Concepts Review

Identify each element of Query Design View shown in FIGURE F-19.

FIGURE F-19

Match each term with the statement that best describes it.

8. **Record Source**
9. **Select query**
10. **Wildcard character**
11. **AND criteria**
12. **Sorting**
13. **OR criteria**

a. Placing the records of a datasheet in a certain order
b. Entered on more than one row of the query design grid
c. Report property that determines what fields and records the report will display
d. Asterisk (*) or question mark (?) used in query criteria
e. Retrieves fields from related tables and displays records in a datasheet
f. Entered on one row of the query design grid

Select the best answer from the list of choices.

14. **The query datasheet can best be described as a:**
    a. Logical view of the selected data from underlying tables.
    b. Duplication of the data in the underlying table's datasheet.
    c. Separate file of data.
    d. Second copy of the data in the underlying tables.

Improving Queries

15. **Queries may *not* be used to:**
    - **a.** Calculate new fields of data.
    - **b.** Set the primary key field for a table.
    - **c.** Enter or update data.
    - **d.** Sort records.
16. **When you update data in a table that is also selected in a query:**
    - **a.** You must relink the query to the table to refresh the data.
    - **b.** The updated data is automatically displayed in the query.
    - **c.** You must also update the data in the query datasheet.
    - **d.** You can choose whether to update the data in the query.
17. **Which of the following is *not* an aggregate function available to a summary query?**
    - **a.** Avg
    - **b.** Subtotal
    - **c.** Count
    - **d.** Max
18. **The order in which records in a query are sorted is determined by:**
    - **a.** The order in which the fields are defined in the underlying table.
    - **b.** The importance of the information in the field.
    - **c.** The alphabetic order of the field names.
    - **d.** The left-to-right position of the fields in the query design grid that contain a sort order choice.
19. **A crosstab query is generally constructed with how many fields?**
    - **a.** 1
    - **b.** 3
    - **c.** 2
    - **d.** More than 5
20. **In a crosstab query, which field is the most likely candidate for the Value position?**
    - **a.** FName
    - **b.** Department
    - **c.** Cost
    - **d.** Country

Skills Review

1. **Create multitable queries.**
   - **a.** Start Access and open the Service-F.accdb database from the location where you store your Data Files, then enable content if prompted.
   - **b.** Create a new select query in Query Design View using the Names and Zips tables.
   - **c.** Add the following fields to the query design grid in this order:
     - FirstName, LastName, and Street from the Names table
     - City, State, and Zip from the Zips table
   - **d.** In Datasheet View, replace the LastName value in the Martin Chen record with *your* last name.
   - **e.** Save the query as **AddressList**, print the datasheet if requested by your instructor, then close the query.
2. **Apply sorts and view SQL.**
   - **a.** Open the AddressList query in Query Design View.
   - **b.** Drag the FirstName field from the Names field list to the third column in the query design grid to make the first three fields in the query design grid FirstName, LastName, and FirstName.
   - **c.** Add an ascending sort to the second and third fields in the query design grid, and uncheck the Show check box in the third column. The query is now sorted in ascending order by LastName, then by FirstName, though the order of the fields in the resulting datasheet still appears as FirstName, LastName.
   - **d.** Click the FILE tab, click Save As, then use Save Object As to save the query as **SortedAddressList**. View the datasheet, print the datasheet if requested by your instructor, then close the SortedAddressList query.
3. **Develop AND criteria.**
   - **a.** Right-click the SortedAddressList query in the Navigation Pane, click Copy, right-click a blank spot in the Navigation Pane, click Paste, then type **KansasC** as the name for the new query.
   - **b.** Open the KansasC query in Design View, then type **C*** (the asterisk is a wildcard) in the LastName field Criteria cell to choose all people whose last name starts with *C*. Access assists you with the syntax for this type of criterion and enters Like "C*" in the cell when you click elsewhere in the query design grid.

Skills Review (continued)

    c. Enter **KS** as the AND criterion for the State field. Be sure to enter the criterion on the same line in the query design grid as the Like "C*" criterion.

    d. View the datasheet. It should select only those people from Kansas with a last name that starts with the letter C.

    e. Enter *your* hometown in the City field of the first record to uniquely identify the printout.

    f. Save the KansasC query, print the datasheet if requested by your instructor, then close the KansasC query.

4. Develop OR criteria.

    a. Right-click the KansasC query in the Navigation Pane, click Copy, right-click a blank spot in the Navigation Pane, click Paste, then type **KansasCD** as the name for the new query.

    b. Open the KansasCD query in Design View, then enter **D*** in the second Criteria row (the or row) of the LastName field.

    c. Enter **KS** as the criterion in the second Criteria row (the or row) of the State field so that those people from KS with a last name that starts with the letter D are added to this query.

    d. View the datasheet. It should select only those people from Kansas with a last name that starts with the letter C or D. Print the datasheet if requested by your instructor, then save and close the query.

5. Create calculated fields.

    a. Create a new select query in Query Design View using only the Names table.

    b. Add the following fields to the query design grid in this order: FirstName, LastName, Birthday.

    c. Create a calculated field called Age in the fourth column of the query design grid by entering the expression: **Age: Int((Now()-[Birthday])/365)** to determine the age of each person in years based on the information in the Birthday field. The Now() function returns today's date. Now()-[Birthday] determines the number of days a person has lived. Dividing that value by 365 determines the number of years a person has lived. The Int() function is used to return the integer portion of the answer. So if a person has lived 23.5 years, Int(23.5) = 23.

    d. Sort the query in descending order on the calculated Age field.

    e. Save the query with the name **AgeCalculation**, view the datasheet, print the datasheet if requested by your instructor, then close the query.

6. Build summary queries.

    a. Create a new select query in Query Design View using the Names and Activities tables.

    b. Add the following fields: FirstName and LastName from the Names table, and Hours from the Activities table.

    c. Add the Total row to the query design grid, then change the aggregate function for the Hours field from Group By to Sum.

    d. Sort in descending order by Hours.

    e. Save the query as **HoursSummary**, view the datasheet, widen all columns so that all data is clearly visible, print the datasheet if requested by your instructor, then save and close the query.

7. Build crosstab queries.

    a. Use Query Design View to create a select query with the City and State fields from the Zips table and the Dues field from the Names table. Save the query as **DuesCrosstab**, then view the datasheet.

    b. Return to Query Design View, then click the Crosstab button to add the Total and Crosstab rows to the query design grid.

Skills Review (continued)

c. Specify City as the crosstab row heading, State as the crosstab column heading, and Dues as the summed value field within the crosstab datasheet.

d. View the datasheet as shown in **FIGURE F-20**, print the datasheet if requested by your instructor, then save and close the DuesCrosstab query.

8. Create a report on a query.

a. Use the Report Wizard to create a report on all of the fields of the SortedAddressList query. View the data by Names, add State as a grouping level, add LastName then FirstName as the ascending sort orders, use a Stepped layout and Landscape orientation, then title the report **Names by State**.

b. In Design View, open the Property Sheet for the report, then open the SortedAddressList query in Design View using the Build button on the Record Source property.

c. Add the Birthday field to the SortedAddressList query then close the query.

d. To the left of the LastName field in the Detail section, add a text box bound to the Birthday field. (*Hint*: Type **Birthday** in place of Unbound or modify the text box's Control Source property to be Birthday.) Delete the label that is automatically created to the left of the text box.

e. In Layout View, resize the City and Zip columns so that all data is clearly visible, as shown in **FIGURE F-21**. Be sure to preview the report to make sure it fits on the paper.

f. If requested by your instructor, print the first page of the Names by State report, save and close it, close the Service-F.accdb database, then exit Access.

FIGURE F-20

City	IA	KS	MO
Blue Springs			$50.00
Bridgewater	$50.00		
Buehler		$50.00	
Des Moines	$25.00		
Dripping Spring		$25.00	
Flat Hills		$50.00	
Fontanelle	$50.00		
Greenfield	$50.00		
Kansas City		$50.00	$100.00
Langguth		$25.00	
Leawood			$50.00
Lee's Summit			$75.00
Lenexa		$25.00	
Manawatta		$25.00	
Manhattan		$25.00	
Overland Park		$100.00	
Red Bridge		$425.00	
Running Deer			$25.00
Shawnee		$200.00	
Student Home		$100.00	

FIGURE F-21

Names by State

	State	LastName	FirstName	Street	City	Zip
IA						
10/6/1961		Goode	Loraine	900 Barnes Road	Greenfield	50265
7/16/1963		Martin	Benjamin	5253 Duck Creek Dr	Des Moines	52240
9/30/1960		May	Jaye	1515 Maple St	Fontanelle	50033
8/19/1980		StudentLastName	Martin	1010 Green St	Bridgewater	50022
KS						
6/4/1979		Alman	Josiah	2505 McGee St	Flat Hills	64141
10/1/1989		Bovier	Mary	110 College Blvd	Manhattan	66031
9/4/1961		Browning	Forrest	8206 Marshall Drive	Dripping Springs	66214
1/1/1954		Cabriella	Holly	52520 W. 505 Terr	Student Home Town	66215
6/19/1960		Camel	Mark	66020 King Street	Red Bridge	66210
6/12/1958		Custard	Mildred	66900 College Blvd	Red Bridge	66210

Independent Challenge 1

As the manager of a music store's instrument rental program, you have created a database to track rentals to schoolchildren. Now that several rentals have been made, you want to query the database for several different datasheet printouts to analyze school information.

   a. Start Access and open the MusicStore-F.accdb database from the location where you store your Data Files, then enable content if prompted.

   b. In Query Design View, create a query with the following fields in the following order:

     • SchoolName field from the Schools table

     • RentalDate field from the Rentals table

     • Description field from the Instruments table

     (*Hint*: Although you don't use any fields from the Customers table, you need to add the Customers table to this query to make the connection between the Schools table and the Rentals table.)

   c. Sort in ascending order by SchoolName, then in ascending order by RentalDate.

   d. Save the query as **SchoolRentals**, view the datasheet, replace Lincoln Elementary with *your* elementary school name, print the datasheet if requested by your instructor, then close the datasheet.

   e. Copy and paste the SchoolRentals query as **SchoolCount**, then open the SchoolCount query in Query Design View.

   f. Modify the SchoolCount query by deleting the Description field. Use the Totals button to group the records by SchoolName and to count the RentalDate field. Print the datasheet if requested by your instructor, then save and close the SchoolCount query.

   g. Create a crosstab query named **SchoolCrosstab** based on the SchoolRentals query. (*Hint*: Select the SchoolRentals query in the Show Table dialog box.) Use Description as the column heading position and SchoolName in the row heading position. Count the RentalDate field.

   h. View the SchoolCrosstab query in Datasheet View. Resize each column to best fit the data in that column, then print the datasheet if requested by your instructor. Save and close the SchoolCrosstab query.

   i. Copy and paste the SchoolRentals query as **ElementaryRentals**. Modify the ElementaryRentals query in Query Design View so that only those schools with the word **Elementary** in the SchoolName field are displayed. (*Hint*: You have to use wildcard characters in the criteria.)

   j. View the ElementaryRentals query in Datasheet View, print it if requested by your instructor, then save and close the datasheet.

   k. Close the MusicStore-F.accdb database, then exit Access.

Independent Challenge 2

As the manager of a music store's instrument rental program, you have created a database to track rentals to schoolchildren. You can use queries to analyze customer and rental information.

   a. Start Access and open the MusicStore-F.accdb database from the location where you store your Data Files, then enable content if prompted.

   b. In Query Design View, create a query with the following fields in the following order:

     • Description and MonthlyFee fields from the Instruments table

     • LastName, Zip, and City fields from the Customers table

     (*Hint*: Although you don't need any fields from the Rentals table in this query's datasheet, you need to add the Rentals table to this query to make the connection between the Customers table and the Instruments table.)

Independent Challenge 2 (continued)

c. Add the Zip field to the first column of the query grid, and specify an ascending sort order for this field. Uncheck the Show check box for the first Zip field so that it does not appear in the datasheet.

d. Add an ascending sort order to the Description field.

e. Save the query as **ZipAnalysis**.

f. View the datasheet, replace Johnson with *your* last name in the LastName field, print the datasheet if requested by your instructor, then save and close the datasheet. (*Note:* If you later view this query in Design View, note that Access changes the way the sort orders are specified but in a way that gives you the same results in the datasheet.)

g. In Query Design View, create a query with the following fields in the following order:
- Description and MonthlyFee fields from the Instruments table
- LastName, Zip, and City fields from the Customers table

(*Hint:* You'll need to add the Rentals table.)

h. Add criteria to find the records where the Description is equal to **viola**. Sort in ascending order based on the Zip then City fields. Save the query as **Violas**, view the datasheet, print it if requested by your instructor, then close the datasheet.

i. Copy and paste the Violas query as **DesMoinesViolas**, then modify the DesMoinesViolas query with AND criteria to further specify that the City must be **Des Moines**. View the datasheet, print it if requested by your instructor, then save and close the datasheet.

j. Copy and paste the DesMoinesViolas query as **DesMoinesOrViolas**, then modify the DesMoinesOrViolas query so that all records with a Description equal to Violas or a City value of **Des Moines** are selected. View the datasheet, print it if requested by your instructor, then save and close the datasheet.

k. Close the MusicStore-F.accdb database, then exit Access.

Independent Challenge 3

As a real estate agent, you use an Access database to track residential real estate listings in your area. You can use queries to answer questions about the real estate properties and to analyze home values.

a. Start Access and open the RealEstate-F.accdb database from the location where you store your Data Files, then enable content if prompted.

b. In Query Design View, create a query with the following fields in the following order:
- AgencyName from the Agencies table
- RFirst and RLast from the Realtors table
- SqFt and Asking from the Listings table

c. Sort the records in descending order by the Asking field.

d. Save the query as **AskingPrice**, view the datasheet, enter *your* last name instead of Dell for the most expensive listing, then print the datasheet if requested by your instructor.

e. In Query Design View, modify the AskingPrice query by creating a calculated field that determines price per square foot. The new calculated field's name should be **SquareFootCost**, and the expression should be the asking price divided by the square foot field, or **[Asking]/[SqFt]**.

f. Remove any former sort orders, sort the records in descending order based on the SquareFootCost calculated field, and view the datasheet. Save and close the AskingPrice query. ###### means the data is too wide to display in the column. You can make the data narrower and also align it by applying a Currency format.

g. Reopen the AskingPrice query in Query Design View, right-click the calculated SquareFootCost field, click Properties, then change the Format property to Currency. View the datasheet, print it if requested by your instructor, then save and close the AskingPrice query.

h. Copy and paste the AskingPrice query as **CostSummary**.

Independent Challenge 3 (continued)

i. In Design View of the CostSummary query, delete the RFirst, RLast, and SqFt fields.

j. View the datasheet, then change the Sun and Ski Realtors agency name to *your* last name followed by **Realtors**.

k. In Design View, add the Total row, then sum the Asking field and use the Avg (Average) aggregate function for the SquareFootCost calculated field.

l. In Datasheet View, add the Total row and display the sum of the SumOfAsking field. Widen all columns as needed, as shown in FIGURE F-22.

m. If requested by your Instructor, print the CostSummary query, then save and close it.

n. Close the RealEstate-F.accdb database, then exit Access.

FIGURE F-22

AgencyName	SumOfAsking	SquareFootCost
Four Lakes Realtors	$2,359,512.00	$88.02
Marvin and Pam Realtors	$477,800.00	$77.42
StudentLastName Realtors	$1,629,350.00	$66.24
Total	$4,466,662.00	

Independent Challenge 4: Explore

You're working with the local high school guidance counselor to help him with an Access database used to record college scholarship opportunities. You help him with the database by creating several queries. (*Note: To complete this Independent Challenge, make sure you are connected to the Internet.*)

a. Start Access, open the Scholarships-F.accdb database from the location where you store your Data Files, then enable content if prompted.

b. Conduct research on the Internet or at your school to find at least five new scholarships relevant to your major, and enter them into the Scholarships table.

c. Conduct research on the Internet or at your school to find at least one new scholarship relevant to a Business major as well as a Science major, and enter the two records into the Scholarships table.

d. Create a query called **Business** that displays all fields from the Scholarships table that selects all records with a Business major. If requested by your instructor, print the Business query then save and close it.

e. Copy and paste the Business query as **BusinessOrScience**. Add OR criteria to the BusinessOrScience query to select all scholarships in the Business or Science majors. If requested by your instructor, print the BusinessOrScience query then save and close it.

Independent Challenge 4: Explore (continued)

f. Create a new query that selects the ScholarshipName, DueDate, and Amount from the Scholarships table, and sorts the records in ascending order by DueDate, then descending order by Amount. Name the query **ScholarshipMasterList**. If requested by your instructor, print the ScholarshipMasterList query then save and close it.

g. Use the Report Wizard to create a report on the ScholarshipMasterList, do not add any grouping levels, sort the records in ascending order by ScholarshipName, use a Tabular layout and a Portrait orientation, and title the report **Scholarship Master List**.

h. In Design View of the Scholarship Master List report, open the Property Sheet, and use the Record Source Build button to open the ScholarshipMasterList query in Design View. Add the Major field to the query, save and close it.

i. In Report Design View, open the Group, Sort, and Total pane, add the Major field as a grouping field, then move it above the Sort by ScholarshipName sort field.

j. Add a text box to the Major Header section, and bind it to the Major field. (*Hint*: Type **Major** in place of Unbound or modify the text box's Control Source property to be Major.) Delete the label that is automatically created to the left of the text box. Preview the report, as shown in **FIGURE F-23**, then print it if requested by your instructor.

k. Save and close the Scholarship Master List report, close the Scholarships-F.accdb database, then exit Access.

FIGURE F-23

ScholarshipName	DueDate	Amount
Scholarship Master List		
All Majors		
Achievement Community Scholarship	2/16/2013	$2,000.00
Alpha Kappa Alpha	3/30/2013	$1,000.00
Balanced Man Scholarship Sigma Phi	3/29/2014	$1,000.00
Delta Sigma Phi Fraternity at K-State Scholarship	3/26/2013	$500.00
Great Plains Associations of College Admissions Counseling	2/27/2013	$1,000.00
Hispanic Scholarship of Greater Kansas City	3/1/2014	$1,000.00
Kohl's Kids Who Care	3/13/2014	$1,000.00
Masonic Grand Lodge of AF & AM of Kansas	10/30/2013	$500.00

Visual Workshop

Open the Training-F.accdb database from the location where you store your Data Files, then enable content if prompted. In Query Design View, create a new select query with the DeptName field from the Departments table, the CourseCost field from the Courses table, and the Description field from the Courses table. (*Hint*: You will also have to add the Employees and Enrollments tables to Query Design View to build relationships from the Departments table to the Courses table.) Save the query with the name **DepartmentCrosstab**, then display it as a crosstab query, as shown in **FIGURE F-24**. Print the DepartmentCrosstab query if requested by your instructor, save and close it, then close the Training-F.accdb database.

FIGURE F-24

Description	Accounting	Engineering	Executive	Human Resc	Information	Legal	Marketing	Operations	Research	Shipping	Training
Access Case Problems	$400.00	$200.00	$200.00			$600.00	$200.00	$200.00			$200.00
Computer Fundamentals	$200.00	$200.00	$200.00	$400.00	$200.00	$800.00	$600.00		$400.00	$400.00	$400.00
Dynamite Customer Service Skills			$100.00	$100.00	$100.00	$100.00	$200.00		$100.00		
Employee Benefits Made Clear		$50.00	$50.00	$100.00	$50.00	$150.00	$150.00	$50.00	$100.00	$100.00	$50.00
Excel Case Problems	$200.00		$200.00	$200.00				$400.00	$200.00	$400.00	$200.00
Intermediate Access	$800.00	$400.00	$400.00			$1,200.00	$400.00	$400.00			$400.00
Intermediate Excel	$400.00		$200.00	$200.00		$200.00		$400.00	$200.00	$400.00	$200.00
Intermediate Internet Explorer	$400.00		$400.00	$400.00	$200.00	$800.00	$400.00	$200.00	$200.00	$200.00	$400.00
Intermediate Phone Skills	$300.00		$150.00			$300.00		$300.00	$150.00		$150.00
Intermediate PowerPoint	$400.00	$200.00	$200.00	$200.00		$600.00	$200.00	$200.00	$200.00	$200.00	$400.00
Intermediate Tax Planning	$100.00		$100.00	$50.00	$50.00	$50.00		$50.00	$100.00	$100.00	$50.00
Intermediate Windows			$200.00	$400.00	$200.00	$200.00	$400.00		$400.00	$400.00	$200.00
Intermediate Word			$200.00	$200.00	$200.00	$200.00	$400.00		$200.00		
Internet Fundamentals		$200.00	$200.00	$400.00	$200.00	$600.00	$600.00		$400.00	$400.00	$400.00
Introduction to Access	$400.00	$200.00	$200.00	$200.00		$600.00	$400.00	$200.00			$200.00
Introduction to Excel	$400.00		$400.00	$200.00		$200.00		$400.00	$400.00	$400.00	$200.00
Introduction to Insurance Planning	$150.00	$75.00	$75.00	$75.00		$225.00	$75.00	$75.00	$75.00	$150.00	$150.00
Introduction to Internet Explorer	$400.00	$200.00	$400.00	$400.00	$200.00	$800.00	$600.00	$200.00	$400.00	$200.00	$400.00
Introduction to Networking		$200.00	$200.00	$400.00	$200.00	$400.00	$600.00		$400.00	$400.00	$200.00
Introduction to Outlook	$400.00	$200.00		$400.00		$600.00	$400.00	$400.00	$200.00	$400.00	$400.00
Introduction to Phone Skills	$300.00	$150.00	$150.00			$450.00	$150.00	$300.00	$150.00	$150.00	$150.00
Introduction to PowerPoint	$400.00	$200.00	$200.00	$400.00	$200.00	$800.00	$600.00	$200.00	$200.00	$200.00	$400.00
Introduction to Project	$1,200.00	$800.00	$1,200.00	$400.00		$2,000.00	$1,600.00	$1,600.00	$1,200.00	$1,600.00	$1,200.00
Introduction to Tax Planning	$100.00		$100.00	$50.00	$50.00	$100.00	$50.00	$50.00	$100.00	$100.00	$50.00
Introduction to Windows		$200.00	$200.00	$400.00	$200.00	$600.00	$600.00	$200.00	$400.00	$400.00	$400.00

Record: 1 of 31 | No Filter | Search

Enhancing Forms

CASE ▶ Samantha Hooper wants to improve the usability of the forms in the QuestTravel database. You will build and improve forms by working with subforms, combo boxes, option groups, and command buttons to enter, find, and filter data.

Unit Objectives

After completing this unit, you will be able to:

- Use Form Design View
- Add subforms
- Align control edges
- Add a combo box for data entry

- Add a combo box to find records
- Add command buttons
- Add option groups
- Add tab controls

Files You Will Need

QuestTravel-G.accdb
Service-G.accdb
MusicStore-G.accdb

RealEstate-G.accdb
Scholarships-G.accdb
Baseball-G.accdb

©Tumanyan/Shutterstock

Use Form Design View

A **form** is a database object designed to make data easy to find, enter, and edit. You create forms by using **controls**, such as labels, text boxes, combo boxes, and command buttons, which help you manipulate data more quickly and reliably than working in a datasheet. A form that contains a **subform** allows you to work with related records in an easy-to-use screen arrangement. For example, using a form/subform combination, you can display customer data and all of the orders placed by that customer at the same time. **Design View** of a form is devoted to working with the detailed structure of a form. The purpose of Design View is to provide full access to all of the modifications you can make to the form. **CASE** ▷ *Samantha Hooper has asked you to create a customer entry form. You create this form from scratch in Form Design View.*

STEPS

1. **Start Access, then open the** QuestTravel-G.accdb database **from the location where you store your Data Files, enable content if prompted, click the** CREATE tab **on the Ribbon, then click the** Form Design button **in the Forms group**

   A blank form is displayed in Design View. Your first step is to connect the blank form to an underlying **record source**, a table or query that contains the data you want to display on the form. The fields in the record source populate the **Field List**, a small window that lists the fields in the record source. The Customers table should be the record source for the CustomerEntry form.

2. **Double-click the** form selector button ■ **to open the form's Property Sheet, click the** Data tab **in the Property Sheet, click the** Record Source list arrow, **then click** Customers

   The Record Source property lists all existing tables and queries. With the record source selected, you're ready to add controls to the form. Recall that bound controls, such as text boxes and combo boxes, display data from the record source, and unbound controls, such as labels and lines, clarify information for the person using the form.

3. **Click the** Add Existing Fields button **in the Tools group to open the Field List, click** CustNo **in the Field List, press and hold** [Shift], **click** Photo **in the Field List, then drag the selection to the form at about the** 1" **mark on the horizontal ruler**

   The fields of the Customers table are added to the form, as shown in **FIGURE G-1**. The FirstContact field is added as a combo box because it has Lookup properties. The other fields are text boxes except for the Photo field, which is inserted as an **Attachment** control given the Photo field has an Attachment data type. Labels are created for each bound control and are captioned with the field name. You can rearrange the controls by moving them.

4. **Click the** form **to deselect all controls, click the** Phone text box, **press and hold** [Ctrl], **click the** FirstContact combo box **and** Photo Attachment box **to add them to the selection, then release** [Ctrl]

   Selected controls will move as a group.

5. **Use the** ⁺ℛ **pointer to drag the selected controls up and to the right to position them about** 0.25" **to the right of the name and address controls, then click the** View button ▦ **to switch to Form View**

   The new form in Form View is shown in **FIGURE G-2**. You will improve and enhance it in later lessons.

6. **Click the** Save button ▦ **on the Quick Access toolbar, type** CustomerEntry **as the form name, click** OK, **then close the CustomerEntry form**

FIGURE G-1: Adding fields in Form Design View

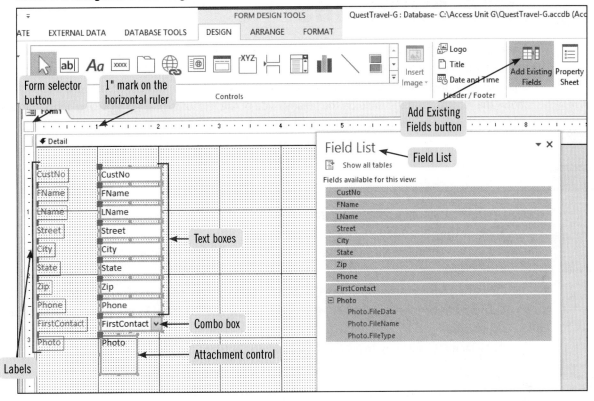

FIGURE G-2: New form in Form View

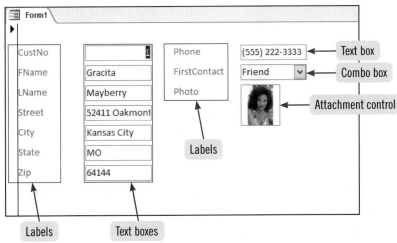

Add Subforms

Learning
Outcomes
• Add a subform to
  a form
• Resize columns in
  a subform
• Define form layouts

A **subform** is a form within a form. The form that contains the subform is called the **main form**. A main form/subform combination displays the records of two tables that are related in a one-to-many relationship. The main form shows data from the table on the "one" side of the relationship, and the subform shows the records from the table on the "many" side of the relationship. **CASE** *You decide to add a subform to the CustomerEntry form to show related sales for each customer.*

STEPS

1. **Open the** CustomerEntry form **in Design View, then close the Field List and Property Sheet if they are open**

   You add new controls to a form by dragging fields from the Field List or selecting the control on the DESIGN tab of the Ribbon.

TROUBLE
If the SubForm
Wizard doesn't start,
click the More but-
ton in the Controls
group, then click Use
Control Wizards to
toggle it on.

2. **Click the** More button ▾ **in the Controls group to view all of the form controls, click the** Subform/Subreport button ▦**, then click below the** Zip label **in the form, as shown in** FIGURE G-3

   The Subform Wizard opens to help you add a subform control to the form.

QUICK TIP
To remove a form
layout, you must
work in Form
Design View.

3. **Click** Next **to use existing Tables and Queries as the data for the subform, click the** Tables/Queries list arrow, **click** Query: SalesInfo, **click the** Select All Fields button >> **, click** Next, **click** Next **to accept the option Show SalesInfo for each record in Customers using CustNo, then click** Finish **to accept SalesInfo subform as the name for the new subform control**

   A form **layout** is the general way that the data and controls are arranged on the form. By default, subforms display their controls in a columnar layout in Design View, but their **Default View property** is set to Datasheet. See **TABLE G-1** for a description of form layouts. The difference in form layout is apparent when you view the form in Form View.

4. **Click the** View button ▦ **to switch to Form View, then navigate to** CustNo 6, Kristen Collins, **who has purchased four different tours, as shown in the subform**

   Sales information appears in the subform in a datasheet layout. As you move through the customer records of the main form, the information changes in the subform to reflect sales for each customer. The main form and subform are linked by the common CustNo field. Resize the columns of the subform to make the information easier to read.

QUICK TIP
Double-click the line
between field names
to automatically
adjust the width of
the column to the
widest field entry.

5. **Point to the line between field names in the subform and use the** ↔ **pointer to resize the column widths of the subform, as shown in** FIGURE G-4

   The CustomerEntry form displays two navigation bars. The inside bar is for the subform records, and the outside bar is for the main form records.

6. **Right-click the** CustomerEntry form tab, **click** Close, **then click** Yes **when prompted to save changes to both form objects**

FIGURE G-3: Adding a subform control

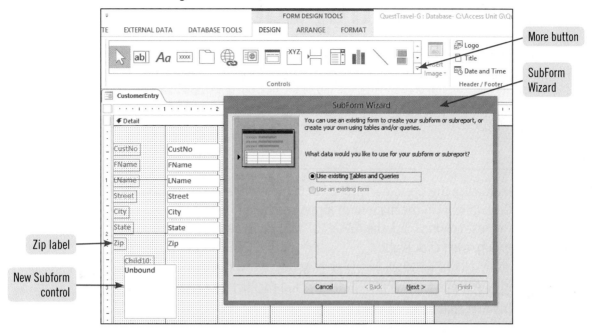

FIGURE G-4: CustomerEntry form and SalesInfo subform

TABLE G-1: Form layouts

layout	description
Columnar	Default view for main forms; each field appears on a separate row with a label to its left
Tabular	Each field appears as an individual column, and each record is presented as a row
Datasheet	Default view for subforms; fields and records are displayed as they appear in a table or query datasheet

©2014 Cengage Learning

Linking the form and subform

If the form and subform do not appear to be correctly linked, examine the subform's Property Sheet, paying special attention to the **Link Child Fields** and **Link Master Fields** properties on the Data tab. These properties tell you which field serves as the link between the main form and subform.

Align Control Edges

Learning
Outcomes
• Select multiple
controls together
• Align the edges of
controls

Well-designed forms are logical, easy to read, and easy to use. Aligning the edges of controls can make a big difference in form usability. To align the left, right, top, or bottom edges of two or more controls, use the Align button on the ARRANGE tab of the Ribbon. **CASE** ▶ *Samantha Hooper asks you to align and rearrange the controls in the main form to make it easier to read, and to resize the Photo box so it is much larger.*

STEPS

QUICK TIP
To select multiple
controls, click the
first control, then
press and hold either
[Ctrl] or [Shift] to
add more controls to
the selection.

1. **Right-click the CustomerEntry form in the Navigation Pane, click Design View, click the CustNo label in the main form, press and hold [Shift] while clicking the other labels in the first column, click the ARRANGE tab, click the Align button in the Sizing & Ordering group, then click Right**

   Aligning the right edges of these labels makes them easier to read and closer to the data they describe.

2. **Click the CustNo text box, press and hold [Shift] while clicking the other text boxes in the first column, then drag a middle-left sizing handle to the left**

   Leave only a small amount of space between the labels in the first column and the bound controls in the second column, as shown in **FIGURE G-5**.

3. **Click the form to deselect the selected controls, press and hold [Shift] to select the three labels in the third column of the main form, click the Align button in the Sizing & Ordering group, then click Right**

   With the main form's labels and text boxes better sized and aligned, you decide to delete the Photo label, and move and resize the Photo box to make it much larger.

TROUBLE
The Undo button
↺ will undo multi-
ple actions in Form
Design View.

4. **Click the form to deselect any selected controls, click the Photo label, press [Delete], click the Photo box to select it, use the ⬚ pointer to move it to the upper-right corner of the form, use the ⤢ pointer to drag the lower-left sizing handle to fill the space, right-click the CustomerEntry form tab, then click Form View to review the changes**

   The final CustomerEntry form should look like **FIGURE G-6**. Use the subform to enter a new sale to Gracita Mayberry.

5. **Click the SaleDate field in the second record of the subform, use the Calendar Picker to choose 8/1/14, press [Tab], enter 3 for the TourNo, then press [Tab]**

   Once you identify the correct TourNo, the rest of the fields describing that tour are automatically added to the record. Continue to make additional enhancements in Form Design View as needed to match **FIGURE G-6**.

6. **Save and close the CustomerEntry form**

Anchoring, margins, and padding

Anchoring means to position and tie a control to other controls so they move or resize together. The control **margin** is the space between the content inside the control and the outside border of the control. Control **padding** is the space between the outside borders of adjacent controls. To apply anchoring, margins, or padding, work in Form Design View. Click the ARRANGE tab, select the control(s) you want to modify, and choose the Control Margins, Control Padding, or Anchoring buttons in the Position group.

FIGURE G-5: Aligning and resizing controls

FIGURE G-6: Final CustomerEntry form

Add a Combo Box for Data Entry

Learning Outcomes
• Add a combo box to a form
• Modify combo box properties
• Use a combo box for data entry

If a finite set of values can be identified for a field, using a combo box instead of a text box control on a form allows the user to select a value from the list, which increases data entry accuracy and speed. Both the **list box** and **combo box** controls provide a list of values from where the user can choose an entry. A combo box also allows the user to type an entry from the keyboard; therefore, it is a "combination" of the list box and text box controls. You can create a combo box by using the **Combo Box Wizard**, or you can change an existing text box or list box into a combo box. Fields with Lookup properties are automatically created as combo boxes on new forms. Foreign key fields are also good candidates for combo boxes. **CASE** *Samantha Hooper asks you to change the TourNo field in the subform of the CustomerEntry form into a combo box so that when a customer purchases a new tour, users can choose the tour from a list instead of entering the TourNo value from the keyboard.*

STEPS

1. **Open the CustomerEntry form in Design View, click the TourNo text box in the subform to select it, right-click the TourNo text box, point to Change To on the shortcut menu, then click Combo Box**

   Now that the control has been changed from a text box to a combo box, you need to populate the list with the appropriate values.

   QUICK TIP
   A brief description of the property appears in the status bar.

2. **Click the Property Sheet button in the Tools group, click the Data tab in the Property Sheet, click the Row Source property box, then click the Build button [...]**

   Clicking the Build button for the **Row Source property** opens the Query Builder window, which allows you to select the field values you want to display in the combo box list. You want to select the TourNo and TourName fields for the list, which are both stored in the Tours table.

3. **Double-click Tours, then click Close in the Show Table dialog box**

4. **Double-click TourNo in the Tours field list to add it to the query grid, double-click TourName, click the Sort list arrow for the TourName field, click Ascending, click the Close button on the DESIGN tab, then click Yes to save the changes**

   The beginning of a SELECT statement is displayed in the Row Source property, as shown in **FIGURE G-7**. This is an SQL (Structured Query Language) statement and can be modified by clicking the Build button [...]. If you save the query with a name, the query name will appear in the Row Source property.

   QUICK TIP
   The title bar of the Property Sheet identifies the name of the control with which you are currently working.

5. **With the TourNo combo box still selected, click the Format tab in the Property Sheet, click the Column Count property, change 1 to 2, click the Column Widths property, type 0.5;2, click the List Width property and change Auto to 2.5, save the form, then display it in Form View**

   Entering 0.5;2 sets the width of the first column to 0.5 inches and the width of the second column to 2 inches. To test the new combo box, you add another new sales record in the subform.

6. **Move to the second record for CustNo 2, click the TourNo list arrow in the second record in the subform, scroll as needed and click Franklin Family Reunion on the list, press [Tab], enter 9/1/14 as the SaleDate value, then press [Enter]**

   The new record is entered as shown in **FIGURE G-8**. Selecting a specific TourNo automatically fills in the correct Tour fields for that TourNo number.

FIGURE G-7: Changing the TourNo field to a combo box

Format tab

SELECT SQL statement in Row Source property

TourNo field changed to combo box

FIGURE G-8: Using the TourNo combo box to enter a new record

CustNo 2

TourNo field now functions as a combo box

Choosing between a combo box and a list box

The list box and combo box controls are very similar, but the combo box is more popular for two reasons. While both provide a list of values from which the user can choose to make an entry in a field, the combo box also allows the user to make a unique entry from the keyboard (unless the **Limit To List property** is set to Yes). More important, however, is that most users like the drop-down list action of the combo box.

Add a Combo Box to Find Records

**Learning
Outcomes**
• Add a combo box
  to find records
• Modify the Row
  Source property
• Search for data
  with a combo box

Most combo boxes are used to enter data; however, you can also use a combo box to find records. Often, controls used for navigation are placed in the Form Header section to make them easy to find. **Sections** determine where controls appear on the screen and print on paper. See **TABLE G-2** for more information on form sections. **CASE** *You decide to add a combo box to the Form Header section to quickly locate customers in the CustomerEntry form.*

STEPS

1. **Right-click the CustomerEntry form tab, click Design View, close the Property Sheet if it is open, then click the Title button in the Header/Footer group on the DESIGN tab**

   The **Form Header** section opens and displays a label captioned with the name of the form. You modify and resize the label.

2. **Click between the words Customer and Entry in the label in the Form Header, press the [Spacebar], then use the ←→ pointer to drag the middle-right sizing handle to the left to about the 3" mark on the horizontal ruler**

   Now you have space on the right side of the Form Header section to add a combo box to find records.

3. **Click the Combo Box button 📋 in the Controls group, click in the Form Header at about the 5" mark on the horizontal ruler, click the Find a record option button in the Combo Box Wizard, click Next, double-click LName, double-click FName, click Next, click Next to accept the column widths and hide the key column, type Find Customer: as the label for the combo box, then click Finish**

   The new combo box is placed in the Form Header section, as shown in **FIGURE G-9**. The accompanying label is hard to read because of the text color. You modify the label and widen the combo box.

4. **Click the Find Customer: label, click the HOME tab, click the Font Color button arrow
   🅰 ▾, click the Dark Blue, Text 2 color box (top row, fourth from the left), click the Unbound combo box, use the ←→ pointer to drag the middle-right sizing handle to the right edge of the form to widen the combo box, then click the View button 📄**

   You test the combo box in Form View.

5. **Click the Find Customer: list arrow, then click Braven, Samantha**

   The combo box works to find the customer named Samantha Braven as intended, but the combo box list entries are not in alphabetical order. You fix this in Form Design View by working with the Property Sheet of the combo box.

6. **Right-click the CustomerEntry form tab, click Design View, double-click the edge of the Unbound combo box in the Form Header to open its Property Sheet, click the Data tab, click SELECT in the Row Source property, then click the Build button ⋯**

   The Query Builder opens, allowing you to modify the fields or sort order of the values in the combo box list.

7. **Click the Sort cell for LName, click Ascending, click Ascending in the Sort cell for FName, click the Close button on the DESIGN tab, click Yes when prompted to save changes, click the View button 📄, then click the Find Customer: list arrow**

   This time, the combo box list is sorted in ascending order by last name, then by first name, as shown in **FIGURE G-10**.

8. **Scroll and click Taylor, Tim to test the combo box again, then save and close the CustomerEntry form**

   To modify the number of items displayed in the list, use the **List Rows property** on the Format tab.

Enhancing Forms

FIGURE G-9: Adding a combo box to find records

Form Header section

Customer Entry label has been modified

3" mark · Controls · 5" mark

Combo Box button

New combo box

Form Header
Customer Entry · Find Customer: · Unbound

Detail
Photo
CustNo · CustNo · Phone · Phone
FName · FName · FirstContact · FirstContact

FIGURE G-10: Using a combo box to find customers

Customer Entry · Find Customer: · Braven

Combo box is resized

Font color is easier to read

		Braven	Samantha
CustNo	1	Phone	(555) 222-3333	Cabriella	Daniel
FName	Gracita	FirstContact	Friend	Camel	Tom
LName	Mayberry			Collins	Kristen
Street	52411 Oakmont Rd			Diverman	Nancy
City	Kansas City			Dotey	Kathryn
State	MO			Duman	Anne
Zip	64144			Eahlie	Brad

Combo box values are sorted by last name, then first name

Eckert · Mary Jane
Edwards · Hannah
Edwards · Marcus
Goode · Kris
Goode · Lois
Hammer · Jose
Hope · Kelsey
Hopper · Ralph

SalesInfo subform

CustNo	TourNo	SaleDate	TourName	Tour
1	2	7/1/2014	Red Reef Scuba	
1	3	8/1/2014	Ames Ski Club	01/02/2015	7 Breckenridge
*				

TABLE G-2: Form sections

section	description
Detail	Appears once for every record
Form Header	Appears at the top of the form and often contains command buttons or a label with the title of the form
Form Footer	Appears at the bottom of the form and often contains command buttons or a label with instructions on how to use the form
Page Header	Appears at the top of a printed form with information such as page numbers or dates
Page Footer	Appears at the bottom of a printed form with information such as page numbers or dates

Access 2013

Add Command Buttons

You use a **command button** to perform a common action in Form View such as printing the current record, opening another form, or closing the current form. Command buttons are often added to the Form Header or Form Footer sections. **CASE** ▶ *You add command buttons to the Form Footer section of the CustomerEntry form to help other Quest Specialty Travel employees print the current record and close the form.*

STEPS

1. **Right-click the CustomerEntry form in the Navigation Pane, click Design View, close the Property Sheet if it is open, then scroll to the bottom of the form to display the Form Footer section**

   Good form design gives users everything they need in a logical location. You decide to use the Form Footer section for all of your form's command buttons.

2. **Click the Button button 🔲 in the Controls group, then click in the Form Footer at the 1" mark**

   The Command Button Wizard opens, listing 28 of the most popular actions for the command button, organized within six categories, as shown in **FIGURE G-11**.

3. **Click Record Operations in the Categories list, click Print Record in the Actions list, click Next, click the Text option button, click Next to accept the default text of Print Record, type PrintRecord as the meaningful button name, then click Finish**

   Adding a command button to print only the current record prevents the user from using the Print option on the File tab, which prints *all* records. You also want to add a command button to close the form.

4. **Click the Button button 🔲 in the Controls group, then click to the right of the Print Record button in the Form Footer section**

5. **Click Form Operations in the Categories list, click Close Form in the Actions list, click Next, click the Text option button, click Next to accept the default text of Close Form, type CloseForm as the meaningful button name, then click Finish**

   To test your command buttons, you switch to Form View.

6. **Click the Save button 🔲 on the Quick Access toolbar, click the View button 🔲 to review the form, as shown in FIGURE G-12, click the Print Record button you added in the Form Footer section, then click OK to confirm that only one record prints**

7. **Click the Close Form button in the Form Footer section to close the form**

Shape effects

Shape effects provide a special visual impact (such as shadow, glow, soft edges, and bevel) to command buttons. To apply a shape effect, work in Form Design View. Click the FORMAT tab, select the command button you want to modify, then click the Shape Effects button in the Control Formatting group to display the options.

FIGURE G-11: Command Button Wizard

FIGURE G-12: Final Customer Entry form with two command buttons

Add Option Groups

Learning Outcomes
• Add an option group to a form
• Add option buttons to an option group
• Use option buttons to edit data

An **option group** is a bound control used in place of a text box when only a *few* values are available for a field. You add one **option button** control within the option group box for each possible field value. Option buttons within an option group are mutually exclusive; only one can be chosen at a time. **CASE** ▶ *Samantha Hooper asks you to build a new form to view tours and sales information. You decide to use an option group to work with the data in the Duration field because there are only a handful of possible duration values for Quest tours.*

STEPS

1. **Click the Tours table in the Navigation Pane, click the CREATE tab, then click the Form button in the Forms group**

   A form/subform combination is created and displayed in Layout View, showing tour information in the main form and sales records in the subform. You delete the Duration text box and resize the controls to provide room for an option group.

   TROUBLE
   The blank place-holder is where the Duration text box formerly appeared.

2. **Click the Duration text box, press [Delete], click the blank placeholder, press [Delete], click the right edge of any text box, then use the ↔ pointer to drag the right edge of the controls to the left so they are about half as wide**

   You add the Duration field back to the form as an option group control using the blank space on the right that you created.

3. **Right-click the Tours form tab, click Design View, click the DESIGN tab on the Ribbon, click the Option Group button [XYZ] in the Controls group, then click to the right of the TourNo text box**

   The Option Group Wizard starts and prompts for label names. All the tours sold by Quest Specialty Travel have a duration of 3, 4, 5, 7, 10, or 14 days, so the labels and values will describe this data.

   TROUBLE
   FIGURE G-13 shows the completed Label Names and Values in the Option Group Wizard at the end of Step 4.

4. **Enter the Label Names shown in FIGURE G-13, click Next, click the No, I don't want a default option button, click Next, then enter the Values to correspond with their labels, as shown in FIGURE G-13**

   The Values are the actual data that are entered into the field and correspond with the **Option Value property** of each option button. The Label Names are clarifying text.

5. **Click Next, click the Store the value in this field list arrow, click Duration, click Next, click Next to accept Option buttons in an Etched style, type Duration as the caption for the option group, then click Finish**

   View and work with the new option group in Form View.

6. **Click the View button [≡] to switch to Form View, click the Next record button [▶] in the navigation bar for the main form twice to move to the Ames Ski Club tour, then click the 5 days option button**

   Your screen should look like FIGURE G-14. You changed the duration of this tour from 7 to 5 days.

7. **Right-click the Tours form tab, click Close, click Yes when prompted to save changes, then click OK to accept Tours as the form name**

Enhancing Forms

FIGURE G-13: Option Group Label Names and Values

FIGURE G-14: Tours form with option group for Duration field

Duration label

Tours	

Tours

TourNo	3
TourName	Ames Ski Club
TourStartDate	01/02/2015
City	Breckenridge
StateAbbrev	CO
Category	Adventure
Price	$850

Duration
- ○ 3 days
- ○ 4 days
- ● 5 days
- ○ 7 days
- ○ 10 days
- ○ 14 days

Option buttons → **Label names**

	SalesNo	SaleDate	CustNo
⊞	3	4/30/2014	6
⊞	8	5/1/2014	7
⊞	53	7/11/2014	26
⊞	54	7/11/2014	19
⊞	55	7/12/2014	20
⊞	56	7/12/2014	24
⊞	57	7/12/2014	21

Record: I◄ ◄ 3 of 51 ► ►I ►▣ | ▚ No Filter | Search

Access 2013

Protecting data

You may not want to allow all users who view a form to change all the data that appears on that form. You can design forms to limit access to certain fields by changing the Enabled and Locked properties of a control. The **Enabled property** specifies whether a control can have the focus in Form View. The **Locked property** specifies whether you can edit data in a control in Form View.

Add Tab Controls

Learning
Outcomes
• Add a tab control
  to a form
• Modify tab control
  properties

You use the **tab control** to create a three-dimensional aspect to a form so that many controls can be organized and displayed by clicking the tabs. You have already used tab controls because many Access dialog boxes use tabs to organize information. For example, the Property Sheet uses tab controls to organize properties identified by categories: Format, Data, Event, Other, and All. **CASE** *Samantha Hooper asks you to organize database information based on two categories: Tours and Customers. You create a new form with tab controls to organize command buttons for easy access to tour and customer information.*

STEPS

1. **Click the CREATE tab, click the Blank Form button in the Forms group, close the Field List if it is open, click the Tab Control button 🗂 in the Controls group, then click the form**

   A new tab control is automatically positioned in the upper-left corner of the new form with two tabs. You rename the tabs to clarify their purpose.

2. **Click the Page1 tab to select it, click the Property Sheet button in the Tools group, click the Other tab in the Property Sheet, double-click Page1 in the Name property, type Customers, then press [Enter]**

   You also give Page2 a meaningful name.

3. **Click Page2 to open its Property Sheet, click the Other tab (if it is not already selected), double-click Page2 in the Name property text box, type Tours, then press [Enter]**

   Now that the tab names are meaningful, you're ready to add controls to each page. In this case, you add command buttons to each page.

4. **Click the Customers tab, click the Button button ⌧ in the Controls group, click in the middle of the Customers page, click the Form Operations category, click the Open Form action, click Next, click CustomerEntry, click Next, then click Finish**

   You add a command button to the Tours tab to open the Tours form.

5. **Click the Tours tab, click the Button button ⌧, click in the middle of the Tours page, click the Form Operations category, click the Open Form action, click Next, click Tours, click Next, then click Finish**

   Your new form should look like **FIGURE G-15**. To test your command buttons, you must switch to Form View.

6. **Click the View button 🖩 to switch to Form View, click the command button on the Tours tab, right-click the Tours form tab, click Close, click the Customers tab in Form1, click the command button on the Customers tab, then click the Close Form command button at the bottom of the CustomerEntry form**

   Your screen should look like **FIGURE G-16**. The two command buttons opened the CustomerEntry and Tours forms and are placed on different pages of a tab control in the form. In a fully developed database, you would add many more command buttons to make all of the database objects (tables, queries, forms, and reports) that users need to access very easy to find and open.

7. **Right-click the Form1 form tab, click Close, click Yes to save changes, type Form Navigation as the form name, click OK, then close the QuestTravel-G.accdb database**

   To add or delete a page, right-click a tab and choose Insert Page or Delete Page.

FIGURE G-15: Adding command buttons to a tab control

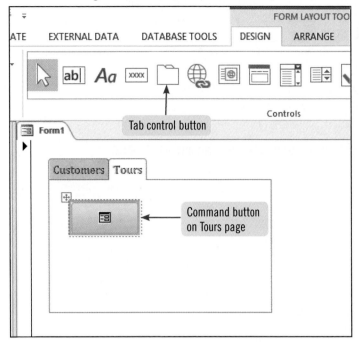

FIGURE G-16: Form Navigation form

Practice

Concepts Review

Identify each element of Form Design View shown in FIGURE G-17.

FIGURE G-17

Match each term with the statement that best describes it.

8. **Command button**
9. **Subform**
10. **Tab control**
11. **Option group**
12. **Combo box**

a. A bound control that displays a few mutually exclusive entries for a field
b. A control that provides a three-dimensional aspect to a form used to organize other controls
c. A bound control that is really both a list box and a text box
d. A control that shows records that are related to one record shown in the main form
e. An unbound control that executes an action when it is clicked

Select the best answer from the list of choices.

13. **Which control works best to display three choices—1, 2, or 3—for a Rating field?**
    a. Option group
    b. Label
    c. Text box
    d. Command button

14. **Which control would you use to initiate a print action?**
    a. Option group
    b. Command button
    c. Text box
    d. List box

15. **Which control would you use to display a drop-down list of 50 states?**
    a. Check box
    b. Field label
    c. Combo box
    d. List box

16. **To view many related records within a form, use a:**
    a. Subform.
    b. List box.
    c. Design template.
    d. Link control.

17. **Which of the following form properties defines the fields and records that appear on a form?**
    a. Record Source
    b. Default View
    c. Row Source
    d. List Items Edit Form

18. **Which is a popular layout for a main form?**
    a. Datasheet
    b. Global
    c. Columnar
    d. Justified

19. **Which is a popular layout for a subform?**
    a. Columnar
    b. Justified
    c. Global
    d. Datasheet

20. **To align controls on their left edges, first:**
    a. Click the LAYOUT tab on the Ribbon.
    b. Select the controls whose edges you want to align.
    c. Click the DESIGN tab on the Ribbon.
    d. Align the data within the controls.

21. **Which control is most commonly used within an option group?**
    a. Command button
    b. Toggle button
    c. Option button
    d. Check box

Skills Review

1. **Use Form Design View.**
   a. Start Access and open the Service-G.accdb database from the location where you store your Data Files. Enable content if prompted.
   b. Create a new form in Form Design View, open the Property Sheet for the new form, then choose Names as the Record Source.
   c. Open the Field List, then add all fields from the Names table to Form Design View.
   d. Move the Birthday, Dues, MemberNo, CharterMember, and StatusNo controls to a second column, about an inch to the right of the FirstName, LastName, Street, and Zip fields.
   e. Save the form with the name **MemberActivity**.

2. **Add subforms.**
   a. In Form Design View of the MemberActivity form, use the SubForm Wizard to create a subform below the Zip label.
   b. Use all three fields in the Activities table for the subform. Show Activities for each record in Names using MemberNo, and name the subform **Activities**.
   c. Drag the bottom edge of the form up to just below the subform control.
   d. View the MemberActivity form in Form View, and move through several records. Note that the form could be improved with better alignment, and that the Street text box is too narrow to display the entire value in the field.

Skills Review (continued)

3. Align control edges.

   a. Switch to Form Design View, then edit the FirstName, LastName, MemberNo, CharterMember, and StatusNo labels in the main form to read **First Name**, **Last Name**, **Member No**, **Charter Member**, and **Status No**.

   b. Select the four labels in the first column (First Name, Last Name, Street, and Zip) together, and align their right edges.

   c. Move the Charter Member label between the Member No and Status No labels. (*Hint*: Point to the upper-left corner of the Charter Member label to move the label without moving the label and its associated check box.)

   d. Select the five labels in the third column (Birthday, Dues, Member No, Charter Member, and Status No) together, and align their right edges.

   e. Select the First Name label, the FirstName text box, the Birthday label, and the Birthday text box together. Align their top edges.

   f. Select the Last Name label, the LastName text box, the Dues label, and the Dues text box together. Align their top edges.

   g. Select the Street label, the Street text box, the Member No label, and the MemberNo text box together. Align their top edges.

   h. Select the Zip label, the Zip text box, the Charter Member label, and the CharterMember check box together. Align their top edges.

   i. Select the FirstName text box, the LastName text box, the Street text box, and the Zip text box together. Align their left edges and resize them to be wider and closer to the corresponding labels in the first column.

   j. Align the left edges of the Birthday, Dues, MemberNo, and StatusNo text box controls.

   k. Resize the Street text box to be about twice as wide as its current width.

   l. Save the MemberActivity form.

4. Add a combo box for data entry.

   a. In Form Design View, right-click the Zip text box, then change it to a combo box control.

   b. In the Property Sheet of the new combo box, click the Row Source property, then click the Build button.

   c. Select only the Zips table for the query, then double-click the Zip field and the City field to add them to the query grid.

   d. Close the Query Builder window, and save the changes.

   e. On the Format tab of the Property Sheet for the Zip combo box, change the Column Count property to **2**, the Column Widths property to **0.5;2**, and the List Width property to **2.5**.

   f. Close the Property Sheet, then save and view the MemberActivity form in Form View.

   g. In the first record for Micah Mayberry, change the Zip to **64153** using the new combo box.

5. Add a combo box to find records.

   a. Display the MemberActivity form in Design View.

   b. Open the Form Header section by clicking the Title button in the Header/Footer section on the DESIGN tab.

   c. Modify the label to read **Member Activity**, then narrow the width of the label to be only as wide as needed.

   d. Add a combo box to the right side of the Form Header, and choose the "Find a record on my form..." option in the Combo Box Wizard.

   e. Choose the MemberNo, LastName, and FirstName fields in that order.

   f. Hide the key column.

   g. Label the combo box **FIND MEMBER:**.

   h. Move and widen the new combo box to be at least 2" wide, change the FIND MEMBER: label text color to black so it is easier to read, save the MemberActivity form, then view it in Form View.

   i. Use the FIND MEMBER combo box to find the Patch Mullins record. Notice that the entries in the combo box are not alphabetized on last name.

   j. Return to Form Design View, and use the Row Source property and Build button for the FIND MEMBER combo box to open the Query Builder. Add an ascending sort order to the LastName and FirstName fields.

   k. Close the Query Builder, saving changes. View the MemberActivity form in Form View, and find the record for Benjamin Martin. Note that the entries in the combo box list are now sorted in ascending order first by the LastName field, then by the FirstName field.

Skills Review (continued)

6. Add command buttons.

a. Display the MemberActivity form in Design View.

b. Use the Command Button Wizard to add a command button to the middle of the Form Footer section.

c. Choose the Print Record action from the Record Operations category.

d. Choose the Text option button, type **Print Current Record**, then name the button **PrintButton**.

e. Use the Command Button Wizard to add a command button to the right side of the Form Footer section.

f. Choose the Close Form action from the Form Operations category.

g. Choose the Text option button, type **Close**, then name the button **CloseButton**.

h. Select both command buttons then align their top edges.

i. Save the form, display it in Form View, navigate through the first few records, then close the MemberActivity form using the new Close command button.

7. Add option groups.

a. Open the MemberActivity form in Form Design View.

b. Because the dues are always $25 or $50, the Dues field is a good candidate for an option group control. Delete the existing Dues text box and label.

c. Click the Option Group button in the Controls group on the DESIGN tab, then click the form just to the right of the Birthday text box.

d. Type **$25** and **$50** for Label Names, do not choose a default value, and enter **25** and **50** for corresponding Values.

e. Store the value in the Dues field, use option buttons, use the etched style, and caption the option group **Initiation Dues:**.

f. Save the MemberActivity form, and view it in Form View. Move and align the other form controls as needed to match **FIGURE G-18**.

g. Use the FIND MEMBER: combo box to find the record for Roberto Maxim, change his first and last names to *your* name, then change the Initiation Dues to $50 using the new option group. Print this record if requested by your instructor.

h. Use the Close command button to close the MemberActivity form.

FIGURE G-18

8. Add tab controls.

a. Create a new blank form, and add a tab control to it.

b. Open the Property Sheet, then use the Name property to rename Page1 to **Member Info** and Page2 to **Activity Info**.

c. Right-click the Activity Info tab, click Insert Page, and use the Name property to rename the third page to **Dues Info**.

d. On the Member Info tab, add a command button with the Preview Report action from the Report Operations category. Choose the MemberListing report, choose Text on the button, type **Preview Member Listing Report** as the text, and name the button **MemberListingButton**.

e. On the Activity Info tab, add a command button with the Open Form action from the Form Operations category. Choose the MemberActivity form, choose to open the form and show all the records, choose Text on the button, type **Open Member Activity Form** as the text, and name the button **MemberActivityButton**.

f. On the Activity Info tab, add a second command button with the Preview Report action from the Report Operations category. Choose the ActivityAnalysis report, choose Text on the button, type **Preview Activity Analysis Report** as the text, and name the button **ActivityAnalysisButton**.

Skills Review (continued)

g. Widen the command buttons on the Activity Info tab as needed so that all of the text on the command buttons is clearly visible, as shown in **FIGURE G-19**.

h. On the Dues Info tab, add a command button with the Preview Report action from the Report Operations category. Choose the DuesAnalysis report, choose Text on the button, type **Preview Dues Analysis Report** as the text, and name the button **DuesAnalysisButton**.

i. Save the form with the name **Database Navigation**, then view it in Form View.

j. Test each button on each tab of the Navigation form to make sure it works as intended.

k. Close all open objects, then close the Service-G.accdb database.

Independent Challenge 1

As the manager of a music store's instrument rental program, you have created a database to track instrument rentals to schoolchildren. You want to build an enhanced form for data entry.

a. Start Access, then open the database MusicStore-G.accdb from the location where you store your Data Files. Enable content if prompted.

b. Using the Form Wizard, create a new form based on all of the fields in the Customers and Rentals tables.

c. View the data by Customers, choose a Datasheet layout for the subform, then accept the default form titles of **Customers** for the main form and **Rentals Subform** for the subform.

d. Add another record to the rental subform for Amanda Smith by typing **888335** as the SerialNo entry and **10/1/15** as the RentalDate entry. Note that no entry is necessary in the RentalNo field because it is an AutoNumber field. No entry is necessary in the CustNo field as it is the foreign key field that connects the main form to the subform and is automatically populated when the forms are in this arrangement.

e. Change Amanda Smith's name to *your* name.

f. Open the Customers form in Design View. Right-align the text within each label control in the first column of the main form. (*Hint*: Use the Align Right button on the HOME tab.)

g. Resize the Zip, CustNo, and SchoolNo text boxes to as wide as the State text box.

h. Move the CustNo and SchoolNo text boxes and their accompanying labels to the upper-right portion of the form, directly to the right of the FirstName and LastName text boxes.

i. Modify the FirstName, LastName, CustNo, and SchoolNo labels to read First Name, Last Name, Cust No, and School No.

j. Delete the RentalNo and CustNo fields from the subform.

FIGURE G-20

k. Open the Field List, and drag the Description field from the Instruments table to the subform above the existing text boxes. (*Hint*: Show all tables, then look in the Fields available in related tables section of the Field List.)

l. Move the subform up, and continue moving and resizing fields as needed so that your form in Form View looks similar to **FIGURE G-20**.

m. Save and close the Customers form, close the MusicStore-G.accdb database, then exit Access.

Independent Challenge 2

As the manager of a community effort to provide better access to residential real estate listings across a regional area, you have developed a database to track listings by realtor and real estate agency. You want to develop a form/subform system to see all listings within each realtor as well as within each real estate agency.

a. Start Access, then open the database RealEstate-G.accdb from the location where you store your Data Files. Enable content if prompted.

b. Using the Form Wizard, create a new form based on all of the fields in the Agencies, Realtors, and Listings tables.

c. View the data by Agencies, choose a Datasheet layout for each of the subforms, and accept the default titles of **Agencies**, **Realtors Subform**, and **Listings Subform**.

d. In Form Design View, use the Combo Box Wizard to add a combo box to the Form Header to find a record. Choose the AgencyName field, hide the key column, and enter the label **FIND AGENCY:**.

e. Change the text color of the FIND AGENCY: label to black, and widen the combo box to about twice its current size.

f. Add a command button to a blank spot on the main form to print the current record. Use the Print Record action from the Record Operations category. Use a picture on the button, and give the button the meaningful name of **PrintButton**.

g. Use your skills to modify, move, resize, align text, and align control edges, as shown in **FIGURE G-21**. Note that several labels have been modified, resized, and aligned. Note that the subforms have also been resized and moved.

h. Save the form, view it in Form View, then use the combo box to find Four Lakes Realtors.

i. Resize the columns of the subforms to view as much data as possible, as shown in **FIGURE G-21**, change Tom Hall's name in the first record of the Realtors subform to *your* name, then if requested by your instructor, print only the current record using the new command button.

FIGURE G-21

j. Save and close the Agencies form, close the RealEstate-G.accdb database, and exit Access.

Independent Challenge 3

As the manager of a community effort to provide better access to residential real estate listings across a regional area, you have developed a database to track listings by realtor and real estate agency. You want to develop a navigation form to help find queries and reports in your database much faster.

   a. Start Access, then open the database RealEstate-G.accdb from the location where you store your Data Files. Enable content if prompted.

   b. Create a new blank form, and add a tab control to it.

   c. Open the Property Sheet and use the Name property to rename Page1 to **Realtors** and Page2 to **Listings**.

   d. On the Realtors tab, add a command button with the Preview Report action from the Report Operations category. Choose the CurrentRealtors report, choose Text on the button, type **Preview Current Realtors** as the text, and name the button **cmdCurrentRealtors**. (Note that *cmd* is the three-character prefix sometimes used to name command buttons.)

   e. On the Listings tab, add a command button with the Run Query action from the Miscellaneous category. Choose the AllListings query, choose Text on the button, type **Open All Listings query** as the text, and name the button **cmdAllListings**.

   f. On the Listings tab, add a second command button with the Preview Report action from the Report Operations category. Choose the ListingReport report, choose Text on the button, type **Preview Listing Report** as the text, and name the button **cmdListingReport**.

   g. Save the form with the name **Real Estate Navigation System**, then view it in Form View. The new form with the Listings tab selected should look like FIGURE G-22.

   h. Test each command button on both the Realtors and Listings tabs.

   i. Close all open objects, then close the RealEstate-G.accdb database and exit Access.

FIGURE G-22

Independent Challenge 4: Explore

You have created an Access database to help manage college scholarship opportunities. You can keep the database updated more efficiently by creating some easy-to-use forms.

a. Start Access and open the Scholarships-G.accdb database from the location where you store your Data Files. Enable content if prompted.

b. Create a split form for the Scholarships table. Save and name the form **Scholarships**.

c. In Form Design View, narrow the label in the Form Header section to about half of its current size, then use the Combo Box Wizard to add a combo box to the Form Header section to find a scholarship based on the ScholarshipName field. Hide the key column, and use the label **FIND SCHOLARSHIP:**.

d. In Form Design View, widen the combo box as necessary so that all of the scholarship names in the list are clearly visible in Form View. Change the color of the FIND SCHOLARSHIP: text to black, and move and resize the label and combo box as necessary to clearly view them. Switch between Form View and Form Design View to test the new combo box control.

e. In Form Design View, change the combo box's List Rows property (on the Format tab) to **50** and use the Build button to modify the Row Source property to add an ascending sort order based on the ScholarshipName field.

f. Save the form, and in Form View, use the combo box to find the Papa Johns Scholarship. Change Papa Johns to *your* name as shown in **FIGURE G-23**, then, if requested by your instructor, print only that record by using the Selected Record(s) option on the Print dialog box.

FIGURE G-23

Scholarships		

Scholarships		FIND SCHOLARSHIP:	Papa Johns Scholarship	

ID	6
ScholarshipName	Student Name Scholarship
DueDate	1/29/2015
Amount	$1,000.00
Major	Business

ID	ScholarshipName	DueDate	Amount	Major
3	Siemens Westinghouse Competition	9/29/2015	$100,000.00	Science
4	Target All-Around Scholarship	10/30/2015	$10,000.00	Any
5	All-Ink.com College Scholarship Program	12/29/2015	$1,000.00	English
6	Papa Johns Scholarship	1/29/2015	$1,000.00	Business
7	Scholarships for Military Children	1/30/2015	$1,500.00	Military
8	Young Women In Business Affairs	1/30/2015	$1,000.00	Political Science
9	National Peace Essay Contest	1/31/2015	$1,000.00	Any
11	Achievement Community Scholarship	2/16/2015	$2,000.00	Any

Record: ◄ ◄ 4 of 59 ► ►► ►► No Filter Search

g. Save and close the Scholarships form, close the Scholarships-G.accdb database, then exit Access.

Visual Workshop

Open the Baseball-G.accdb database from the location where you store your Data Files. Enable content if prompted. Use Form Design View to create a form based on the Players table named **PlayersEntry**. Use your skills to modify, move, resize, align text, and align control edges as shown in **FIGURE G-24**. Note that both the PlayerPosition as well as the TeamNo fields are presented as option groups. The values that correspond with each Position label can be found in the Field Description of the PlayerPosition field in Table Design View of the Players table. The Position option group is tied to the PlayerPosition field. The values that correspond with each Team label can be found by reviewing the TeamNo and TeamName fields of the Teams table. The Team option group is tied to the TeamNo field. Do not choose default values for either option group. Change Louis Gehrig's name to *your* name, change the Position value to Pitcher, and change the Team to Yellow Jackets. If requested by your instructor, print only that record.

FIGURE G-24

Analyzing Data with Reports

CASE ▶ Samantha Hooper asks you to create and enhance reports to analyze, clarify, and format important information at Quest Specialty Travel.

Unit Objectives

After completing this unit, you will be able to:

- Use Report Design View
- Create parameter reports
- Apply conditional formatting
- Add lines

- Use the Format Painter and themes
- Add subreports
- Modify section properties
- Create summary reports

Files You Will Need

QuestTravel-H.accdb
RealEstate-H.accdb
MusicStore-H.accdb

Scholarships-H.accdb
Baseball-H.accdb

© Tumanyan/Shutterstock

Use Report Design View

Learning
Outcomes
• Modify report
properties
• Modify group and
sort orders

Although you can print data in forms and datasheets, **reports** give you more control over how data is printed and greater flexibility in presenting summary information. To create a report, you include text boxes to display data and use calculations and labels, lines, and graphics to clarify the data. **Report Design View** allows you to work with a complete range of report, section, and control properties. Because Report Design View gives you full control of all aspects of a report, it is well worth your time to master. **CASE** ▶ *Samantha Hooper asks you to build a report that shows all tours grouped by category and sorted in descending order by price. You use Report Design View to build this report.*

STEPS

1. **Start Access, open the** QuestTravel-H.accdb database **from the location where you store your Data Files, enable content if prompted, click the** CREATE tab, **then click the** Report Design button **in the Reports group**

   The first step to building a report in Report Design View is identifying the record source.

2. **If the Property Sheet is not open, click the** Property Sheet button **in the Tools group, click the** Data tab **in the Property Sheet, click the** Record Source list arrow, **then click** Tours

   The Record Source can be an existing table, query, or SQL SELECT statement. The **Record Source** identifies the fields and records that the report can display. To build a report that shows tours grouped by category, you'll need to add a Category Header section. See **TABLE H-1** for a review of report sections.

3. **Scroll down in the report to view the Page Footer section, use the** ✛ **pointer to drag the** top edge of the Page Footer section **up to about the 1" mark on the vertical ruler, then click the** Group & Sort button **in the Grouping & Totals group to open the Group, Sort, and Total pane if it is not already open**

   The Group, Sort, and Total pane gives you the ability to specify grouping and sorting fields and open group headers and footers.

4. **Click the** Add a group button **in the Group, Sort, and Total pane; click** Category; **click the** Add a sort button **in the Group, Sort, and Total pane; click** Price; **click the** from smallest to largest button arrow; **then click** from largest to smallest, **as shown in FIGURE H-1**

   With the grouping and sorting fields specified, you're ready to add controls to the report.

5. **Click the** Add Existing Fields button **in the Tools group, click** TourNo **in the Field List, press and hold** [Shift] **as you click** Price **in the Field List to select all fields in the Tours table, drag the** selected fields **to the Detail section of the report, then close the Field List window**

   Next, you move the Category controls to the Category Header section.

6. **Click the** report **to remove the current selection, right-click the** Category text box, **click** Cut **on the shortcut menu, right-click the** Category Header section, **then click** Paste **on the shortcut menu**

   If the data is self-explanatory, it doesn't need descriptive labels. Delete the labels, and position the text boxes across the page to finalize the report.

7. **Click** each label **and press** [Delete] **to delete each label in the first column of the Detail section, then move and resize the remaining text boxes and shorten the Detail section, as shown in FIGURE H-2**

8. **Click the** Save button 🖫 **on the Quick Access toolbar, type** ToursByCategory **as the new report name, click** OK, **preview the first page of the report, as shown in FIGURE H-3, then close the report**

FIGURE H-1: Creating a report in Report Design View

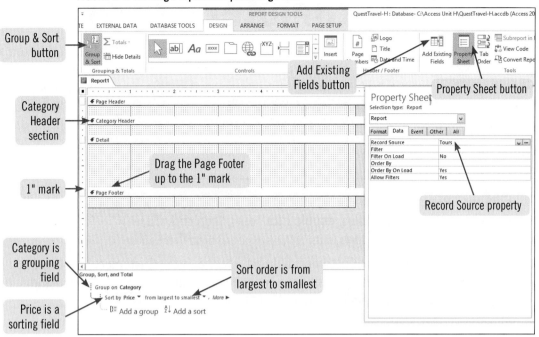

Group & Sort button

Category Header section

1" mark

Category is a grouping field

Price is a sorting field

Add Existing Fields button

Property Sheet button

Record Source property

Sort order is from largest to smallest

FIGURE H-2: Moving and resizing the text box controls in the Detail section

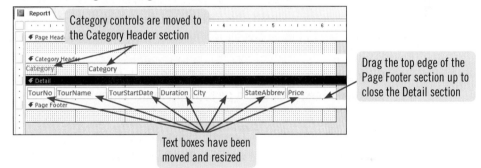

Category controls are moved to the Category Header section

Drag the top edge of the Page Footer section up to close the Detail section

Text boxes have been moved and resized

FIGURE H-3: Previewing the ToursByCategory report

Records are grouped by Category

Records are sorted in descending order by Price

TABLE H-1: Review of report sections

section	where does this section print?	what is this section most commonly used for?
Report Header	At the top of the first page of the report	To print a title or logo
Page Header	At the top of every page (but below the Report Header on page 1)	To print titles, dates, or page numbers
Group Header	Before every group of records	To display the grouping field value
Detail	Once for every record	To display data for every record
Group Footer	After every group of records	To calculate summary statistics on groups of records
Page Footer	At the bottom of every page	To print dates or page numbers

Access 2013

Create Parameter Reports

A **parameter report** prompts you for criteria to determine the records to use for the report. To create a parameter report, you base it on a parameter query. The report's **Record Source** property determines what table or query provides the fields and records for the report. **CASE** *Samantha Hooper requests a report that shows all tour sales for a given period. You use a parameter query to prompt the user for the dates, then build the report on that query.*

STEPS

1. **Click the CREATE tab, click the Query Design button in the Queries group, double-click Customers, double-click Sales, double-click Tours, then click Close**

   You want fields from all three tables in the report, so you add them to the query.

2. **Double-click FName in the Customers field list, LName in the Customers field list, and SaleDate in the Sales field list; resize the Tours field list; then double-click Price and TourName in the Tours field list**

   To select only those tours sold in a given period, you add parameter criteria to the SaleDate field.

3. **Click the Criteria cell for the SaleDate field, type Between [Enter start date] and [Enter end date], then widen the SaleDate column to see the entire entry, as shown in FIGURE H-4**

   To test the query, run it and enter dates in the parameter prompts. **Parameter criteria** are text entered in [square brackets] that prompt the user for an entry each time the query is run. In this case, the user will be prompted for the start and end date.

4. **Click the View button [icon] on the DESIGN tab to run the query, type 6/1/15 in the Enter start date box, click OK, type 6/30/15 in the Enter end date box, then click OK**

   Eight records are displayed in the datasheet, each with a SaleDate value in June 2015.

5. **Click the Save button [icon] on the Quick Access toolbar, type SalesParameter as the new query name, click OK, then close the SalesParameter query**

   You use the Report button on the CREATE tab to quickly build a report on the SalesParameter query.

6. **Click the SalesParameter query in the Navigation Pane, click the CREATE tab, click the Report button in the Reports group, type 6/1/15 in the Enter start date box, click OK, type 6/30/15 in the Enter end date box, then click OK**

   The report is displayed in Layout View with records in June 2015. You decide to preview and save the report.

7. **Work in Layout and Design View to narrow the report so that it fits within the margins of a single page and to increase the height of the calculated field in the Report Footer, save the report with the name SalesDateParameter, then preview it, as shown in FIGURE H-5, entering 6/1/15 as the start date and 6/30/15 as the end date**

FIGURE H-4: Entering parameter criteria in a query

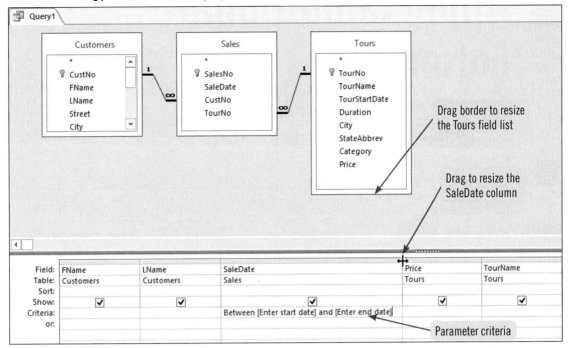

FIGURE H-5: Previewing the SalesDateParameter report

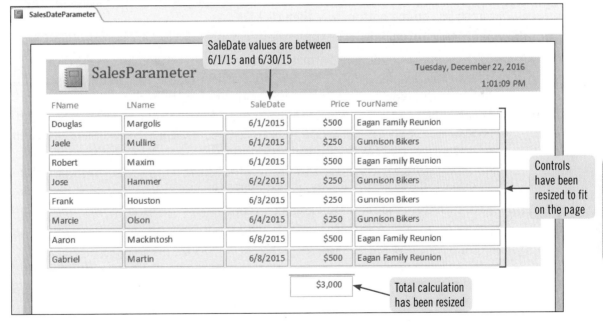

Parameter criteria

In Query Design View, you must enter parameter criteria within [square brackets]. Each parameter criterion you enter appears as a prompt in the Enter Parameter Value dialog box. The entry you make in the Enter Parameter Value box is used as the criterion for the field that contains the parameter criteria.

Apply Conditional Formatting

Conditional formatting allows you to change the appearance of a control on a form or report based on criteria you specify. Conditional formatting helps you highlight important or exceptional data on a form or report. **CASE** *You want to apply conditional formatting to the SalesDateParameter report to emphasize different tour Price levels.*

STEPS

1. **Right-click the** SalesDateParameter report tab, **then click** Design View

2. **Click the** Price text box **in the Detail section, click the** FORMAT tab, **then click the** Conditional Formatting button **in the Control Formatting group**

   The Conditional Formatting Rules Manager dialog box opens, asking you to define the conditional formatting rules. You want to format Price values between 500 and 1000 with a yellow background color.

3. **Click** New Rule, **click the** text box to the right of the between arrow, **type** 500, **click the** and box, **type** 999, **click the** Background color button arrow ⬛ ▾, **click the** Yellow box **on the bottom row, then click** OK

   You add the second conditional formatting rule to format Price values greater than or equal to 1000 with a light green background color.

4. **Click** New Rule, **click the** between list arrow, **click** greater than or equal to, **click the** value box, **type** 1000, **click the** Background color button arrow ⬛ ▾, **click the** Light Green box **on the bottom row, then click** OK

   The Conditional Formatting Rules Manager dialog box with two rules should look like **FIGURE H-6**.

5. **Click** OK **in the Conditional Formatting Rules Manager dialog box, right-click the** SalesDateParameter report tab, **click** Print Preview, **type** 7/1/15 **in the Enter start date box, click** OK, **type** 7/31/15 **in the Enter end date box, then click** OK

   Conditional formatting rules applied a light green background color to the Price text box for two tours because the Price value is greater than 1000, as shown in **FIGURE H-7**. Conditional formatting applied a yellow background color to the Price text box for one tour because the Price value is between 500 and 1000. Default formatting was not applied to the Price text box for two tours because they do not meet any of the conditions in the Conditional Formatting Rules Manager dialog box.

6. **Save then close the** SalesDateParameter report

FIGURE H-6: Conditional Formatting Rules Manager dialog box

New Rule
button

First rule

Second rule

Formatting
for first rule

Formatting for
second rule

FIGURE H-7: Conditional formatting applied to SalesDateParameter report

FName	LName	SaleDate	Price	TourName
Brad	Langguth	7/1/2015	$1,050	Bear Valley Adventures
Nancy	Langguth	7/1/2015	$1,050	Bear Valley Adventures
Kris	Goode	7/14/2015	$455	Bigfoot Rafting Club
Lois	Goode	7/14/2015	$455	Bigfoot Rafting Club
Elsie	Lang	7/15/2015	$525	Black Sheep Hiking Club

SalesDateParameter

SalesParameter

Tuesday, December 22, 2016
1:27:12 PM

Cost is greater than
or equal to 1000

Default formatting

$3,535

Cost is between
500 and 1000

Access 2013

Conditional formatting using data bars

A recent feature of Access allows you to compare the values
of one column to another with small data bars. To use this
feature, use the "Compare to other records" rule type
option in the New Formatting Rule dialog box, as shown
in **FIGURE H-8**.

FIGURE H-8: Conditional formatting with data bars

Add Lines

Lines are often added to a report to highlight information or enhance its clarity. For example, you might want to separate the Report Header and Page Header information from the rest of the report with a horizontal line. You can also use short lines to indicate subtotals and grand totals. **CASE** Samantha Hooper likes the data on the CategoryRevenue report, which has already been created in the QuestTravel-H database, but she asks you to enhance the report by adding a grand total calculation and separating the categories more clearly. Lines will help clarify the information.

STEPS

QUICK TIP
Recall that Report
View does not show
page margins or
individual pages of
the report.

1. **Double-click the** CategoryRevenue report **in the Navigation Pane to open it in Report View, then scroll to the end of the report**

   The report needs lines separating the tour categories and a new grand total calculation on the last page of the report. You use Report Design View to make these improvements.

2. **Right-click the** CategoryRevenue report tab, **click** Design View, **right-click the =Sum([Revenue]) text box in the Category Footer section, click** Copy, **right-click the Report Footer section, click** Paste, **press [→] enough times to position the expression directly under the one in the Category Footer, click** Subtotal: **in the Report Footer section to select it, double-click** Subtotal: **in the label to select it, type** Grand Total:, **then press [Enter]**

   The =Sum([Revenue]) expression in the Report Footer section sums the Revenue values in the entire report, whereas the same expression in the Category Footer section sums Revenue values in each category. With the calculations in place, you add clarifying lines.

TROUBLE
Lines can be difficult
to find in Report
Design View. See the
"Line troubles" box in
this lesson for tips on
working with lines.

3. **Click the** More button ⟱ **in the Controls group to show all controls, click the** Line button ◰, **press and hold [Shift], drag from the upper-left edge of =Sum([Revenue]) in the Category Footer section to its upper-right edge, press [Ctrl][C] to copy the line, click the** Report Footer section, **press [Ctrl][V] two times to paste the line twice, then move the lines just below the =Sum([Revenue]) expression in the Report Footer section**

   Pressing [Shift] while drawing a line makes sure that the line remains perfectly horizontal or vertical. The single line above the calculation in the Category Footer section indicates that the calculation is a subtotal. Double lines below the calculation in the Report Footer section indicate that it is a grand total. You also want to add a line to visually separate the categories.

QUICK TIP
Use the Rectangle
▢ button to
insert a rectangle
control on a form
or report.

4. **Click the** More button ⟱ **in the Controls group to show all controls, click the** Line button ◰, **press and hold [Shift], then drag along the bottom of the Category Footer section**

   The final CategoryRevenue report in Report Design View is shown in **FIGURE H-9**.

QUICK TIP
As a final report
creation step, print
preview a report to
make sure it fits on
the paper.

5. **Right-click the** CategoryRevenue report tab, **click** Print Preview, **then navigate to the last page of the report**

   The last page of the CategoryRevenue report shown in **FIGURE H-10** displays the Category Footer section line as well as the subtotal and grand total lines.

FIGURE H-9: Adding lines to a report

New line at the bottom of the Category Footer section

Subtotal and grand total lines

FIGURE H-10: Previewing the last page of the CategoryRevenue report

Sale Date	Tour Name	Revenue
5/5/2014	Golden Footsteps	$100.00
5/5/2014	Golden Footsteps	$100.00
5/5/2014	Golden Footsteps	$600.00
5/5/2014	Golden Footsteps	$200.00
5/5/2014	Golden Footsteps	$200.00
5/5/2014	Golden Footsteps	$200.00
7/7/2014	Bright Lights Expo	$200.00
7/7/2014	Bright Lights Expo	$100.00
7/7/2014	Bright Lights Expo	$50.00
7/7/2014	Bright Lights Expo	$150.00
	Subtotal:	$1,900.00
	Grand Total:	$25,650.00

Subtotal line

Line at the bottom of the Category Footer section

Grand total lines

Line troubles

Sometimes lines are difficult to find in Report Design View because they are placed against the edge of a section or the edge of other controls. To find lines that are positioned next to the edge of a section, drag the section bar to expand the section and expose the line. Recall that to draw a perfectly horizontal line, you hold [Shift] while creating or resizing the line. It is easy to accidentally widen a line beyond the report margins, thus creating extra unwanted pages in your printout. To fix this problem, narrow any controls that extend beyond the margins of the printout, and drag the right edge of the report to the left. Note that the default left and right margins for an 8.5 × 11-inch sheet of paper are often 0.25 inches each, so a report in portrait orientation must be no wider than 8 inches, and a report in landscape orientation must be no wider than 10.5 inches.

Use the Format Painter and Themes

The **Format Painter** is a tool you use to copy multiple formatting properties from one control to another in Design or Layout View for forms and reports. **Themes** are predefined formats that you apply to the database to set all of the formatting enhancements, such as font, color, and alignment on all forms and reports. **CASE** ▶ *You think the CategoryRevenue report can be improved with a few formatting embellishments. You can use the Format Painter to quickly change the characteristics of labels in the Page Header section, then apply a built-in theme to the entire report.*

STEPS

1. **Right-click the** CategoryRevenue report tab, **click** Design View, **click the** Category Revenue Report label **in the Report Header, click the** HOME tab, **click the** Format Painter button, **then click the** Sale Date label **in the Page Header section**

   The Format Painter applied several formatting characteristics, including font face, font color, and font size from the label in the Report Header section to the Sale Date label in the Page Header section. You like the new font face and color, but the font size is too large.

2. **Click the** Sale Date label, **click the** Font Size list arrow 18 ▾ **in the Text Formatting group, click** 12, **double-click the** Format Painter button, **click the** Tour Name label **in the Page Header section, click the** Revenue label **in the Page Header section, then press** [Esc] **to release the Format Painter pointer**

   Now that you've mastered the Format Painter, you're ready to see how themes affect the formatting of the report.

3. **Click the** DESIGN tab, **click the** Themes button, **point to several themes to observe the changes in the report, then click** Organic, **as shown in FIGURE H-11**

   The Organic theme gives the Report Header section a gray background. All text now has a consistent font face, controls in the same section are the same font size, and all controls have complementary font colors. You preview the report to review the changes as they will appear on a printout.

4. **Right-click the** CategoryRevenue report tab, **click** Layout View, **then resize the** left edge **of the Tour Name label and text box, as shown in FIGURE H-12, to better position the data on the newly formatted report**

   The first page of the CategoryRevenue report is shown in **FIGURE H-12**.

5. **Save and close the CategoryRevenue report**

FIGURE H-11: Applying a theme to a report

FIGURE H-12: Organic theme applied to the CategoryRevenue report

Add Subreports

A **subreport** control displays a report within another report. The report that contains the subreport control is called the **main report**. You can use a subreport control when you want to connect two reports together. **CASE** ▸ *You want the CategoryRevenue report to automatically print at the end of the ToursByCategory report. You use a subreport in the Report Footer section to accomplish this.*

STEPS

1. **Right-click the** ToursByCategory report **in the Navigation Pane, click** Design View, **right-click the** Page Header section bar, **then click** Report Header/Footer **on the shortcut menu to open the Report Header and Footer sections**

   With the Report Footer section open, you're ready to add the CategoryRevenue subreport.

2. **Click the** More button ▼ **in the Controls group, click the** Subform/Subreport **button** ⊞, **then click the left side of the Report Footer to start the SubReport Wizard, as shown in** FIGURE H-13

   The first question of the SubReport Wizard asks what data you want to use for the subreport.

3. **Click the** Use an existing report or form option button **in the SubReport Wizard, click** CategoryRevenue **if it is not already selected, click** Next, **click** None **when asked how you want the reports to be linked, click** Next, **then click** Finish **to accept the default name**

   The Report Footer section contains the CategoryRevenue report as a subreport. Therefore, the CategoryRevenue report will print after the ToursByCategory report prints. You don't need the label that accompanies the subreport so you delete it.

TROUBLE
You may need to move the subreport control to see the CategoryRevenue label.

4. **Click the new** CategoryRevenue label **associated with the subreport, then press** [Delete]

   If the subreport pushes the right edge of the main report beyond the 8" mark on the ruler, you may see a green error indicator in the report selector button because the report width is greater than the page width. Narrow the subreport and main report to make sure the right edge is to the left of the 8" mark.

TROUBLE
Selecting the subreport control can be tricky. Refer to FIGURE H-14 as you perform this step.

5. **Click the** edge of the subreport control **to select it, use the** ↔ **pointer to drag the middle-right sizing handle of the subreport to the left of the 8" mark on the main ruler, then use the** ↔ **pointer to drag the** right edge of the main report **to the left of the 8" mark on the main ruler**

   Report Design View should look similar to FIGURE H-14. Preview your changes.

6. **Right-click the** ToursByCategory report tab, **click** Print Preview, **then navigate through the pages of the report**

   The ToursByCategory report fills the first two pages. The CategoryRevenue subreport starts at the top of page three. There should be no blank pages between the printed pages of the report.

7. **Save and close the ToursByCategory report**

FIGURE H-13: SubReport Wizard dialog box

Left side of the Report
Footer section

FIGURE H-14: Subreport in Report Design View

Modify Section Properties

Report **section properties**, the characteristics that define each section, can be modified to improve report printouts. For example, you might want each new Group Header to print at the top of a page. Or, you might want to modify section properties to format that section with a background color. **CASE** Samantha Hooper asks you to modify the SalesByTour report so that each tour prints at the top of a page.

STEPS

1. **Right-click the SalesByTour report in the Navigation Pane, then click Design View**

   To force each new tour to start printing at the top of a page, you open and modify the TourName Footer.

2. **Click the Group & Sort button to open the Group, Sort, and Total pane if it is not open; click the TourName More Options button in the Group, Sort, and Total pane; click the without a footer section list arrow; click with a footer section; then double-click the TourName Footer section bar to open its Property Sheet**

   You modify the **Force New Page** property of the TourName Footer section to force each tour to start printing at the top of a new page.

3. **Click the Format tab in the Property Sheet, click the Force New Page property list arrow, then click After Section, as shown in FIGURE H-15**

   You also move the Report Header controls into the Page Header so they print at the top of every page. First, you need to create space in the upper half of the Page Header section to hold the controls.

4. **Close the Property Sheet, drag the top edge of the TourName Header down to expand the Page Header section to about twice its height, click the vertical ruler to the left of the TourName label in the Page Header section to select all of the controls in that section, then use ⟨k to move the labels down to the bottom of the Page Header section**

   With space available in the top half of the Page Header section, you cut and paste the controls from the Report Header section to that new space.

5. **Drag down the vertical ruler to the left of the Report Header section to select all controls in that section, click the HOME tab, click the Cut button in the Clipboard group, click the Page Header section bar, click the Paste button, then drag the top of the Page Header section up to close the Report Header section, as shown in FIGURE H-16**

   Preview the report to make sure that each page contains the new header information and that each tour prints at the top of its own page.

6. **Right-click the SalesByTour report tab, click Print Preview, navigate back and forth through several pages to prove that each new TourName value prints at the top of a new page, then navigate and zoom into the second page, as shown in FIGURE H-17**

   Each tour now starts printing at the top of a new page, and the former Report Header section controls now print at the top of each page too, because they were moved to the Page Header section.

7. **Save and close the SalesByTour report**

FIGURE H-15: Changing section properties

FIGURE H-16: Moving controls from the Report Header to the Page Header

FIGURE H-17: Second page of SalesByTour report

Create Summary Reports

Learning Outcomes
• Use rulers to select controls in Report Design View

Summary reports are reports that show statistics on groups of records rather than details for each record. You create summary reports by using Access functions such as Sum, Count, or Avg in expressions that calculate the desired statistic. These expressions are entered in text boxes most commonly placed in the Group Footer section. **CASE** ▶ *Samantha Hooper asks for a report to summarize the revenue for each tour category. You create a copy of the CategoryRevenue report and modify it to satisfy this request.*

STEPS

1. **Right-click the** CategoryRevenue report **in the Navigation Pane, click** Copy **on the shortcut menu, right-click below the report objects in the Navigation Pane, click** Paste**, type** CategorySummary **as the report name, then click** OK

   Summary reports may contain controls in the Group Header and Group Footer sections, but because they provide summary statistics instead of details, they do not contain controls in the Detail section. You delete the controls in the Detail section and close it.

2. **Right-click the** CategorySummary report **in the Navigation Pane, click** Design View**, click the** vertical ruler **to the left of the Detail section to select all controls in the Detail section, press** [Delete]**, then drag the top of the** Category Footer **section up to close the Detail section**

   You can also delete the labels in the Page Header section.

3. **Click the** vertical ruler **to the left of the Page Header section to select all controls in the Page Header section, press** [Delete]**, then drag the top of the** Category Header **section up to close the Page Header section**

   Because the Page Header and Page Footer sections do not contain any controls, those section bars can be toggled off to simplify Report Design View.

4. **Right-click the** Report Header **section bar, then click** Page Header/Footer **on the shortcut menu to remove the Page Header and Page Footer section bars from Report Design View**

   With the unneeded controls and sections removed, as shown in **FIGURE H-18**, you preview the final summary report.

5. **Right-click the** CategorySummary report **tab, then click** Print Preview

   You could make this report look even better by moving the Category text box into the Category Footer section and deleting the Subtotal label and line.

QUICK TIP
If you make a mistake, click Undo ↶ and try again.

6. **Right-click the** CategorySummary report **tab, click** Design View**, drag the** Category text box **down from the Category Header section to the Category Footer section, click the** Subtotal label **in the Category Footer section, press** [Delete]**, click the** subtotal line **just above the =Sum([Revenue]) text box in the Category Footer section, press** [Delete]**, right-click the** CategorySummary report **tab, then click** Print Preview

   The summarized revenue for each category is shown in the one-page summary report in **FIGURE H-19**.

QUICK TIP
Be sure to review all reports in Print Preview to make sure that the report is not too wide, that no labels are cut off, and that all numbers and dates are clearly visible.

7. **Save and close the CategorySummary report, then close QuestTravel-H.accdb and exit Access**

FIGURE H-18: Design View of the CategorySummary report

Page Header and Page Footer sections are removed

All controls in the Detail section are deleted and the Detail section is closed

Category Revenue Report

Subtotal: =Sum([Revenue])

Grand Total: =Sum([Revenue])

FIGURE H-19: Preview of the CategorySummary report

Category Revenue Report — Report Header section

Adventure	$11,000.00
Educational	$10,300.00
Family	$1,200.00
Service	$1,250.00
Site Seeing	$1,900.00
Grand Total	$25,650.00

Category Footer section

Report Footer section

Practice

Concepts Review

Identify each element of Report Design View shown in FIGURE H-20.

FIGURE H-20

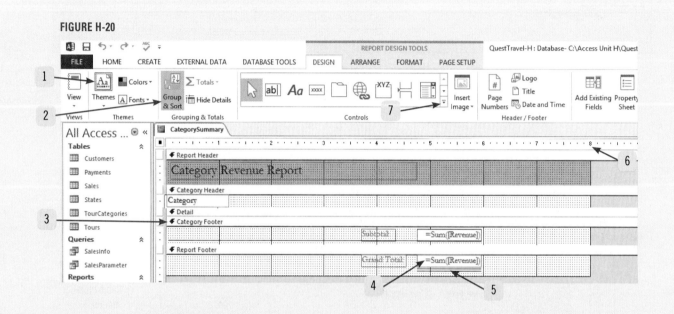

Match each term with the statement that best describes it.

8. **Summary report**
9. **Parameter report**
10. **Conditional formatting**
11. **Format Painter**
12. **Theme**

a. Used to copy multiple formatting properties from one control to another in Report Design View

b. Provides predefined formats that you apply to an entire form or report

c. Prompts the user for the criteria for selecting the records for the report

d. A way to change the appearance of a control on a form or report based on criteria you specify

e. Used to show statistics on groups of records

Select the best answer from the list of choices.

13. Which control would you use to visually separate groups of records on a report?
- **a.** Line
- **b.** Bound Object Frame
- **c.** Option group
- **d.** Image

14. Which property would you use to force each group of records to print at the top of the next page?
- **a.** Paginate
- **b.** Calculate
- **c.** Display When
- **d.** Force New Page

15. What feature allows you to apply the formatting characteristics of one control to another?
- **a.** Theme
- **b.** AutoContent Wizard
- **c.** Report Layout Wizard
- **d.** Format Painter

16. Which key do you press when creating a line to make it perfectly horizontal?
- **a.** [Ctrl]
- **b.** [Alt]
- **c.** [Shift]
- **d.** [Home]

17. Which feature allows you to apply the same formatting characteristics to all the controls in a report at once?
- **a.** Format Wizard
- **b.** AutoPainting
- **c.** Themes
- **d.** Palletizing

18. In a report, an expression used to calculate values is entered in which type of control?
- **a.** Text Box
- **b.** Label
- **c.** Combo Box
- **d.** Command Button

19. Which section most often contains calculations for groups of records?
- **a.** Page Header
- **b.** Detail
- **c.** Page Footer
- **d.** Group Footer

20. Which control would you use to combine two reports?
- **a.** Subreport
- **b.** List Box
- **c.** Combo Box
- **d.** Group & Sort Control

Skills Review

1. Use Report Design View.
a. Open the RealEstate-H.accdb database from the location where you store your Data Files and enable content if prompted.

b. Open the RealtorList query, and then change the RLast value for Sara Johnson to *your* last name. Close the query.

c. Create a new report in Report Design View based on the RealtorList query.

d. Select AgencyName as a grouping field and RLast as a sort field.

e. Add the AgencyName field to the AgencyName Header. Delete the accompanying AgencyName label, position the AgencyName text box on the left side of the AgencyName Header, then resize it to be about 3" wide.

f. Add the RealtorNo, RFirst, RLast, and RPhone fields to the Detail section. Delete all labels and position the text boxes horizontally across the top of the Detail section.

g. Drag the top edge of the Page Footer section up to remove the blank space in the Detail section.

h. Save the report with the name **RealtorList**, then preview it, as shown in FIGURE H-21. The width and spacing of the controls in your report may differ. Use Layout View to resize each control so it is wide enough to view all data.

i. Save and close the RealtorList report.

FIGURE H-21

RealtorList			
Four Lakes Realtors			
8	Mary	Dell	555-888-7777
2	Phil	Kirkpatrick	555-111-9900
1	Sara	Student Last	555-222-8877
9	Deb	Trumpet	555-333-0123
Marvin and Pam Realtors			
7	Trixie	Angelina	555-220-4466
6	Shari	Duncan	555-228-5577
5	Jane Ann	Welch	555-223-0044
Ridgedale Real Estate			
10	Cy	Clone	555-888-9999
11	Rob	Zacharias	555-888-1111
Sun and Ski Realtors			
3	Jessica	Polar	555-333-3344
4	Malika	Thompson	555-444-7788

2. Create parameter reports.
a. Create a query in Query Design View, including the RFirst, RLast, and RPhone fields from the Realtors table. Include the Type, Area, SqFt, and Asking fields from the Listings table.

b. In the Asking field, include the following parameter criteria: **<[Enter maximum asking price]**.

Skills Review (continued)

c. Test the query by switching to Datasheet View, enter **200,000** in the Enter maximum asking price box, then click OK. The query should display 21 records, all with an AskingPrice of less than $200,000. Save the query as **AskingParameter**, then close it.

d. Click the AskingParameter query in the Navigation Pane, then click Report on the CREATE tab. Enter **250,000** in the Enter maximum asking price box, then click OK.

e. Work in Layout View to narrow each column to be only as wide as necessary and to fit all columns across a single sheet of paper in portrait orientation.

f. In Report Design View, add a label with *your* name to the Report Header section.

g. In Report Design View, drag the right edge of the report to the left to make sure the report is no wider than 8 inches. This may include moving controls in the Page Footer or Report Footer to the left as well.

h. Preview the report again to make sure it is not too wide to fit on the paper, enter **250,000** in the prompt, then print the report if requested by your instructor.

i. Save the report with the name **AskingParameter**, then close it.

3. Apply conditional formatting.

a. Open the AskingParameter report in Report Design View, click the Asking text box, then open the Conditional Formatting Rules Manager dialog box.

b. Add a rule to format all Asking field values between **0** and **99999** with a light green background color.

c. Add a rule to format all Asking field values between **100000** and **199999** with a yellow background color.

d. Add a rule to format all Asking field values greater than or equal to **200000** with a red background color.

e. Test the report in Print Preview, entering a value of **400,000** when prompted.

4. Add lines.

a. Open the AskingParameter report in Design View, then use the Group, Sort, and Total pane to add a sort order. Sort the fields in descending (largest to smallest) order on the Asking field.

b. Add a label to the Report Footer section directly to the left of the =Sum([Asking]) text box. Enter **Grand Total:** as the label text.

c. Expand the vertical size of the Report Footer section to about twice its current height and resize the =Sum([Asking]) text box in the Report Footer to better read the contents.

d. Draw two short horizontal lines just below the =Sum([Asking]) calculation in the Report Footer section to indicate a grand total.

e. Save the report, then switch to Print Preview to review the changes using a value of **150,000** when prompted.

5. Use the Format Painter and themes.

a. Open the AskingParameter report in Layout View.

b. Change the AskingParameter label in the Report Header section to **Asking Price Analysis**.

c. Apply the Retrospect theme. Review and resize the columns and the calculated field in the Report Footer to see all data as needed.

d. Change the font color of the RFirst label in the Page Header section to Automatic (black).

e. Use the Format Painter to copy the format from the RFirst label to the RLast, RPhone, Type, and Area labels in the Page Header section.

f. Change the font color of the SqFt label in the Page Header section to red.

g. Use the Format Painter to copy the format from the SqFt label to the Asking label.

h. Save and close the AskingParameter report.

Skills Review (continued)

6. Add subreports.

   a. Open the ListingReport in Layout View, and resize any text boxes that are not wide enough to show all data. Be careful to not extend the right edge of the report beyond one sheet of paper. Resize and align the SqFt, LakeFt, and BR labels to better fit above the columns of data they describe.

   b. Open the RealtorList report in Layout View, and resize any text boxes that are not wide enough to show all data. Again be careful to not extend the right edge of the report beyond one sheet of paper. Save and close the RealtorList report.

   c. Display the ListingReport in Design View. Expand the Report Footer section, and add the RealtorList report as a subreport using the SubReport Wizard. Choose None when asked to link the main form to the subform (you may have to scroll), and accept the default name of RealtorList.

   d. Delete the extra RealtorList label in the Report Footer. (*Hint*: It will be positioned near the upper-left corner of the subreport, but it may be mostly hidden by the subreport.)

   e. Preview each page of the report to make sure all data is clearly visible. Widen any controls that do not clearly display information, again being careful not to extend the report beyond the right margin.

   f. Narrow the width of the report if necessary in Report Design View, then save and close it.

7. Modify section properties.

   a. In Report Design View of the ListingReport, modify the Realtors.RealtorNo Footer section's Force New Page property to After Section. (*Note*: The RealtorNo field is included in two tables, Realtors and Listings. Access uses the *tablename.fieldname* convention to specify that the RealtorNo grouping field is from the Realtors table.)

   b. Open the Page Footer section, and add a label, **Created by *Your* Name**.

   c. Save and preview the ListingReport to make sure that the new section property forces each new realtor group of records to print on its own page, as shown in **FIGURE H-22**. Also check that a label identifying you as the report creator appears at the bottom of each page. Remember that you must print preview the report (rather than display it in Report View) to see how the report prints on each page.

   d. Print the report if requested by your instructor, then save and close the report.

FIGURE H-22

ListingNo	Type	Area	SqFt	LakeFt	BR	Bath	Garage	Pool	Asking
2	New	Ridgedale	3000	65	2	3	0	☐	$129,000.00
3	New	Ridgedale	2900	180	3	2.5	2	☐	$135,000.00
11	Ranch	Ridgedale	1215	80	3	2	0	☐	$85,000.00
1	Ranch	Ozark Mountain	3400	150	4	4	2	☐	$90,000.00

ListingReport

Master Listing Report

Sara   Student Last   555-222-8877

Skills Review (continued)

8. Create summary reports.

a. Right-click the ListingReport, click Copy, right-click the Navigation Pane, click Paste, then type **ListingSummary**.

b. Open the ListingSummary report in Design View, then delete the subreport from the Report Footer, all the controls in the Detail section, and all the labels in the Realtors.RealtorNo Header section. (*Note*: Be careful not to delete the three text boxes for RFirst, RLast, and RPhone in the Realtors.RealtorNo Header section.)

c. Close the extra space in the Detail and Realtors.RealtorNo Header sections.

d. Expand the size of the Realtors.RealtorNo Footer section, move the line to the bottom of that section, then add a text box to the right side of the section with the following expression: **=Sum([Asking])**.

e. Modify the new label to read **Subtotal of Asking Price:**, then move and resize the controls as needed so that both the label and text box can be clearly read in Report Design View.

f. Open the Property Sheet for the =Sum([Asking]) text box, click the Format tab, then choose **Currency** for the Format property, and **0** for the Decimal Places property.

g. Copy the =Sum([Asking]) text box to the Report Footer section, move it directly under the =Sum([Asking]) text box in the Realtors.RealtorNo Footer section, then change the label to be **Grand Total:**.

h. Draw two short lines under the =Sum([Asking]) text box in the Report Footer section to indicate a grand total.

i. Change the Force New Page property of the Realtors.RealtorNo Footer section to None.

j. Position all controls within the 8" mark on the ruler so that the width of the paper is no wider than 8". Drag the right edge of the report as far to the left as possible so that it does not extend beyond 8".

k. Preview the report. Switch to Portrait orientation, and resize sections and move controls in Design View so the report matches FIGURE H-23. Print the report if requested by your instructor, then save and close the report.

l. Close the RealEstate-H.accdb database, and exit Access.

FIGURE H-23

Master Listing Report

Sara	Student Last	555-222-8877		
			Subtotal of Asking Price:	$439,000
Phil	Kirkpatrick	555-111-9900		
			Subtotal of Asking Price:	$1,158,613
Jessica	Polar	555-333-3344		
			Subtotal of Asking Price:	$584,350
Malika	Thompson	555-444-7788		
			Subtotal of Asking Price:	$1,045,000
Jane Ann	Welch	555-223-0044		
			Subtotal of Asking Price:	$252,800
Shari	Duncan	555-228-5577		
			Subtotal of Asking Price:	$120,000
Trixie	Angelina	555-220-4466		
			Subtotal of Asking Price:	$105,000
Mary	Dell	555-888-7777		
			Subtotal of Asking Price:	$761,899
			Grand Total:	$4,466,662

Independent Challenge 1

As the manager of a music store's instrument rental program, you created a database to track instrument rentals to school-children. Now that several instruments have been rented, you need to create a report listing the rental transactions for each instrument.

a. Start Access, open the MusicStore-H.accdb database from the location where you store your Data Files, and enable content if prompted.

b. Use the Report Wizard to create a report based on the FirstName and LastName fields in the Customers table, the RentalDate field from the Rentals table, and the Description and MonthlyFee fields from the Instruments table.

c. View the data by Instruments, do not add any more grouping levels, sort the data in ascending order by RentalDate, use a Stepped layout and Portrait orientation, and title the report **Instrument Rental Report**.

d. Open the report in Design View, change the first grouping level from SerialNo to Description so that all instruments with the same description are grouped together, and open the Description Footer section.

e. Add a new text box to the Description Footer section with the expression **=Count([LastName])**. Change the label to **Customers:**.

f. Change the Force New Page property of the Description Footer section to After Section.

g. Add *your* name as a label to the Report Header section, and use the Format Painter to copy the formatting from the Instrument Rental Report label to your name. Double-click a corner sizing handle of the label with your name to resize it to show your entire name.

h. Save and preview the report, as shown in **FIGURE H-24**. Move, resize, and align controls as needed to match the figure, make sure all controls fit within the margins of one sheet of paper, then print the report if requested by your instructor.

i. Save and close the Instrument Rental Report, close the MusicStore-H.accdb database, then exit Access.

FIGURE H-24

Instrument Rental Report		Student Name		
Description	MonthlyFee	RentalDate	FirstName	LastName
Bass	$65.00			
		3/29/2015	Kathryn	Johnson
		7/29/2015	Kathryn	Johnson
Customers:		2		

Independent Challenge 2

As the manager of a music store's instrument rental program, you have created a database to track instrument rentals to schoolchildren. Now that the rental program is under way, you need to create a summary report that shows how many instruments have been rented by each school.

a. Start Access, open the MusicStore-H.accdb database from the location where you store your Data Files, and enable content if prompted.

b. Build a query in Query Design View with the following fields: SchoolName from the Schools table and RentalDate from the Rentals table. (*Hint*: Include the Customers table to build the proper relationships between the Schools and the Rentals table.) Save the query with the name **SchoolSummary**, then close it.

c. Create a new report in Report Design View. Use the SchoolSummary query as the Record Source property.

d. Add SchoolName as a grouping field, and add the SchoolName field to the left side of the SchoolName Header section. Delete the SchoolName label, and widen the SchoolName text box to about 4".

e. Drag the top edge of the Page Footer section up to completely close the Detail section.

f. Add a label to the Page Header section with *your* name. Format the label with an Arial Black font and 14-point font size. Resize the label to display all the text.

g. Add a label to the Report Header section that reads **New student musicians per school**.

h. Add a text box to the right side of the SchoolName Header section with the expression **=Count([RentalDate])**. Delete the accompanying label.

i. Align the top edges of the two text boxes in the SchoolName Header.

j. Use the Format Painter to copy the formatting from the label with your name to the new label in the Report Header section, the SchoolName text box, and the =Count([RentalDate]) expression in the SchoolName Header section. Switch back and forth between Print Preview and Design View to resize the text boxes in the SchoolName Header section as needed to show all information in each box.

k. Open the Report Footer section, then copy and paste the =Count([RentalDate]) text box to the same position in the Report Footer section.

l. Add one short line above and two short lines below the =Count([RentalDate]) text box in the Report Footer section to indicate a subtotal and grand total.

m. Save the report with the name **SchoolSummary**, then preview it, as shown in FIGURE H-25.

n. Close the SchoolSummary report, close the MusicStore-H.accdb database, then exit Access.

FIGURE H-25

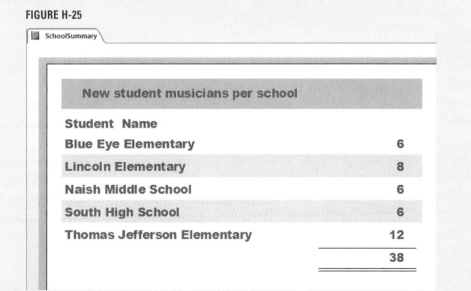

Independent Challenge 3

As the manager of a music store's instrument rental program, you have created a database to track instrument rentals to schoolchildren. Now that the rental program is under way, you need to create a parameter report for each instrument type.

a. Start Access, open the MusicStore-H.accdb database from the location where you store your Data Files, and enable content if prompted.

b. Create a query with the RentalDate field from the Rentals table, the Description and MonthlyFee fields from the Instruments table, and the FirstName and LastName fields from the Customers table.

c. Enter the parameter criteria **Between [Enter start date] And [Enter end date]** for the RentalDate field and **[Enter instrument type such as cello]** for the Description field.

d. Save the query with the name **RentalParameter**, test it with the dates **3/1/15** and **3/31/15** and the type **bass**. These criteria should select one record. Close the RentalParameter query.

e. Use the Report Wizard to create a report on all fields in the RentalParameter query. View the data by Instruments, do not add any more grouping levels, sort the records in ascending order by RentalDate, and use an Outline layout and a Portrait orientation. Title the report **Instrument Lookup**.

f. To respond to the prompts, enter **1/1/15** for the start date and **6/30/15** for the end date. Enter **viola** for the instrument type prompt.

g. In Report Design View, apply the Ion Boardroom theme. Resize the report title in the Report Header to display all the text.

h. Add *your* name as a label to the Report Header section. Change the font color to black so that it is clearly visible.

i. Add spaces between all words in the labels in the Description Header section: MonthlyFee, RentalDate, FirstName, and LastName to change them to **Monthly Fee**, **Rental Date**, **First Name**, and **Last Name**. Be sure to change the *labels* control and not the *text box* controls.

j. Open the Description Footer section.

k. Add a text box to the Description Footer section that contains the expression **=Count([LastName])*[MonthlyFee]**. Change the accompanying label to read **Monthly Revenue:**, then move the text box with the expression below the LastName text box and resize both so that their contents are clearly visible.

l. Open the Property Sheet for the new expression. On the Format tab, change the Format property to **Currency** and the Decimal Places property to **0**.

m. Display the report for RentalDates **1/1/15** through **3/31/15**, instrument type **cello**. Your report should look like FIGURE H-26.

n. Save the Instrument Lookup report, print it if requested by your instructor, close the MusicStore-H.accdb database, then exit Access.

FIGURE H-26

Independent Challenge 4: Explore

You have created an Access database to help manage college scholarship opportunities. You analyze scholarships by building a report with conditional formatting.

a. Start Access and open the Scholarships-H.accdb database from the location where you store your Data Files. Enable content if prompted.

b. Use the Report Wizard to create a report based on the Scholarships table. Include all of the fields. Add Major then Amount as the grouping levels, then click the Grouping Options button in the Report Wizard. Choose 5000s as the Grouping interval for the Amount field. Sort the records by DueDate in a descending order. Use a Stepped layout and a Landscape orientation. Title the report **Scholarships By Major**.

c. Preview the report, then add *your* name as a label next to the report title.

d. In Layout View, add spaces to the DueDate and ScholarshipName labels to read **Due Date** and **Scholarship Name**.

e. Delete the ID column.

f. Resize and narrow the columns to fit on a single sheet of landscape paper, then drag the right edge of the report to the left in Report Design View to make sure it is within the 10.5" mark on the horizontal ruler.

g. Expand the Page Header section to about twice its height, move the labels in the Page Header section to the bottom of the Page Header section, move the labels from the Report Header section to the top of the Page Header section, then close up the Report Header section.

h. Open the Major Footer section, then change the Force New Page property of the Major Footer section to After Section.

i. Click the Amount text box in the Detail section, then apply a new rule of conditional formatting. Use the Compare to other records rule type, and change the Bar color to green.

j. Preview page 3 of the report for the Business majors, as shown in **FIGURE H-27**.

k. Save and close the Scholarships By Major report and the Scholarships-H.accdb database.

FIGURE H-27

Major	Amount by 5000s	Due Date	Scholarship Name	Amount
Business			Student Name	
	0 - 5000			
		10/29/2016	Toyota Community Scholars	$1,000.00
		3/27/2016	Brown Foundation Goodyear Scholarship	$3,000.00
		3/19/2016	Shelter Insurance Scholarship	$1,500.00
		3/12/2016	Certified Public Accountants Scholarship	$200.00
		1/29/2016	Discover Card Scholarship	$1,000.00
		1/18/2016	Wal-Mart Stores Sam Walton Community Scholarship	$1,000.00
		4/28/2015	Tylenol Scholarship	$150.00
		3/17/2015	Monster Scholarship for Business	$2,500.00
		3/13/2015	NFIB Business Scholarships	$1,000.00
		3/7/2015	Executive Women International	$1,000.00
		1/29/2015	Pizza Hut Scholarship	$1,000.00
	5000 - 10000			
		2/26/2016	Kodak Scholarship	$6,000.00
		9/29/2015	SAL Commander's Scholarship	$5,000.00
		4/2/2015	International Trade Essay Contest	$5,000.00
	20000 - 25000			
		10/28/2016	Coca-Cola Scholars Program Scholarship	$20,000.00

Visual Workshop

Open the Baseball-H.accdb database from the location where you store your Data Files and enable content if prompted. Using the Report Wizard, build a report on the PlayerLName field from the Players table, and the AtBats and Hits fields from the Player Stats table. View the data by Players, do not add any more grouping or sorting fields, and use a Stepped layout and Portrait orientation. Enter **Batting Average** as the name of the report. In Report Design View, open the PlayerNo Footer section and move the PlayerLName text box to the same position in the PlayerNo Footer section. Add new text boxes to the PlayerNo Footer section to sum the AtBats, sum the Hits, and calculate the overall batting average per player. The expression to find the batting average is **=Sum([Hits])/Sum([AtBats])**. Delete any extra labels that are created when you add the text boxes, and delete all of the controls in the Detail section. Close the PlayerNo Header and Detail sections and resize the PlayerNo Footer section to remove blank space. Modify the Decimal Places property of the batting average calculation to show **3** digits to the right of the decimal point, and modify the Format property to be Standard. Apply a conditional format to the batting average expression so that if it is greater than or equal to **0.5**, the background color is yellow. Add a label to the Page Header section to identify the batting average, add a label to the Report Header section with *your* name, and then edit the labels and align the controls, as shown in **FIGURE H-28**. As a final step, change the Group on field from PlayerNo to PlayerLName so the records are sorted by player last name, as shown in **FIGURE H-28**. Save the Batting Average report, print the report if requested by your instructor, and then close it.

FIGURE H-28

PlayerLName	AtBats	Hits	Batting Average
Arno	6	2	0.333
Campanella	8	5	0.625
Dean	8	3	0.375
Douglas	8	8	1.000
Friedrichsen	6	3	0.500
Hammer	8	4	0.500
Kelsey	8	4	0.500
Langguth	8	4	0.500
Mantle	8	2	0.250

Working in the Cloud

CASE In your job for the Vancouver branch of Quest Specialty Travel, you travel frequently, you often work from home, and you also collaborate online with colleagues and clients. You want to learn how you can use SkyDrive with Office 2013 to work in the Cloud so that you can access and work on your files anytime and anywhere. (*Note*: SkyDrive and Office Web Apps are dynamic Web pages, and might change over time, including the way they are organized and how commands are performed. The steps and figures in this appendix reflect these pages at the time this book was published.)

Unit Objectives

After completing this unit, you will be able to:

- Understand Office 2013 in the Cloud
- Work Online
- Explore SkyDrive
- Manage Files on SkyDrive

- Share Files
- Explore Office Web Apps
- Complete a Team Project

Files You Will Need

WEB-1.pptx
WEB-2.docx

Learning
Outcomes
• Describe Office
  2013 Cloud
  Computing
  features
• Define SkyDrive
• Define Office
  Web Apps

Understand Office 2013 in the Cloud

The term **cloud computing** refers to the process of working with files and apps online. You may already be familiar with Web-based e-mail accounts such as Gmail and outlook.com. These applications are **cloud-based**, which means that you do not need a program installed on your computer to run them. Office 2013 has also been designed as a cloud-based application. When you work in Office 2013, you can choose to store your files "in the cloud" so that you can access them on any device connected to the Internet. **CASE** *You review the concepts related to working online with Office 2013.*

DETAILS

- **How does Office 2013 work in the Cloud?**

  When you launch an Office application such as Word or Excel, you might see your name and maybe even your picture in the top right corner of your screen. This information tells you that you have signed in to Office 2013, either with your personal account or with an account you are given as part of an organization such as a company or school. When you are signed in to Office and click the FILE tab in any Office 2013 application such as Word or Excel, you see a list of the files that you have used recently on your current computer and on any other connected device such as a laptop, a tablet or even a Windows phone. The file path appears beneath each filename so that you can quickly identify its location as shown in **FIGURE WEB-1**. Office 2013 also remembers your personalized settings so that they are available on all the devices you use.

- **What are roaming settings?**

  A **roaming setting** is a setting that travels with you on every connected device. Examples of roaming settings include your personal settings such as your name and picture, the files you've used most recently, your list of connected services such as Facebook and Twitter, and any custom dictionaries you've created. Two particularly useful roaming settings are the Word Resume Reading Position setting and the PowerPoint Last Viewed Slide setting. For example, when you open a PowerPoint presentation that you've worked on previously, you will see a message similar to the one shown in **FIGURE WEB-2**.

- **What is SkyDrive?**

  SkyDrive is an online storage and file sharing service. When you are signed in to your computer with your Microsoft account, you receive access to your own SkyDrive, which is your personal storage area on the Internet. On your SkyDrive, you are given space to store up to 7 GB of data online. A SkyDrive location is already created on your computer as shown in **FIGURE WEB-3**. Every file you save to SkyDrive is synced among your computers and your personal storage area on SkyDrive.com. The term **synced** (which stands for synchronized) means that when you add, change or delete files on one computer, the same files on your other devices are also updated.

- **What are Office Web Apps?**

  Office Web Apps are versions of Microsoft Word, Excel, PowerPoint, and OneNote that you can access online from your SkyDrive. An Office Web App does not include all of the features and functions included with the full Office version of its associated application. However, you can use the Office Web App from any computer that is connected to the Internet, even if Microsoft Office 2013 is not installed on that computer.

- **How do SkyDrive and Office Web Apps work together?**

  You can create a file in Office 2013 using Word, Excel, PowerPoint, or OneNote and then save it to your SkyDrive. You can then open the Office file saved to SkyDrive and edit it using your Office 2013 apps. If you do not have Office 2013 installed on the computer you are using, you can edit the file using your Web browser and the corresponding Office Web App. You can also use an Office Web App to create a new file, which is saved automatically to SkyDrive while you work and you can download a file created with an Office Web App and work with the file in the full version of the corresponding Office application.

FIGURE WEB-1: FILE tab in Microsoft Excel

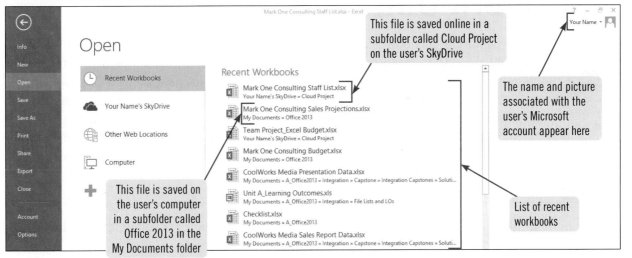

FIGURE WEB-2: PowerPoint Last Viewed Slide setting

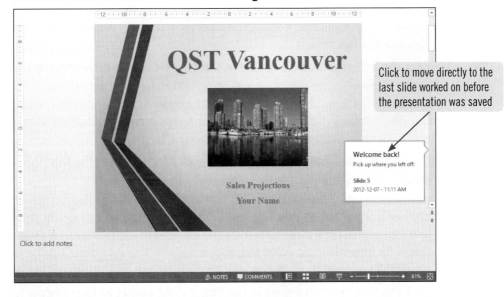

FIGURE WEB-3: Saving a Word file on SkyDrive

Work Online

Learning Outcomes
- View Microsoft account settings
- Sign out of a Microsoft account
- Switch Microsoft accounts

When you work on your own computer, you are usually signed in to your Microsoft account automatically. When you use another person's computer or a public computer, you will be required to enter the password associated with your Microsoft account to access files you have saved on Windows SkyDrive. You know you are signed in to Windows when you see your name and possibly your picture in the top right corner of your screen. *Note*: To complete the steps below, you need to be signed in to your Microsoft account. If you do not have a Microsoft account, see "Getting a Microsoft account" in the yellow box. **CASE** ▶ *You explore the settings associated with your account, learn how to switch accounts, and sign out of an account.*

STEPS

1. **Sign in to Windows, if necessary, launch Word, click** Blank document, **then verify that your name appears in the top right corner of your screen**

2. **Click the** list arrow **to the right of your name, as shown in** FIGURE WEB-4, **then click** About me **and sign in if prompted**

   Internet Explorer opens and your Profile page appears. Here, you can add or edit your contact information and information about your workplace. You can also change the name and picture that appear in the top right corner of your window.

3. **Click the** list arrow **next to Profile in the top left corner of your screen, above the picture**

   The tiles representing the services your Windows account is connected to appear as shown in FIGURE WEB-5. Note that if you have connected your Microsoft account to accounts in other services such as Facebook, LinkedIn, or outlook.com, you will see these connections in the appropriate app. For example, your connections to Facebook and LinkedIn appear in the People app.

4. **Click a blank area below the apps tiles, click** Your Name **in the top right corner, then click** Account settings

   Either you are taken directly to the Microsoft account screen or, depending on your security settings, a Sign in screen appears. To make changes to your account, you might need to enter the password associated with your account. You can also choose to sign in with a different Microsoft account. Once you sign in, you can change the information associated with your account such as your name, email address, birth date, and password. You can also choose to close your Microsoft account, which deletes all the data associated with it.

5. **Click the** Close button ▨ **in the upper right corner of the window to remove the Sign-in window, click** Close all tabs **to return to Word, then click the** list arrow ▼ **next to Your Name in the top right corner of the Word window**

   To sign out of your account, you can click Sign Out at the top of the Accounts dialog box that appears when you click Account Settings. When you are working on your own computers, you will rarely need to sign out of your account. However, if you are working on a public computer, you may want to sign out of your account to avoid having your files accessible to other users.

6. **Click** Switch account

   You can choose to sign into another Microsoft account or to an account with an organization.

7. **Click the** Close button ▨

   You are returned to a blank document in Word.

8. **Exit Word**

FIGURE WEB-4: Viewing Windows account options in Word

FIGURE WEB-5: Connected services associated with a Profile

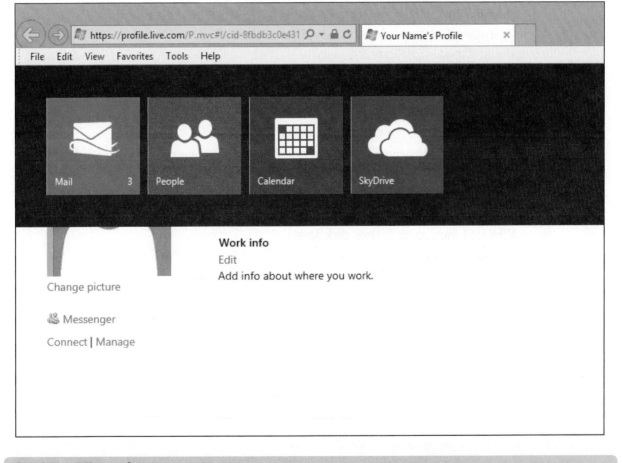

Getting a Microsoft account

If you have been working with Windows and Office 2013, you might already have a Microsoft account, which was previously referred to as a Windows Live ID. You also have an account if you use outlook.com (formerly Hotmail), SkyDrive, Xbox LIVE, or have a Windows Phone. A Microsoft account consists of an email address and a password. If you wish to create a new Microsoft account, go to https://signup.live.com/ and follow the directions provided.

Explore SkyDrive

Learning Outcomes
- Save a file to SkyDrive
- Create a folder on SkyDrive

SkyDrive works like the hard drive on your computer. You can save and open files from SkyDrive, create folders, and manage your files. You can access the files you save on SkyDrive from any of your connected devices and from anywhere you have a computer connection. **CASE** ▶ *You open a PowerPoint presentation, save the file to your SkyDrive, then create a folder.*

STEPS

1. **Start PowerPoint, then open the file** WEB-1.pptx **from the location where you store your Data Files**

QUICK TIP

If you are signed in with your own account, you will see Your Name's Sky-Drive (for example, "Tom's SkyDrive").

2. **Click the** FILE **tab, click** Save As, **then click** Your Name's SkyDrive **(top selection) if it is not already selected**

3. **Click the** Browse button

   The Save As dialog box opens, showing the folders stored on your SkyDrive. You may have several folders already stored there or you may have none.

4. **Click** New folder, **type** Cengage, **then press** [Enter]

5. **Double-click** Cengage, **select** WEB-1.pptx **in the File name text box, type** WEB-QST Vancouver 1 **as shown in** FIGURE WEB-6, **then click** Save

   The file is saved to the Cengage folder on the SkyDrive that is associated with your Microsoft account. The PowerPoint window reappears.

6. **Click the** FILE **tab, click** Close, **click the** FILE **tab, then click** Open

   WEB-QST Vancouver 1.pptx appears as the first file listed in the Recent Presentations list, and the path to your Cengage folder on your SkyDrive appears beneath it.

7. **Click** WEB-QST Vancouver 1.pptx **to open it, then type your name where indicated on the title slide**

8. **Click** Slide 2 **in the Navigation pane, select** 20% **in the third bullet, type** 30%, **click the** FILE **tab, click** Save As, **click** Cengage **under Current Folder, change the file name to** WEB-QST Vancouver 2, **then click** Save

9. **Exit PowerPoint**

   A new version of the presentation is saved to the Cengage folder that you created on SkyDrive.

How to disable default saving to Skydrive

You can specify how you want to save files from Office 2013 applications. By default, files are saved to locations you specify on your SkyDrive. You can change the default to be a different location. In Word, PowerPoint, or Excel, click the FILE tab, then click Options. Click Save in the left sidebar, then in the Save section, click the Save to Computer by default check box, as shown in FIGURE WEB-7. Click OK to close the PowerPoint Options dialog box. The Save options you've selected will be active in Word, PowerPoint, and Excel, regardless of which application you were using when you changed the option.

FIGURE WEB-6: Saving a presentation to SkyDrive

FIGURE WEB-7: Changing the default Save location in PowerPoint

Save to Computer by default check box

Manage Files on SkyDrive

Learning Outcomes
- Access SkyDrive from Internet Explorer
- Rename, Delete, and Move files in SkyDrive

You are automatically connected to SkyDrive when you sign into your Microsoft account and launch an Office 2013 application. You can also access SkyDrive through your Web browser or from the SkyDrive App in Windows 8. When you start the SkyDrive App, you can upload and download files, create folders, and delete files. You can also download the SkyDrive app to your tablet or other mobile device so you can access files wherever you have an Internet connection. When you access SkyDrive from Internet Explorer, you can do more file management tasks, including renaming and moving files. **CASE** *You explore how to work with SkyDrive from your Web browser and from the SkyDrive App.*

STEPS

1. **Launch Internet Explorer or another Web browser, type** skydrive.com **in the Address box, then press [Enter]**

   If you are signed in to your Microsoft account, your SkyDrive opens. If you are not signed in, the login page appears where you can enter the email address and password associated with your Microsoft account.

2. **Sign in if necessary, click the blue tile labeled** Cengage, **then right-click** WEB-QST Vancouver 1.pptx **as shown in** FIGURE WEB-8

   You can open the file in the PowerPoint Web App or in PowerPoint, download the file to your computer, share it, embed it, and perform other actions such as renaming and deleting.

3. **Click** Download, **click** Open **in the bar at the bottom of the screen, then click** Enable Editing

   The presentation opens in PowerPoint where you can save it to your computer hard drive or back to SkyDrive.

4. **Click the** DESIGN **tab, click the** More button ⌄ **in the Themes group, select the** Wisp **theme, click the** FILE **tab, click** Save As, **click** Computer, **click** Browse, **navigate to a location on your computer or on an external drive such as a USB flash drive, click** Save, **then exit PowerPoint**

5. **Launch PowerPoint, then notice the files listed in the left pane under Recent**

   The file you just saved to your computer or external drive appears first and the file saved to the Cengage folder on SkyDrive appears second.

6. **Click the second listing, notice that the file is not updated with the Wisp design, then exit PowerPoint**

   When you download a file from SkyDrive, changes you make are not saved to the version on SkyDrive. You can also access SkyDrive from your Windows 8 screen by using the SkyDrive app.

TROUBLE
If prompted, enter your log in information in the Add your Microsoft account screen. Note that you can only complete steps 7 to 9 if you are working on Windows 8.

7. **Show the Windows 8 Start screen, click the** SkyDrive tile, **open the Cengage folder, right-click** WEB-QST Vancouver 1, **view the buttons on the taskbar as shown in** FIGURE WEB-9, **click the** Delete button **on the taskbar, then click** Delete

8. **Right-click** WEB-QST Vancouver 2, **click the** New Folder button **on the taskbar, type** Illustrated, **then click** Create folder

   You can rename and move files in SkyDrive through Internet Explorer.

9. **Move the mouse pointer to the top of the screen until it becomes the hand pointer, drag to the bottom of the screen to close the SkyDrive App, click the** Internet Explorer **tile on the Start screen, go to** skydrive.com, **right-click** WEB-QST Vancouver 2 **on the SkyDrive site, click** Move to, **click the** ⊳ **next to Cengage, click** Illustrated, **then click** Move

FIGURE WEB-8: File management options on SkyDrive

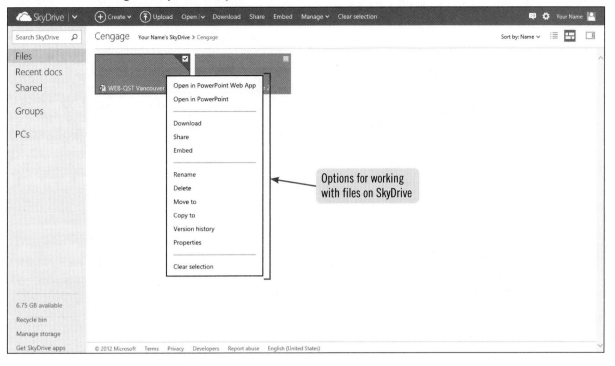

Options for working with files on SkyDrive

FIGURE WEB-9: File management options on SkyDrive App

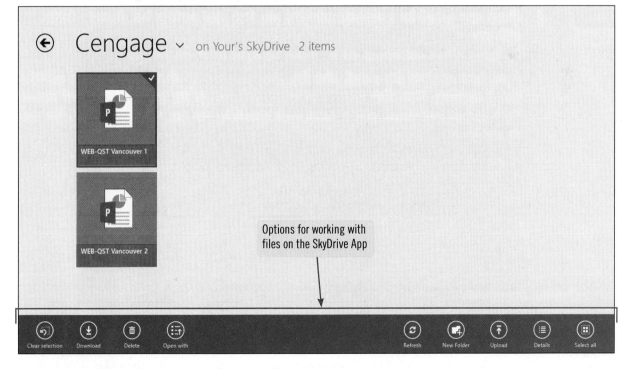

Options for working with files on the SkyDrive App

Share Files

One of the great advantages of working with SkyDrive is that you can share your files with others. Suppose, for example, that you want a colleague to review a presentation you created in PowerPoint and then add a new slide. You can, of course, e-mail the presentation directly to your colleague who can then make changes and e-mail the presentation back. Alternatively, you can share the PowerPoint file directly from SkyDrive. Your colleague can edit the file using the PowerPoint Web App or the full version of PowerPoint, and then you can check the updated file on SkyDrive. In this way, you and your colleague are working with just one version of the presentation that you both can update. **CASE** ▶ *You have decided to share files in the Illustrated folder that you created in the previous lesson with another individual. You start by sharing files with your partner and your partner can share files with you.*

STEPS

TROUBLE
If you cannot find a partner, you can email the file to yourself.

1. **Identify a partner with whom you can work, and obtain his or her e-mail address; you can choose someone in your class or someone on your e-mail list, but it should be someone who will be completing these steps when you are**

2. **Right-click the Illustrated folder, then click Sharing as shown in FIGURE WEB-10**

3. **Type the e-mail address of your partner**

4. **Click in the Include a personal message box, then type Here's the presentation we're working on together as shown in FIGURE WEB-11**

5. **Verify that the Recipients can edit check box is selected, then click Share**
   Your partner will receive a message advising him or her that you have shared the WEB-QST Vancouver 2.pptx file. If your partner is completing the steps at the same time, you will receive an e-mail from your partner.

TROUBLE
If you do not receive a message, your partner has not yet completed the steps to share the folder.

6. **Check your e-mail for a message advising you that your partner has shared a folder with you**
   The subject of the e-mail message will be "[Name] has shared documents with you."

7. **If you have received the e-mail, click the Show content link that appears in the warning box, if necesary, then click WEB-QST Vancouver 2.pptx in the body of the e-mail message**
   The PowerPoint presentation opens in the Microsoft PowerPoint Web App. You will work in the Web App in the next lesson.

Co-authoring documents

You can work on a document, presentation, or workbook simultaneously with a partner. First, save the file to your SkyDrive. Click the FILE tab, click Share, then click Invite People. Enter the email addresses of the people you want to work on the file with you and then click Share. Once your partner has received, opened, and started editing the document, you can start working together. You will see a notification in the status bar that someone is editing the document with you. When you click the notification, you can see the name of the other user and their picture if they have one attached to their Windows account. When your partner saves, you'll see his or her changes in green shading which goes away the next time you save. You'll have an opportunity to co-author documents when you complete the Team Project at the end of this appendix.

FIGURE WEB-10: Sharing a file from SkyDrive

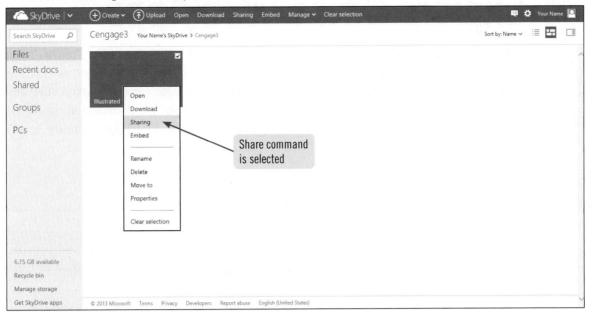

FIGURE WEB-11: Sharing a file with another person

Send email	Send a link to "WEB-QST Vancouver 2.pptx" in email
Post to [f] [y] [in]	To
Get a link	PartnerName@partneremail.com ✕
	Here's the presentation we're working on together.
	✔ Recipients can edit
	☐ Require everyone who accesses this to sign in
Help me choose how to share	Share Cancel

Explore Office Web Apps

Learning
Outcomes
• Edit a presentation
  with PowerPoint
  Web App
• Open a presenta-
  tion from
  PowerPoint
  Web App

As you have learned, a Web App is a scaled-down version of an Office program. Office Web Apps include Word, Excel, PowerPoint, and OneNote. You can use the Office Web Apps to create and edit documents even if you don't have Office 2013 installed on your computer and you can use them on other devices such as tablets and smartphones. From SkyDrive, you can also open the document in the full Office application if the application is installed on the computer you are using. **CASE** ▶ *You use the PowerPoint Web App and the full version of PowerPoint to edit the presentation.*

STEPS

1. **Click EDIT PRESENTATION, then click Edit in PowerPoint Web App**

   Presentations opened using the PowerPoint Web App have the same look and feel as presentations opened using the full version of PowerPoint. However, like all of the Office Web Apps, the PowerPoint Web App has fewer features available than the full version of PowerPoint.

2. **Review the Ribbon and its tabs to familiarize yourself with the commands you can access from the PowerPoint Web App**

   TABLE WEB-1 summarizes the commands that are available.

   TROUBLE
   You need to click the
   text first, click it
   again, then drag to
   select it.

3. **Click Slide 3, click the text Hornby Island, click it again and select it, then type Tofino so the bullet item reads Tofino Sea Kayaking**

4. **Click outside the text box, click the DESIGN tab, then click the More Themes list arrow ▼ to show the selection of designs available**

   A limited number of designs are available on the PowerPoint Web App. When you want to use a design or a command that is not available on the PowerPoint Web App, you open the file in the full version of PowerPoint.

5. **Click on a blank area of the slide, click OPEN IN POWERPOINT at the top of the window, then click Yes in response to the message**

6. **Click the DESIGN tab, click the More button ▼ in the Themes group to expand the Themes gallery, select the Quotable design as shown in FIGURE WEB-12, click the picture on Slide 1, then press [Delete]**

7. **Click the Save button ⬚ on the Quick Access toolbar**

   The Save button includes a small icon indicating you are saving to SkyDrive and not to your computer's hard drive or an external drive.

8. **Click the Close button ✕ to exit PowerPoint**

   You open the document again to verify that your partner made the same changes.

9. **Launch PowerPoint, click WEB-QST Vancouver 2.pptx at the top of the Recent list, verify that the Quotable design is applied and the picture is removed, then exit PowerPoint**

Exploring other Office Web Apps

Three other Office Web Apps are Word, Excel, and OneNote. You can share files on SkyDrive directly from any of these applications using the same method you used to share files from PowerPoint. To familiarize yourself with the commands available in an Office Web App, open the file and then review the commands on each tab on the Ribbon. If you want to perform a task that is not available in the Web App, open the file in the full version of the application.

FIGURE WEB-12: Selecting the Quotable design

TABLE WEB-1: **Commands on the PowerPoint Web App**

tab	category/group	options
FILE	Info	• Open in PowerPoint (also available on the toolbar above the document window)
		• Previous Versions
	Save As	• Where's the Save Button?: In PowerPoint Web App, the presentation is being saved automatically so there is no Save button
		• Download: use to download a copy of the presentation to your computer
	Print	• Create a printable PDF of the presentation that you can then open and print
	Share	• Share with people - you can invite others to view and edit your presentation
		• Embed - include the presentation in a blog on Web site
	About	• Try Microsoft Office, Terms of Use, and Privacy and Cookies
	Help	• Help with PowerPoint questions, Give Feedback to Microsoft, and modify how you can view the presentation (for example, text only)
	Exit	• Close the presentation and exit to view SkyDrive folders
HOME	Clipboard	• Cut, Copy, Paste, Format Painter
	Delete	• Delete a slide
	Slides	• Add a new slide, duplicate a slide, hide a slide
	Font	• Change the font, size, style, and color of selected text
	Paragraph	• Add bullets and numbering, indent text, align text, and change text direction
	Drawing	• Add text boxes and shapes, arrange them on the slide, apply Quick Styles, modify shape fill and outline, and duplicate a shape
INSERT	Slides	• Add new slides with selected layout
	Images	• Add pictures from your computer, online pictures, or screen shots
	Illustrations	• Add shapes, SmartArt, or charts
	Links	• Add links or actions to objects
	Text	• Add comments, text boxes, headers and footers, and other text elements
	Comments	• Add comments
DESIGN	Themes	• Apply a limited number of themes to a presentation and apply variants to a selected theme
		• Apply variants to a selected theme
ANIMATIONS	Animation	• Apply a limited number of animation effects to a slide element and modify existing timings
TRANSITIONS	Transitions to This Slide	• Apply a limited number of transition effects to slides and chose to apply the effect to all slides
VIEW	Presentation Views	• You can view the slide in Editing View, Reading View, Slide Show View, and Notes View and you can show any comments made by users who worked on PowerPoint using the full version

© 2014 Cengage Learning

Team Project

Introduction

From SkyDrive, you can easily collaborate with others to produce documents, presentations, and spreadsheets that include each user's input. Instead of emailing a document to colleagues and then waiting for changes, you can both work on the document at the same time online. To further explore how you can work with SkyDrive and Office 2013, you will work with two other people to complete a team project. The subject of the team project is the planning of a special event of your choice, such as a class party, a lecture, or a concert. The special event should be limited to a single afternoon or evening.

Follow the guidelines provided below to create the files required for the team project. When you have completed the project, the team will submit a Word document containing information about your project, as well as three files related to the project: a Word document, a PowerPoint presentation, and an Excel workbook.

Project Setup

As a team, work together to complete the following tasks.

a. Share email addresses among all three team members.

b. Set up a time (either via email, an online chat session, Internet Messaging, or face to face) when you will get together to choose your topic and assign roles.

c. At your meeting, complete the table below with information about your team and your special event.

Team Name (last name of one team member or another name that describes the project.)
Team Members
Event type (for example, party, lecture, concert, etc.)
Event purpose (for example, fundraiser for a specific cause, celebrate the end of term, feature a special guest, etc.)
Event location, date, and time
Team Roles indicate who is responsible for each of the following three files (one file per team member)
Word document:
Excel workbook:
PowerPoint presentation:

Document Development

Individually, complete the tasks listed below for the file you are responsible for. You need to develop appropriate content, format the file attractively, and then be prepared to share the file with the other team members.

Word Document

The Word document contains a description of your special event and includes a table listing responsibilities and a time line. Create the Word document as follows:

1. Create a Cloud Project folder on your SkyDrive, then create a new Word document and save it as **Cloud Project_ Word Description** to the Cloud Project folder.

Document Development (continued)

2. Include a title with the name of your project and a subtitle with the names of your team members. Format the title with the Title style and the subtitle with the Subtitle style.

3. Write a paragraph describing the special event—its topics, purpose, the people involved, etc. You can paraphrase some of the information your team discussed in your meeting.

4. Create a table similar to the table shown below and then complete it with the required information. Include up to ten rows. A task could be "Contact the caterers" or "Pick up the speaker." Visualize the sequence of tasks required to put on the event.

Task	Person Responsible	Deadline

5. Format the table using the table style of your choice.

6. Save the document to your SkyDrive. You will share the document with your team members and receive feedback in the next section.

Excel Workbook

The Excel workbook contains a budget for the special event. Create the Excel workbook as follows:

1. Create a new Excel workbook and save it as **Cloud Project_Excel Budget** to the Cloud Project folder on your SkyDrive.

2. Create a budget that includes both the revenues you expect from the event (for example, ticket sales, donations, etc.) and the expenses. Expense items include advertising costs (posters, ads, etc.), food costs if the event is catered, transportation costs, etc. The revenues and expenses you choose will depend upon the nature of the project.

3. Make the required calculations to total all the revenue items and all the expense items.

4. Calculate the net profit (or loss) as the revenue minus the expenses.

5. Format the budget attractively using fill colors, border lines, and other enhancements to make the data easy to read.

6. Save the workbook to your SkyDrive. You will share the workbook with your team members and receive feedback in the next section.

PowerPoint Presentation

The PowerPoint presentation contains a presentation that describes the special event to an audience who may be interested in attending. Create the PowerPoint presentation as follows:

1. Create a new PowerPoint presentation and save it as **Cloud Project_PowerPoint Presentation** to the Cloud Project folder on your SkyDrive.

2. Create a presentation that consists of five slides including the title slide as follows:
   a. Slide 1: Title slide includes the name of the event and your team members
   b. Slide 2: Purpose of the party or event
   c. Slide 3: Location, time, and cost
   d. Slide 4: Chart showing a breakdown of costs (to be supplied when you co-author in the next section)
   e. Slide 5: Motivational closing slide designed to encourage the audience to attend; include appropriate pictures

3. Format the presentation attractively using the theme of your choice.

4. Save the presentation to your SkyDrive. You will share the presentation with your team members and receive feedback.

Co-Authoring on Skydrive

You need to share your file, add feedback to the other two files, then create a final version of your file. When you read the file created by the other two team members, you need to add additional data or suggestions. For example, if you created the Excel budget, you can provide the person who created the PowerPoint presentation with information about the cost breakdown. If you created the Word document, you can add information about the total revenue and expenses contained in the Excel budget to your description. You decide what information to add to each of the two files you work with.

1. Open the file you created.
2. Click the **FILE tab**, click **Share**, then click **Invite People**.
3. Enter the email addresses of the other two team members, then enter the following message: **Here's the file I created for our team project. Please make any changes, provide suggestions, and then save it. Thanks!** See FIGURE WEB-13.

FIGURE WEB-13

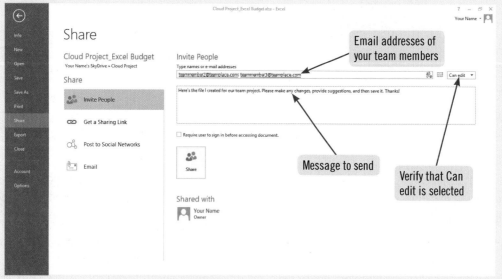

4. Click the **Share button**.
5. Allow team members time to add information and comments to your file. Team members should save frequently. When the file is saved, it is saved directly to your SkyDrive. Note that you can work together on the document or you can work separately. You can also choose to make changes with the full version of the Office 2013 applications or with the Office Web Apps. When someone is working on your file, you will see their user name on the status bar.
6. Decide which changes you want to keep, make any further changes you think are needed to make the document as clear as possible, then save a final version.

Project Summary

When you are pleased with the contents of your file and have provided feedback to your team members, assign a team member to complete the following tasks and then complete your portion as required.

1. Open **WEB-2.docx** from the location where you save your Data Files, then save it to your Cloud Project folder on your SkyDrive as **Cloud Project_Summary**.
2. Read the directions in the document, then enter your name as Team Member 1 and write a short description of your experience working with SkyDrive and Office 2013 to complete the team project.
3. Share the file with your team members and request that they add their own names and descriptions.
4. When all team members have finished working on the document, save all the changes.
5. Make sure you store all four files completed for the project in the Cloud Project appendix on your SkyDrive, then submit them to your instructor on behalf of your team.

Glossary

.accdb The file extension for the Access 2007 – 2013 database file format.

.jpg The file extension for a JPEG file.

.mdb The file extension for the Access 2000 – 2003 database file format.

Aggregate function A function such as Sum, Avg, and Count used in a summary query to calculate information about a group of records.

Alignment command A command used in Layout or Design View for a form or report to either left-, center-, or right-align a value within its control, or to align the top, bottom, right, or left edge of the control with respect to other controls.

Allow Multiple Values A Lookup property that lets you create a multivalued field.

Allow Value List Edits The Lookup field property that determines whether users can add to or edit the list of items.

Alternate Back Color property A property that determines the alternating background color of the selected section in a form or report.

Anchoring A layout positioning option that allows you to tie controls together so you can work with them as a group.

AND criteria Criteria placed in the same row of the query design grid. All criteria on the same row must be true for a record to appear on the resulting datasheet.

Argument Information that a function uses to create the final answer. Multiple arguments are separated by commas. All of the arguments for a function are surrounded by a single set of parentheses.

Asterisk (*) A wildcard character used to search for any number of characters in query criteria.

Attachment A field data type for adding one or more files to a record such as images.

Attachment field A field that allows you to attach an external file such as a Word document, PowerPoint presentation, Excel workbook, or image file to a record.

AutoNumber A field data type in which Access enters a sequential integer for each record added into the datasheet. Numbers cannot be reused even if the record is deleted.

Avg function A built-in Access function used to calculate the average of the values in a given field.

Background image An image that fills an entire form or report, appearing "behind" the other controls.

Backstage view Appears when then FILE tab is clicked. The navigation bar on the left side contains commands to perform actions common to most Office programs, such as opening a file, saving a file, and closing the file.

Backward-compatible Software feature that enables documents saved in an older version of a program to be opened in a newer version of the program.

Bound control A control used in either a form or report to display data from the underlying field; used to edit and enter new data in a form.

Byte A field size that allows entries only from 0 to 255.

Calculated field A field created in Query Design View that results from an expression of existing fields, Access functions, and arithmetic operators. For example, the entry Profit: [RetailPrice]-[WholesalePrice] in the field cell of the query design grid creates a calculated field called Profit that is the difference between the values in the RetailPrice and WholesalePrice fields.

Calculation A new value that is created by entering an expression in a text box on a form or report.

Calendar Picker A pop-up calendar from which you can choose dates for a date field.

Child table The "many" table in a one-to-many relationship.

Clipboard A temporary Windows storage area that holds the selections you copy or cut.

Cloud computing Work done in a virtual environment using data, applications, and resources stored on servers and accessed over the Internet or a company's internal network rather than on users' computers.

Column separator The thin line that separates the field names to the left or right.

Combo box A bound control used to display a list of possible entries for a field in which you can also type an entry from the keyboard. It is a "combination" of the list box and text box controls.

Combo Box Wizard A bound control used to display a list of possible entries for a field in which you can also type an entry from the keyboard.

Command button An unbound control used to provide an easy way to initiate an action.

Compatibility The ability of different programs to work together and exchange data.

Conditional formatting Formatting that is based on specified criteria. For example, a text box may be conditionally formatted do display its value in red if the value is a negative number.

Control Any element on a form or report such as a label, text box, line, or combo box. Controls can be bound, unbound, or calculated.

Control Source property A property of a bound control in a form or report that determines the field to which the control is connected.

Criteria Entries (rules and limiting conditions) that determine which records are displayed when finding or filtering records in a datasheet or form, or when building a query.

Criteria syntax Rules by which criteria need to be entered. For example, text criteria syntax requires that the criteria are surrounded by quotation marks (" "). Date criteria are surrounded by pound signs (#).

Crosstab query A query that represents data in a cross-tabular layout (fields are used for both column and row headings).

Crosstab Query Wizard A wizard used to create crosstab queries and which helps identify fields that will be used for row and column headings, and fields that will be summarized within the datasheet.

Crosstab row A row in the query design grid used to specify the column and row headings and values for the crosstab query.

Current record The record that has the focus or is being edited.

Data type A required property for each field that defines the type of data that can be entered in each field. Valid data types include AutoNumber, Short Text, Number, Currency, Date/Time, and Long Text.

Database designer The person responsible for building and maintaining tables, queries, forms, and reports.

Database user The person primarily interested in entering, editing, and analyzing the data in the database.

Datasheet A spreadsheet-like grid that displays fields as columns and records as rows.

Datasheet View A view that lists the records of the object in a datasheet. Tables, queries, and most form objects have a Datasheet View.

Date function A built-in Access function used to display the current date on a form or report; enter the Date function as Date().

Default View property A form property that determines whether a subform automatically opens in Datasheet or Continuous Forms view.

Design View A view in which the structure of the object can be manipulated. Every Access object (table, query, form, report, macro, and module) has a Design View.

Dialog box launcher An icon you can click to open a dialog box or task pane from which to choose related commands.

Edit List Items button A button you click to add items to the combo box list in Form View.

Edit mode The mode in which Access assumes you are trying to edit a particular field, so keystrokes such as [Ctrl][End], [Ctrl][Home], [↓], and [↑] move the insertion point within the field.

Edit record symbol A pencil-like symbol that appears in the record selector box to the left of the record that is currently being edited in either a datasheet or a form.

Enabled property A control property that determines whether the control can have the focus in Form View.

Error indicator An icon that automatically appears in Design View to indicate some type of error. For example, a green error indicator appears in the upper-left corner of a text box in Form Design View if the text box Control Source property is set to a field name that doesn't exist.

Expression A combination of values, functions, and operators that calculates to a single value. Access expressions start with an equal sign and are placed in a text box in either Form Design View or Report Design View.

Field In a table, a field corresponds to a column of data, a specific piece or category of data such as a first name, last name, city, state, or phone number.

Field list A list of the available fields in the table or query that the field list represents. Also, a pane that opens in Access and lists the database tables and the fields they contain.

Field name The name given to each field in a table.

Field properties Characteristics that further define the field.

Field Properties pane The lower half of Table Design View, which displays field properties.

Field selector button The button to the left of a field in Table Design View that indicates which field is currently selected.

Field selector In Query Design View, the thin gray bar above a field name in the query grid.

Field Size property A field property that determines the number of characters that can be entered in a field.

File A stored collection of data; in Access, the entire database and all of its objects are in one file.

Filter A way to temporarily display only those records that match given criteria.

Filter By Form A way to filter data that allows two or more criteria to be specified at the same time.

Filter By Selection A way to filter records for an exact match.

Find Duplicates Query Wizard A wizard used to create a query that determines whether a table contains duplicate values in one or more fields.

Find Unmatched Query Wizard A wizard used to create a query that finds records in one table that doesn't have related records in another table.

Focus The property that indicates which field would be edited if you were to start typing.

Force New Page A property that forces a report section to start printing at the top of a new page.

Foreign key field In a one-to-many relationship between two tables, the foreign key field is the field in the "many" table that links the table to the primary key field in the "one" table.

Form An Access object that provides an easy-to-use data entry screen that generally shows only one record at a time.

Form Header The section of a form that appears at the beginning of a form and typically displays the form title.

Form section A location in a form that contains controls. The section in which a control is placed determines where and how often the control prints.

Form View View of a form object that displays data from the underlying recordset and allows you to enter and update data.

Form Wizard An Access wizard that helps you create a form.

Format Painter A tool you can use when designing and laying out forms and reports to copy formatting characteristics from one control to another.

Format property A field property that controls how information is displayed and printed.

Formatting Enhancing the appearance of information through font, size, and color changes.

FROM A SQL keyword that determines how tables are joined.

Function A special, predefined formula that provides a shortcut for a commonly used calculation, for example, Sum or Count.

Gallery A visual collection of choices you can browse through to make a selection. Often available with Live Preview.

Graphic image *See* Image.

Grouping A way to sort records in a particular order, as well as provide a section before and after each group of records.

Groups Each tab on the Ribbon is arranged into groups to make features easy to find.

Image A nontextual piece of information such as a picture, piece of clip art, drawn object, or graph. Because images are graphical (and not numbers or letters), they are sometimes referred to as graphical images.

Infinity symbol The symbol that indicates the "many" side of a one-to-many relationship.

Input Mask A field property that provides a visual guide for users as they enter data.

Insertion point A blinking vertical line that appears when you click in a text box; indicates where new text will be inserted.

Integrate To incorporate a document and parts of a document created in one program into another program; for example, to incorporate an Excel chart into a PowerPoint slide, or an Access report into a Word document.

Interface The look and feel of a program; for example, the appearance of commands and the way they are organized in the program window.

Is Not Null A criterion that finds all records in which any entry has been made in the field.

Is Null A criterion that finds all records in which no entry has been made in the field.

Join line The line identifying which fields establish the relationship between two related tables. Also called a link line.

JPEG (Joint Photographic Experts Group) Acronym for Joint Photographic Experts Group, which defines the standards for the compression algorithms that allow image files to be stored in an efficient compressed format. JPEG files use the .jpg filename extension.

Junction table A table created to establish separate one-to-many relationships to two tables that have a many-to-many relationship.

Key symbol The symbol appearing to the left of a primary key field.

Label control An unbound control that displays text to describe and clarify other information on a form or report.

Label Wizard A report wizard that precisely positions and sizes information to print on a vast number of standard business label specifications.

Landscape orientation A way to print or view a page that is 11 inches wide by 8.5 inches tall.

Launch To open or start a program on your computer.

Layout The general arrangement in which a form displays the fields in the underlying recordset. Layout types include Columnar, Tabular, Datasheet, and Chart. Columnar is most popular for a form, and Datasheet is most popular for a subform.

Layout View An Access view that lets you make some design changes to a form or report while you are browsing the data.

Left function An Access function that returns a specified number of characters, starting with the left side of a value in a Text field.

Len function Built-in Access function used to return the number of characters in a field.

Like operator An operator used in a query to find values in a field that match the pattern you specify.

Limit to List A combo box control property that allows you to limit the entries made by that control to those provided by the combo box list.

Line A graphical element that can be added to a report to highlight information or enhance its clarity.

Link Child Fields A subform property that determines which field serves as the "many" link between the subform and main form.

Link line The line identifying which fields establish the relationship between two related tables.

Link Master Fields A subform property that determines which field serves as the "one" link between the main form and the subform.

List box A bound control that displays a list of possible choices for the user. Used mainly on forms.

List Rows A control property that determines how many items can be displayed in a list, such as in a combo box.

Live Preview A feature that lets you point to a choice in a gallery or palette and see the results in the document or object without actually clicking the choice.

Locked property A control property that specifies whether you can edit data in a control in Form View.

Logical view The datasheet of a query is sometimes called a logical view of the data because it is not a copy of the data, but rather, a selected view of data from the underlying tables.

Long Integer The default field size for a Number field.

Lookup field A field that has Lookup properties.

Lookup properties Field properties that allow you to supply a drop-down list of values for a field.

Lookup Wizard A wizard used in Table Design View that allows one field to "look up" values from another table or entered list. For example, you might use the Lookup Wizard to specify that the Customer Number field in the Sales table display the Customer Name field entry from the Customers table.

Macro An Access object that stores a collection of keystrokes or commands.

Main form A form that contains a subform control.

Main report A report that contains a subreport control.

Many-to-many relationship The relationship between two tables in an Access database in which one record of one table relates to many records in the other table and vice versa. You cannot directly create a many-to-many relationship between two tables in Access. To relate two tables with such a relationship, you must establish a third table called junction table that creates separate one-to-many relationships with the two original tables.

Module An Access object that stores Visual Basic for Applications (VBA) programming code that extends the functions of automated Access processes.

Multiuser A characteristic that means more than one person can enter and edit data in the same Access database at the same time.

Multivalued field A field that allows you to make more than one choice from a drop-down list.

Name property A property that uniquely identifies each control on a form or report.

Navigation buttons Buttons in the lower-left corner of a datasheet or form that allow you to quickly navigate between the records in the underlying object as well as add a new record.

Navigation mode A mode in which Access assumes that you are trying to move between the fields and records of the datasheet (rather than edit a specific field's contents), so keystrokes such as [Ctrl][Home] and [Ctrl][End] move you to the first and last field of the datasheet.

Navigation Pane A pane in the Access program window that provides a way to move between objects (tables, queries, forms, reports, macros, and modules) in the database.

Null entry The state of "nothingness" in a field. Any entry such as 0 in a numeric field or a space in a text field is not null. It is common to search for empty fields by using the Null criterion in a filter or query. The Is Not Null criterion finds all records where there is an entry of any kind.

Object A table, query, form, report, macro, or module in a database.

One-to-many line The line that appears in the Relationships or query design window and shows which field is duplicated between two tables to serve as the linking field. The one-to-many line displays a "1" next to the field that serves as the "one" side of the relationship and displays an infinity symbol next to the field that serves as the "many" side of the relationship when referential integrity is specified for the relationship. Also called the one-to-many join line.

One-to-many relationship The relationship between two tables in an Access database in which a common field links the tables together. The linking field is called the primary key field in the "one" table of the relationship and the foreign key field in the "many" table of the relationship.

Online collaboration The ability to incorporate feedback or share information across the Internet or a company network or intranet.

Option button A bound control used to display a limited list of mutually exclusive choices for a field, such as "female" or "male" for a gender field in form or report.

Option group A bound control placed on a form that is used to group together several option buttons that provide a limited number of values for a field.

Option Value An option button property that determines the value entered into a field when the option button is selected.

OR criteria Criteria placed on different rows of the query design grid. A record will appear in the resulting datasheet if it is true for any single row.

ORDER BY A SQL keyword that determines how records in the query result are sorted.

Orphan record A record in the "many" table of a one-to-many relationship that doesn't have a matching entry in the linking field of the "one" table.

Padding The space between controls.

Parameter criteria Text entered in [square brackets] that prompts the user for an entry each time the query is run.

Parameter report A report that prompts you for criteria to determine the records to use for the report.

Parent table The "one" table in a one-to-many relationship.

Pixel (picture element) One pixel is the measurement of one picture element on the screen.

Pmt function Built-in Access function used to calculate the monthly payment on a loan; enter the Pmt function as Pmt([Rate],[Term],[Loan]).

Portrait orientation A way to print or view a page that is 8.5 inches wide by 11 inches tall.

Previewing Prior to printing, seeing onscreen exactly how the printout will look.

Primary key field A field that contains unique information for each record. A primary key field cannot contain a null entry.

Print Preview An Access view that shows you how a report or other object will print on a sheet of paper.

Property A characteristic that further defines a field (if field properties), control (if control properties), section (if section properties), or object (if object properties).

Property Sheet A window that displays an exhaustive list of properties for the chosen control, section, or object within the Form Design View or Report Design View.

Property Update Options A Smart Tag that applies property changes in one field to other objects of the database that use the field.

Query An Access object that provides a spreadsheet-like view of the data, similar to that in tables. It may provide the user with a subset of fields and/or records from one or more tables. Queries are created when the user has a "question" about the data in the database.

Query Datasheet View The view of a query that shows the selected fields and records as a datasheet.

Query design grid The bottom pane of the Query Design View window in which you specify the fields, sort order, and limiting criteria for the query.

Query Design View The window in which you develop queries by specifying the fields, sort order, and limiting criteria that determine which fields and records are displayed in the resulting datasheet.

Question mark (?) A wildcard character used to search for any single character in query criteria.

Quick Access toolbar A small toolbar on the left side of a Microsoft application window's title bar, containing icons that you click to quickly perform common actions, such as saving a file.

Read-only An object property that indicates whether the object can read and display data, but cannot be used to change (write to) data.

Record A row of data in a table.

Record Source A property of a form or report that identifies the table or query containing the data to display.

Referential integrity A set of Access rules that govern data entry and help ensure data accuracy.

Relational database software Software such as Access that is used to manage data organized in a relational database.

Relationship report A printout of the Relationships window that shows how a relational database is designed and includes table names, field names, primary key fields, and one-to-many relationship lines.

Report An Access object that creates a professional printout of data that may contain such enhancements as headers, footers, and calculations on groups of records.

Report Design View An Access view that allows you to work with a complete range of report, section, and control properties.

Report Wizard An Access wizard that helps you create a report.

Ribbon Appears below the title bar in every Office program window, and displays commands you're likely to need for the current task.

Right function Built-in Access function used to return the specified number of characters from the end of a field value.

Row Source A property that defines the values to display in a list, such as in a Lookup field or combo box.

Ruler A vertical or horizontal guide that appears in Form and Report Design View to help you position controls.

Run a query To open a query and view the fields and records that you have selected for the query presented as a datasheet.

Save As command A command on the FILE tab that saves the entire database (and all objects it contains) or only the current object with a new name.

Screen capture An electronic snapshot of your screen, as if you took a picture of it with a camera, which you can paste into a document.

Scrub the database To remove and fix orphan records.

Section A location in a form or report that contains controls. The section in which a control is placed determines where and how often the control prints.

SELECT A SQL keyword that determines what fields a query selects.

Select query The most common type of query that retrieves data from one or more linked tables and displays the results in a datasheet.

Simple Query Wizard An Access wizard that prompts you for information it needs to create a new query.

Sizing handles Small squares at each corner of a selected control in Access. Dragging a handle resizes the control. Also known as handles.

Smart Tag A button that provides a small menu of options and automatically appears under certain conditions to help you work with a task, such as correcting errors. For example, the AutoCorrect Options button, which helps you correct typos and update properties, and the Error Indicator button, which helps identify potential design errors in Form and Report Design View, are Smart Tags.

Sort To reorder records in either ascending or descending order based on the values of a particular field.

Split form A form split into two panes; the upper pane allows you to display the fields of one record in any arrangement, and the lower pane maintains a datasheet view of the first few records.

SQL (Structured Query Language) A language that provides a standardized way to request information from a relational database system.

SQL View A query view that displays the SQL code for the query.

Subdatasheet A datasheet that is nested within another datasheet to show related records. The subdatasheet shows the records on the "many" side of a one-to-many relationship.

Subform A form placed within a form that shows related records from another table or query. A subform generally displays many records at a time in a datasheet arrangement.

Subreport A control that displays a report within another report.

Suite A group of programs that are bundled together and share a similar interface, making it easy to transfer skills and program content among them.

Sum function A mathematical function that totals values in a field.

Summary query A query used to calculate and display information about records grouped together.

Summary report A report that calculates and displays information about records grouped together.

Syntax Rules for entering information such as query criteria or property values.

Tab control An unbound control used to create a three-dimensional aspect to a form so that other controls can be organized and shown in Form View by clicking the "tabs."

Tab Index property A form property that indicates the numeric tab order for all controls on the form that have the Tab Stop property set to Yes.

Tab order property A form property that determines the sequence in which the controls on the form receive the focus when the user presses [Tab] or [Enter] in Form view.

Tab Stop property A form property that determines whether a field accepts focus.

Table A collection of records for a single subject, such as all of the customer records; the fundamental building block of a relational database because it stores all of the data.

Table Design View A view of a table that provides the most options for defining fields.

Template A sample file, such as a database provided within the Microsoft Access program.

Text Align property A control property that determines the alignment of text within the control.

Text box The most common type of control used to display field values.

Theme A predefined set of colors, fonts, line and fill effects, and other formats that can be applied to an Access database and give it a consistent, professional look.

Total row Row in the query design grid used to specify how records should be grouped and summarized with aggregate functions.

Unbound control A control that does not change from record to record and exists only to clarify or enhance the appearance of the form, using elements such as labels, lines, and clip art.

User interface A collective term for all the ways you interact with a software program.

Validation Rule A field property that helps eliminate unreasonable entries by establishing criteria for an entry before it is accepted into the database.

Validation Text A field property that determines what message appears if a user attempts to make a field entry that does not pass the validation rule for that field.

Value field A numeric field, such as Cost, that can be summed or averaged.

View Each Access object has different views for different purposes. For example, you work with data in Datasheet View. You modify the design of the object in Layout and Design Views. You preview a printout in Print Preview.

Wildcard A special character used in criteria to find, filter, and query data. The asterisk (*) stands for any group of characters. For example, the criteria I* in a State field criterion cell would find all records where the state entry was IA, ID, IL, IN, or Iowa. The question mark (?) wildcard stands for only one character.

Zooming in A feature that makes a printout appear larger but shows less of it on screen at once; does not affect the actual size of the printout.

Zooming out A feature that shows more of a printout on screen at once but at a reduced size; does not affect the actual size of the printout.

Index